BETWEEN CITY AND COUNTRY

I0880050

BETWEEN CITY AND COUNTRY

BROOKLINE, MASSACHUSETTS, AND THE ORIGINS OF SUBURBIA

RONALD DALE KARR

UNIVERSITY OF MASSACHUSETTS PRESS
AMHERST & BOSTON

Copyright © 2018 by University of Massachusetts Press
All rights reserved
Printed in the United States of America

ISBN 978-1-62534-304-8 (paper)

Designed by Dennis Anderson
Set in Adobe Caslon Pro by Scribe, Inc.
Printed and bound by Maple Press, Inc.

Cover design by Jack Harrison
Cover art: (Top) Commonwealth of Massachusetts State Archives, digitalcommonwealth.org. (Bottom) National Park Service, Frederick Law Olmsted National Historic Site.

Library of Congress Cataloging-in-Publication Data

Names: Karr, Ronald Dale, author.
Title: Between city and country : Brookline, Massachusetts, and the origins of suburbia / Ronald Dale Karr.
Description: Amherst : University of Massachusetts Press, 2018. | Includes bibliographical references and index.
Identifiers: LCCN 2017038240 | ISBN 9781625343048 (pbk.)
Subjects: LCSH: Brookline (Mass.)—History—19th century. | Suburbs—United States—History—19th century—Case studies. | Urban-rural migration—United States—History—19th century—Case studies. | Suburbs—Social aspects—United States—History. | Suburban life—United States—History.
Classification: LCC F74.B9 K37 2017 | DDC 974.4/7—dc23
LC record available at https://lccn.loc.gov/2017038240

British Library Cataloguing-in-Publication Data
A catalog record for this book is available from the British Library.

Maps 1.1, 2.1, 3.1, 4.1, 4.2, and 7.6 and images 1.2, 4.3, 4.7, and 7.5 have been created by the author.

To Diane
For everything always

It is to be wished, that some person, fitted for the task, would prepare a statistical account of this charming little Town, its rapidly increasing population, its elegant, and, in some instances, princely mansions, its agricultural and horticultural improvements, unparalleled, it is believed, for the size of the place, in the United States.

—Reverend John Pierce, *An Address at the Opening of the Town Hall in Brookline on Tuesday 14 October 1845*

Contents

✦

Preface

✦

ONCE SEEN as an aberration, suburbia has become the American norm. Since the onslaught of mass suburbanization following the Second World War, suburban views on education, politics, and recreation have mostly displaced the urban, rural, and small-town attitudes that previously predominated. The urban preferences of some affluent younger adults notwithstanding, suburbs remain the preferred place to live and raise families because they are believed to combine the best features of cities and country.

As a product of suburbia, I experienced this firsthand. I was born in the city of Pittsburgh after World War II, but my parents lived in the early twentieth-century suburb of Ben Avon, on the banks of the Ohio River. A few years later we moved to a new colonial-revival apartment complex in Drexel Hill, another early twentieth-century suburb in Delaware County, west of Philadelphia. My father, a civil engineer, commuted each workday to his downtown office.

In 1954 we left our apartment for the suburban frontier, my parents having bought a house under construction in Levittown in lower Bucks County, one of the largest and most notorious of the postwar suburbs. We were at the edge of construction when we moved in, and the building around us continued for another four years. Even for a six-year-old, the contrast between the tree-lined streets of Drexel Hill and this raw landscape was obvious and a bit unsettling. With the passing years, the growth of vegetation softened the scenery, and Levittown began to take on the trappings of a settled community. But elsewhere the farmland of lower Bucks County gave way to houses, apartments, gas stations, shopping centers, and express highways, leaving isolated older hamlets and buildings behind to bear witness to what had been before.

In the fall of 1970 I arrived in Brookline after four years at a remote small college town in central Pennsylvania and a summer at my parents' home in Levittown. As a first-year graduate student, my new home initially seemed to be a very urban—and exciting—Boston neighborhood. I was amused whenever someone referred to Brookline as a suburb. Living on busy Beacon Street with a trolley line running by my window, there was little to remind me of the thousands of nearly identical tract houses and endless shopping centers of postwar suburbia, which I had been glad to leave behind. For me, "suburban" had become a pejorative term.

As I explored the streets of Brookline over the four years I lived there, however, I began to realize that something about what I was seeing was familiar after all. Faint memories of Ben Avon and more clearly Drexel Hill reminded me that I had seen these sights before: commercial streets combined with quiet, tree-lined residential streets of large houses. Brookline was indeed suburban, but of an older vintage than the suburbs in which I had lived. As I studied history, especially urban history, I began to ask questions about what I was seeing on my Brookline walks.

First, most of Brookline's buildings dated from the late nineteenth and early twentieth centuries, the same period that saw massive amounts of construction throughout Boston and its inner suburbs. Yet Brookline was different from much of the rest of greater Boston. Why? In the 1970s much of the old suburban belt around Boston looked the same regardless of where you went. Streets in Dorchester, Cambridge, Jamaica Plain, Somerville, Chelsea, Everett, and southern Medford, with their rows of detached wooden two-family and triple-decker houses set on small lots—today surrounded by cars and often set behind chain-link fences—did not vary much from neighborhood to neighborhood, even as the topography changed from flatland to steep slopes. They existed in sharp contrast to the neat stone-and-brick apartment blocks and fine houses on the well-manicured lots of Brookline. Yet all these communities had arisen at the same time, had comparable topography, a similar proximity to Boston, and were subject to the same market forces. What could explain Brookline's distinctive appearance?

Second, I soon learned that not all of Brookline resembled the crowded streets around the commercial center of Coolidge Corner where I lived. South of Route 9, which bisects the town, lay a different realm altogether, featuring great estates with rolling lawns and large Victorian homes. How had this region managed to resist the wave of growth that had swept over the surrounding parts of

Boston and Newton? Who lived there? How did this section relate to the rest of the town?

These questions led me to research the history of Brookline and ultimately to write this book. I learned that American suburbs had their origins before the Civil War, and that Brookline was one of the earliest and best known. Moreover, the attitudes and beliefs with which I was raised in suburbia could be traced back to places like nineteenth-century Brookline, where they had evolved slowly over many decades, often with contention. In a sense, Brookline was an ancestor to Ben Avon, Drexel Hill, and even Levittown.

I was surprised to learn that nineteenth-century commuter suburbs like Brookline were complex communities, which differed in important ways from their almost exclusively affluent twentieth-century counterparts. Sharp inequality, not simply wealth or exclusion of the poor, characterized nearly every aspect of life in the town. Notwithstanding the town's fashionable reputation, low-income Irish Catholics accounted for a significant portion of Brookline's population before 1900, and they frequently made their presence known.

Above all, I discovered that despite the absence of zoning or other land-control laws, the town's appearance, which I had come to admire, was not accidental. It did not result solely from the workings of impersonal market forces that so profoundly shaped nineteenth-century America. Rather, here the political leaders, backed by the wealthy, were able to exert considerable influence over the development of the town, so that the built environment to a large extent came to reflect the preferences of the dominant classes. As Brookline grew, the sentiments of its upper- and middle-class bourgeois residents also evolved, eventually coming to a consensus broadly supported by most of the town's inhabitants, even many of the less affluent. These suburban values, if we may call them that, increasingly set suburbanites apart from urban, rural, and small-town residents, even those of similar socioeconomic status.

Over the forty years in which I have worked on this project, I have owed much to colleagues, librarians, archivists, Brookline officials, and teachers. My initial debt was to Boston University professors the late Robert V. Bruce and James Henretta.

Among the many fellow librarians and archivists who aided me in my research, Deborah Friedman and Rose Patton at the University of Massachusetts O'Leary

Library Interlibrary Loan office have been fielding my requests with great skill for the greatest number of years. I also wish to thank Gary Roberts and David Dearborn of the library of the New England Historic Genealogical Society; the late Leo Flaherty of the Massachusetts Archives; the staff of the Public Library of Brookline, especially Delija P. Karoblis; the staff of the Boston Public Library, especially Charles Longley; the staff of Boston University's Mugar Library, the library of the Massachusetts Historical Society, the Library of Congress, Chicago's Newberry Library, and the library of the American Antiquarian Society; and all of my former colleagues at the Northwestern University Library.

The director of libraries at the University of Massachusetts Lowell, my former colleague George Hart, arranged for a timely grant from the Freeman Trust Fund of the university to help defray publication costs, for which I am extremely grateful.

In Brookline Leslie Larkin and Carla Benka of the Brookline Historical Commission willingly shared their extensive knowledge of Brookline's architectural history and greatly aided my comprehension in interpreting contemporary sources. More recently, Anne Lusk provided leads to locating sources of Brookline photographs. Ken Liss, president of the Brookline Historical Society, kindly provided permission to reproduce photographs from their collection. Archivists Camille Arbogast and Jesus MacLean of the society helped me identify items in their collection. Tom Elwertowski of the Friends of Brookline Preservation conducted a walking tour that taught me about High Street Hill.

Richard Bushman and Michael Ebner have been continual sources of encouragement over the years. Several historians have willingly shared information with me, in person or by correspondence, including David Hackett Fischer; the late Alfred D. Chandler, Jr.; and Joel Tarr. Parts of the manuscript have been read by Mary Blewett; my daughter, Emilie Karr; and anonymous reviewers, and their comments are greatly appreciated.

At the University of Massachusetts Press I want to thank Clark Dougan for shepherding the manuscript through the initial acceptance process. Thanks also go to Matt Becker, who continued the process to publication, and Margaret Hogan, whose skillful copyediting helped complete the process.

Finally, the greatest thanks of all are to my wife, Diane, who has lived with this book from the earliest research through many revisions to its present form. Without her love and advice, I never could have completed it.

BETWEEN CITY AND COUNTRY

Introduction

IN SEARCH OF SUBURBIA

✦

AT THE ONSET of the twenty-first century the U.S. Census Bureau announced that the United States had become a suburban nation, with "half of the U.S. population" now residing "in suburban areas."[1] But what and where were these "suburban areas"? Curiously, as literary critic Karen Tongson observes, there is no official census category of *suburb.* As with such terms as *capitalism* and *social class,* a range of competing definitions of the term *suburban* has been put forward over the years, some emphasizing place, others culture. Advocates of a spatial definition view suburbia as the vast district lying between the city proper and the rural countryside, while those stressing culture would limit the term to those areas sharing a suburban culture.[2]

Although lacking an official definition, the Census Bureau's own analysts clearly embraced the spatial model of suburbia when they informally designated as "suburban" entire metropolitan regions lying outside of central cities. (A metropolitan region is defined as "a large population nucleus, together with adjacent communities that have a high degree of economic and social integration with that nucleus.")[3]

Defining suburbia by political geography means that not only are the inner boundaries of suburban territory fixed by the politics of municipal incorporation but that the metropolitan region's outer boundaries—where the suburbs give way to rural territory—are also determined politically. "Because the Census Bureau is subject to heavy political pressures," notes historian Kenneth T. Jackson, "the way it defines 'suburbs' and 'metropolitan area' serves more to confuse than to enlighten."[4] Indeed, metropolitan areas are delimited not by the Census

Bureau but by the White House–based Office of Management and Budget.[5] Notwithstanding its limitations, however, a political definition has its attractions. If nothing else it is inclusive: by this definition, the American suburban realm encompasses a vast amalgamation of landscapes ranging from industrial slums to upscale enclaves for the very rich, reflecting nearly as much of the economic, ethnic, and racial diversity of the nation as can be found within the boundaries of central cities. Here are residential neighborhoods of single- and multifamily housing, factories, railyards, airports, warehouses, shopping malls, office and industrial parks, high-rise complexes, even prisons, all tied together by ribbons of interstate federal highways.[6] Historian Robert O. Self has shown how these commercial and industrial zones formed integral parts of post–World War II suburban municipalities, which relied on them for tax revenues, jobs, and even political clout.[7]

But a strictly political definition of suburbia runs contrary to the way generations of American critics, novelists, urban historians, journalists, and social scientists—not to mention most ordinary Americans—have used the suburban label. Here suburbia is defined by its distinctive culture, where, according to Jackson, "affluent and middle-class Americans live in suburban areas that are far from their work places, in homes that they own, and in the center of yards that by urban standards elsewhere are enormous."[8] Long ago Frederic Law Olmsted suggested that the term "strictly suburban" be limited to areas of "detached dwellings with sylvan surroundings yet supplied with a considerable share of urban convenience."[9]

Generations of social scientists, popular writers, and journalists have produced an extensive literature, both popular and academic (much of it critical or whimsical), purporting to describe and define the suburbs and the lives led by its privileged inhabitants. In these accounts suburbia is portrayed as a pleasant (if vapid) low-density bourgeois utopia, a world of lawns, shade trees, yards, vegetable gardens, swimming pools, backyard barbeques, and nearly identical detached houses arranged in subdivisions, a place where white children are everywhere but dark-skinned faces seldom seen. Far enough away to escape the crime, poverty, racial minorities, pollution, corrupt politics, and congestion of the city but close enough to enable (male) commuting to the high-paying, white-collar jobs of the city, its residents lead quiet yet busy lives of orderly, middle-class conformity. Countless films, plays, and television shows have reinforced this image.[10]

Both the spatial-political and cultural definitions of suburbia have drawn criticism. The former has been assailed for exaggerating the importance of political boundaries, particularly the city line. Although these bounds have often taken on significance, critics have noted that political borders are frequently invisible on the ground and that the economic structure of the metropolitan region has long ignored city and county lines. For example, the oversimplified model of rich (and white) suburbs surrounding poorer central cities occupied by minorities does not accurately describe the complexity of the American metropolis. Some indisputably suburban neighborhoods, such as Philadelphia's Chestnut Hill and Chicago's Sauganash, are located within city limits, while the slums of most twentieth-century cities, such as Los Angeles and Detroit, consist of mostly low-density housing. At the same time, the metropolitan fringe features nineteenth-century high-density industrial neighborhoods, such as Lynn and Lowell, Massachusetts.[11]

On the other hand, the cultural definition of suburbia, emphasized by the first cohort of suburban historians such as Jackson, Robert Fishman, and John R. Stilgoe, has taken fire from a subsequent generation of scholars for being elitist, even racist or snobbish, since these earlier researchers seemed to imply that suburbs occupied by blue-collar workers or racial minorities were not authentically suburban. Newer urban historians have criticized the earlier studies for unduly focusing on affluent, leafy suburbs and thus ignoring the broader urban fringe where more people actually lived, and produced a series of excellent studies of lower-middle-class, self-built, and black suburbs that demonstrates the complexity of the urban fringe in the twentieth century.[12]

More recently, Becky M. Nicolaides and Andrew Wiese have suggested that "rather than seeing the lack of a scholarly consensus" over the definition of suburban "as a problem, we perceive it more as a virtue, a realistic way of approaching a contested and changing world."[13] I concur. Cultural traits are needed to refine the basic political definition. Over the years numerous studies have documented significant cultural differences between urban and suburban America, mostly (but not exclusively) grounded in socioeconomic class. Of course, there is great variety within these cultures from time to time and place to place, but overall the differences reported between working-class urban and middle-class suburban are striking. These include varied forms of socialization (public street corners, front porches, and bars versus private living rooms and backyards), use of transportation (walking and buses versus private automobile), political styles (ethnic patronage versus ideological disputes), recreational practices (shooting hoops at playgrounds versus shopping at the mall, cycling, and playing golf), religious practices (such as the presence or lack of identity with parishes), kinship relationships, gambling, the informal economy, aesthetic preferences, and many other traits.[14]

Here I propose reserving the suburban label for those low- or medium-density metropolitan neighborhoods, along with nearby ancillary commercial districts, whose residents display suburban cultural behavior. Most of these neighborhoods are politically independent of the city, though some may still be found within the urban bounds.

Throughout most of our national history, suburbia, as here defined, has been a place with an appearance that sets it apart from nearby urban areas, positioned somewhere between city and the rural countryside, mostly consisting of middle-class (however defined) middle- and low-density residential neighborhoods, and displaying distinctive cultural traits that, although showing a considerable variance, can be differentiated from nearby urban and rural cultures. In particular I agree with those who have argued that suburbs have tended to develop their own distinctive landscapes (again distinctive from the rural and the urban), the result of characteristically suburban ethics and aesthetics.[15] To be sure, the cultures of both cities and suburbs often share traits, such as segregation by income and especially by race.[16]

This book attempts to shed light on contemporary suburbia by examining its archeology. Even after decades of scholarship, some may still be surprised to learn that mass suburbanization began at least two decades before the Second World War, spurred on by the expansion of automobile ownership in the 1920s that opened millions of acres far from transit lines to large-lot development.[17] In fact, the first American residential suburbs had appeared a full century earlier, and several were well-established by the time of Abraham Lincoln's election. Among the earliest of these was Brookline, Massachusetts, the subject of this study. By the end of the nineteenth century, this nationally recognized community, less than four miles west of Boston, could count among its celebrated inhabitants the architect Henry H. Richardson, landscape architect Frederick Law Olmsted, industrialist Edward Atkinson, financial publisher Henry Varnum Poor, poetess Amy Lowell, and art collector extraordinaire Isabella Stewart Gardner.

One popular tourist guide called it "the richest suburb of Boston, and in many respects the most attractive, with numerous beautiful estates and tasteful 'villas' and charming drives."[18] Brookline's public schools were renowned, and its government was singled out by reformers as a model worthy of emulation.

It would be hard to find a better place to examine the origins of American suburbanization than here, since it was both exceptionally prominent and yet underwent development not unlike that of other American suburbs. Two of the most-studied nineteenth-century suburbs, Llewelyn Park, New Jersey, and Riverside, Illinois, were atypical planned developments, while Brookline evolved within the market-driven milieu of nineteenth-century American capitalism without centralized direction.[19] The relatively few studies of nineteenth-century suburbanization suggest that Brookline's growth was not unique, and certainly the suburban landscape of the town had its counterparts around most larger American cities, even the new ones on the prairie, like Chicago.[20]

Suburbs like Brookline first began to appear on the outskirts of large eastern American cities in the second quarter of the nineteenth century. Until that time the urban fringe was mostly occupied by persons who needed more land to make their livings than was available in the city: farmers, operators of cattle- and brickyards, soap makers, shopkeepers, blacksmiths, tanners, shipbuilders, and other small manufacturers. Aside from a few villages, the major exception was the country estates of the urban rich, which occupied a significant amount of land, although their numbers were few. But as a result of a convergence of rising (though increasingly unequal) incomes, changing residential fashions inspired by the English elite, urban expansion, the transition to industrial capitalism, the rise of the real-estate industry, and especially the development of rail commuting, an influx of newcomers gave rise to the first wave of suburban development starting in the 1830s and 1840s.[21]

Although the arrival of commuters set these proto-suburbs apart from the rest of the urban fringe, such places differed in several important respects from twentieth-century suburban communities. For one thing, they were more heterogeneous. The commuters may have been affluent—although not truly wealthy like their estate-owning predecessors—but many of their non-commuting neighbors were not. In Brookline, poor Irish immigrants accompanied the first commuters, and the town continued to include many small farmers, farm laborers, craftsmen, and small-business operators. Second, before the middle of the nineteenth century there is little evidence of a suburban consciousness, a sense of living in a community that differed fundamentally from cities or rural communities. Third, because of this, a distinctively suburban style of politics had yet to emerge.[22]

During the final third of the nineteenth century explicitly suburban cultures did evolve on the urban fringes of both well-established northeastern cities and the new metropolises of the Midwest. Upper-middle-class residential districts centered on commuter railroad stations, such as in Brookline, mushroomed. By the first decade of the twentieth century it was clear to many observers that suburban folk lived differently than either their urban or rural compatriots. "The great suburban development stands between the city and the country," noted one writer in 1906. "It is neither the one nor the other, although partaking of the two. It is not agriculture. It is not country life."[23]

Authentic suburbs, so Americans were told, could be distinguished from the urban areas they bordered by their retention of vestiges of country life including fields, streams, and orchards, and house lots of sufficient size to permit owners to maintain gardens for vegetables and flowers, raise chickens, and keep cows, horses, and bees. But as one turn-of-the-century writer was careful to note, here "'the country' does not mean the actual country—farm life, and the giving up of city wages—but the pleasant, often truly country-like districts which surround most of our big cities; the farther suburbs, in other words, where one may have the benefits of the country and still be enabled, by the now excellent train and trolley service, to keep on with city wages."[24] The often elaborate houses and manicured yards of these suburbs readily set them apart from truly rural districts, dominated by working farms.[25]

At the beginning of the twentieth century these "true" suburbs formed a stark contrast with many of the other users with which they shared that vast zone between the city and rural countryside. In 1962 historian Sam Bass Warner coined the term "streetcar suburb" to describe the new residential neighborhoods of modest one- and two-family houses that had sprang up around American cities in the last third of the nineteenth century. Numerous speculative builders constructed hundreds of thousands of single- and two-family houses primarily for white-collar households along the bourgeoning network of horse car and later trolley lines. With their small lawns and freestanding houses, they represented an alternative to the row houses and tenement blocks that had previously housed the urban lower middle class.[26]

At first glance the streetcar suburbs might appear to be scaled-down versions of antebellum suburbs such as Brookline. Indeed, many of these communities had previously been the sites of pre–Civil War commuter suburbs.[27] But on closer look, the new subdivisions had more in common with cities than older suburbs, not to mention truly rural districts. Little served to distinguish streetcar suburbs, though located on the urban fringe, from their more crowded urban antecedents than a bit more space. All that remained of the suburban aesthetic were their detached houses, tiny lawns, a tree or two, and perhaps a backyard chicken coop or vegetable garden plot. Historian John Stilgoe has rightfully questioned whether they should be regarded as suburban at all: "Horsecar and . . . streetcar 'suburbs' deserve another designation, for suburbs they were not, except in fitful pipedreams." Douglas Shand-Tucci has pointed out that the streetcar suburbs represented more an extension of traditional urban forms than a new genre. For that reason most of these communities were subsequently swallowed up by cities and today are considered older urban neighborhoods, even when they kept their municipal independence. Aside from remnants preserved as formal city parks or playgrounds, the original rural scenery of streetcar suburbs quickly vanished without serious effort to preserve it.[28]

Elsewhere on the urban fringe could still be found the same sorts of industrial and commercial uses that had long flourished there. Indeed, new, large-scale factories producing steel, automobiles, railroad equipment, and electrical goods, along with adjacent residential neighborhoods for the families of the factory hands, were being built from coast to coast. These blue-collar communities, notwithstanding their location, clearly displayed a mostly urban culture that set them apart from the older suburbs.[29] Thus, by the early twentieth century in popular usage suburbia referred to a limited portion of the metropolitan region.

This book, then, traces the growth and development of what may be called a true suburb as it evolved from a rural town on the urban fringe of Boston through the arrival of the first middle-class commuters in the 1840s, to its emergence as a partially urbanized suburb at the end of the nineteenth century. As Brookline developed during these six decades, its residents also forged a distinctively suburban ideology, largely in response to their community's growth, one that promoted a suburban ethic of efficient government and a high level of municipal services as well as a suburban aesthetic that sought to preserve what remained of the town's rural ambiance. Even before the twentieth century strengthened the hand of local governments with new land-use controls, such as zoning, Brookline had developed informal means of shaping growth, so that the landscape increasingly reflected the town's suburban ethic and aesthetics.

Places such as Brookline have long been termed *elite suburbs,* but unless used with caution this designation may obscure as much as it reveals.[30] To be sure, the connections between contemporary elite American suburbs and late-nineteenth-century Brookline are many, starting with a number of aspects of the suburban ethic and aesthetic they appear to share. Yet some of these similarities are superficial: social and economic elites dominated the political and economic life of both nineteenth and twentieth century suburbs, but in this they differed little from most American urban places.[31] More importantly, in 1900, Brookline lacked the homogeneity that would become characteristic of twentieth-century elite suburbs, if only because it did not have a practical way of excluding poorer residents. Instead of outright exclusion, which was both impractical and counterproductive, it relied on isolation, economic clout, and politics to keep its potentially unruly working-class immigrants in line.[32]

In the end, despite its distinctiveness, Brookline shared much in common with many other less-favored nineteenth-century American municipalities. As elsewhere, the town's growth reflected the broader national transition from a premodern rural economy to one ultimately driven by markets and industrial production.[33] The burgeoning economy generated the wealth that made possible Brookline's rapid growth after 1840, and the market organized and disciplined the numerous developers, land speculators, builders, and real-estate dealers who built the roads, houses, and commercial buildings that came to define the new suburb.

What ultimately set Brookline apart was the grip that its suburban ideology came to hold over the town. Most nineteenth-century American cities and towns were shaped by market-based capitalism and run by business-friendly political elites anxious to maximize private gain.[34] At least some suburbs were different, even though they were subject to the same market forces. In Brookline the market was manipulated and controlled by a small number of elite individuals and families, nearly all local residents, who did not use their power to maximize potential personal profit (although thanks to rising property values, they hardly suffered). Rather, they sought to shape a community that reflected their collective tastes—a community featuring both elegant neighborhoods and a high level of public services for the affluent commuters, and crowded slums for poor Irish Americans.

The ideology that developed in early suburbs like Brookline had evolved out of a growing popular desire to live closer to nature even as urban growth was beginning to consume the countryside. Unfortunately, however, there seemed to be no easy way of combining the urban with the rural, since urbanization itself quickly threatened to overwhelm the rural countryside and replace sound rural government with corrupt big-city politics. At first there was no easy answer to the question of how a third type of society could be developed that was neither wholly rural nor wholly urban but combined the best traits of both. Between the 1840s and the 1880s Brookline featured a variety of middle- and upper-class residential options, though most of these were not yet distinctively suburban. The fortunate few with ample resources could purchase a traditional country estate. For the rest, most of the new housing, both high and low cost, was built on grid streets laid out adjacent to Brookline Village, houses set squarely facing the street on modest-sized lots. After 1885, however, the development of the town took two paths: the northern end of the town featuring a grand urban boulevard, flanked by high-end streetcar suburbs, while the southern end followed a more modern suburban course, with curvilinear streets and shady yards.

In Brookline, suburbia was made manifest. Its example helped define the vision of the good life eventually embraced by most twentieth-century Americans: ownership of a house and yard on a quiet, safe, leafy street in a physically appealing suburban town convenient to work and featuring good schools and efficient municipal services. No longer could it be doubted that it was possible for a community to remain apart from a nearby city without surrendering either urban amenities or losing rustic charm, and that the advantages of city and country could be combined without suffering the drawbacks of either. As late as 1870 some called it a utopian dream. By 1900 it had become reality.

During the last third of the nineteenth century, at a time when many emerging suburbs throughout urban America were being swallowed up by ambitious cities, Brookline became one of the first to reject annexation and maintain its political independence. By the century's end increasing numbers of suburbs had followed Brookline's lead and were remaining autonomous from their cities. Progressive reformers confronting the broader problems of urban America during the first decades of the twentieth century turned to Brookline and other suburbs when seeking antidotes for the excesses of unbridled capitalism, runaway urban growth, and political corruption. The suburban experience suggested paths to reform that avoided socialism, populism, and other changes odious to the privileged, and many of the government-sponsored innovations of the early twentieth century, such as land-use regulation and housing reforms, came to reflect this suburban outlook.

PART 1

TOWN INTO SUBURB 1790–1850

At the end of the American Revolution Brookline was a small farming town, one of the hundreds of rural New England communities in which the vast majority of the region's inhabitants resided. In retrospect, it is clear that the proximity of Boston was already exerting an influence over the town and its people, although there is little to indicate that those who lived there as yet gave this any thought. Certainly no one yet regarded Brookline as a *suburb* in the modern sense, if by which we mean a community poised between city and country but distinct from either.

By the middle of the nineteenth century Brookline had taken on some of the attributes of a modern American suburb. Early on, some of the richest businessmen of Boston acquired country estates there, and these gentlemen farmers put their stamp of fashion on the town. Every weekday morning hundreds of men left their suburban homes for jobs in the city, leaving wives and children behind. Despite their limited numbers, these commuters were beginning to have a large influence over the town. Their presence had helped to attract more than six hundred Catholic Irish immigrants to settle with them, where they found employment as laborers and domestic servants, joining hundreds of Yankee craftsmen and storekeepers from elsewhere in New England who sold the elite provisions, fixed their carriages, and built their houses.

Perhaps the terms *proto-suburb, quasi-suburb,* or *semi-suburb* might best describe this community, for in 1850 Brookline remained a curious amalgamation of its rural past and an increasingly urban present, facing an uncertain future. Even before the commuters arrived in the 1840s, Brookline had undergone a long process of economic expansion that saw agriculture commercialized and a village develop, part of the advance of an industrial economy that was transforming southern New England. With population growth fueled by industrialization, suburbanization, and immigration, Brookline in 1850 seemed slated to become a Boston neighborhood.

CHAPTER 1

New England Town

✦

The hills and woodlands of Brookline form a considerable part of the scenery presented to the view from the west of Boston common. The town contains some of the finest country seats and best managed lands which adorn the environs of Boston.

—John Warner Barber, *Historical Collections,* 1839

Early American cities began and ended abruptly. As late as 1840 a tourist wandering out of Boston could reach the countryside while the gleaming State House dome atop Beacon Hill was still visible over one's shoulder. Boston may have grown to include nearly 100,000 inhabitants (with even more in surrounding communities), its wharfs may have been crowded with ships and its streets with vehicles, and hazy locomotive smoke may have hung in the air, but a three-mile walk was all it took to leave the metropolis behind. Immediately to the west of Boston, at the end of the long causeway across the Back Bay, lay the boundary of the town of Brookline, population 1,365. Another new road from the causeway brought the traveler to Brookline Village, the sole concentration of population in the town. Although at the doorstep of Boston, our traveler might well have seemed to be in the foothills of the Berkshires a hundred miles to the west. Here was a nondescript rural village of some forty houses, stores, and workshops where one could post a letter, purchase shoes for horses or humans, have a wagon repaired, or take home a new bonnet.[1]

Farmers on the Urban Fringe

Like most New England townships Brookline encompassed more than just the closely settled village. The town's rectangular bounds, unchanged since its incorporation in 1705, measured four miles by less than two. The best lands lay along the three roads that fanned out from the village to the north, northwest, and southwest. The soil in these broad valleys, well-watered by numerous streams and flanked by elongated hills—glacial drumlins—was a rich light loam, well-suited to European-style agriculture. The fringes of Brookline were a different matter. Much of northern Brookline, along the Charles River and the Back Bay, was given over to salt marsh and tidal flats. Since the construction of the great Mill Dam across the bay in 1821, this part of Brookline was closest to Boston proper, but as yet no roads penetrated this region. The extreme southwestern corner of the town was a wilderness of rocks and swamps that would remain largely unused until the twentieth century (fig. 1.1).[2]

The town's rustic appearance was not an illusion; census takers that year reported that fully three out four adult males in Brookline worked the soil for a living.[3] Fields, orchards, and pastures dominated the view on any road out of the village. Farm houses and barns, many predating the American Revolution, were never far from sight, but except for their various outbuildings, a few mansions, two churches, three schoolhouses, and a tannery or two, they were the only structures visible. Since nearly all of these lay close to the roads, the landscape beyond was largely devoid of buildings. Urban conveniences seemed far away. As yet, no ready form of transportation tied the town to Boston save a private carriage, a sporadic omnibus, or one's own legs. Even if Bostonians still wanted to take a stab at living in Brookline, they faced the difficulty of finding suitable housing or even a lot to purchase, since most of the land was tied up in farms and infrequently sold.

Rural though the town may have been, Brookline was both literally and figuratively a long way from the Berkshires. For more than two centuries its economic, political, and social life had been strongly influenced by the city it bordered. Like all of the initial Puritan settlements in Massachusetts Bay launched by John Winthrop in 1630, Boston was intended as a rural village with homes clustered around a town center surrounded by fields. Nature thwarted this scheme. The narrow Shawmut Peninsula did not contain enough land for the many who wished to settle in the Puritan capital. The town fathers reluctantly granted fields to Bostonians on the mainland at Muddy River (Brookline) and Rumney Marsh (Chelsea), the choicest parcels going to the socially prominent, while "the poorer sort of the Inhabitants such as are members or likely so to be, and have Noe Cattell" received the remainder in small plots.[4]

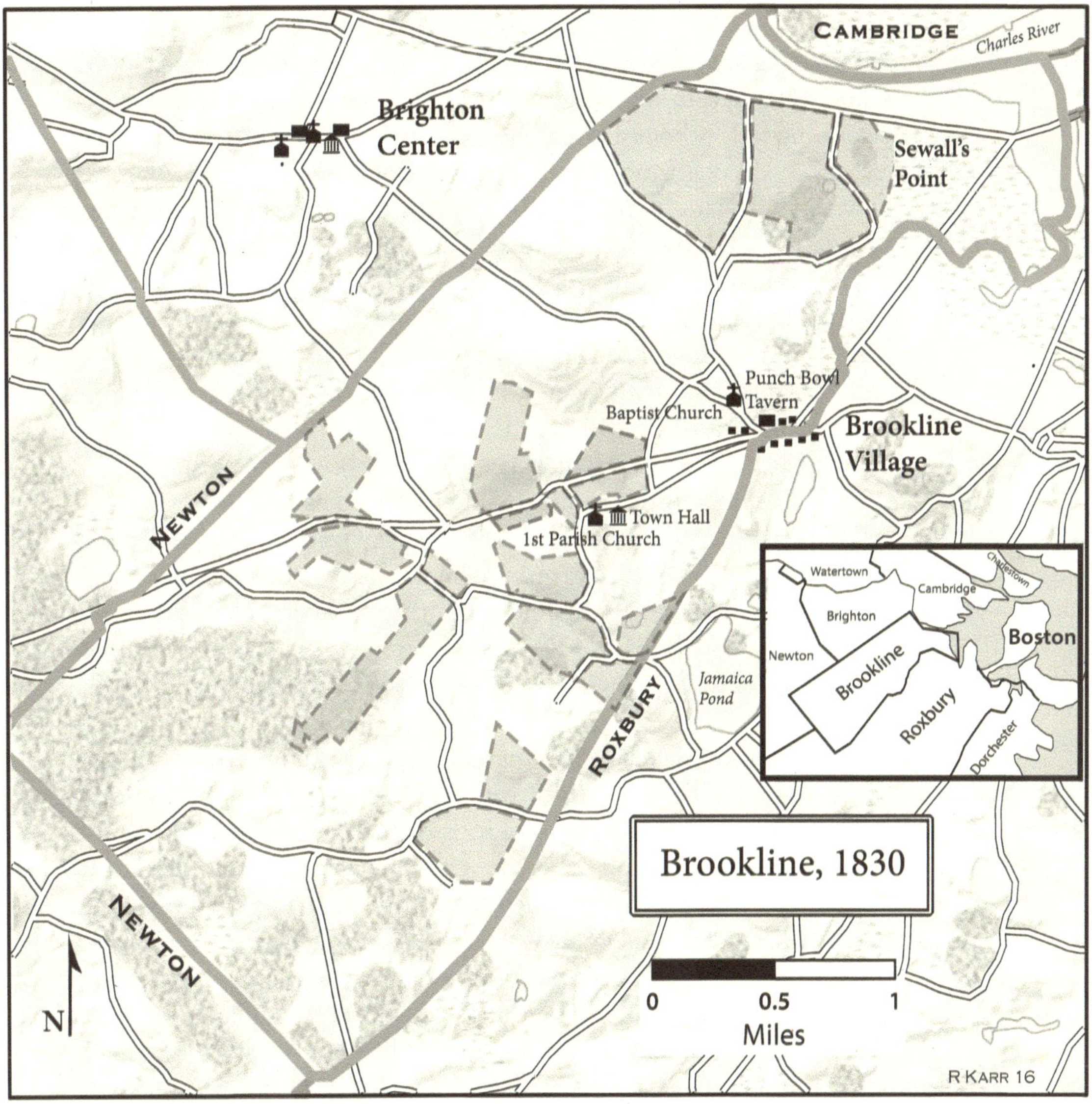

FIGURE I.I. Map of Brookline, 1830, showing areas of land ownership by elite Boston families.

The new owners found their lands remote from Boston, and few made use of their holdings for either agriculture or residences. Most of the initial grants were sold to others, and by 1650 an irregular community of twenty-five families, none of them original grantees, had appeared at Muddy River. Such spontaneous settlement went against the Puritan grain. The earliest New England communities were intended to be villages of inhabitants hived around covenanted churches, forming tightly bound assemblies presided over by ever-watchful elders and magistrates. Although most settlements did not measure up to the standard, few were as deviant as Muddy River. Here the settlers were miles away from church or constable, with each family living on its own farm. Many Boston Puritans found this troubling, and for good reason: Muddy River anticipated the ultimate abandonment of the nucleated village and the rise of the "outlivers," families living on the physical and social fringes of the community.[5]

Over the next half century, however, Brookline backed away from its frontier origins and fell into line with the Puritan order. Closer ties were forged with its immediate neighbors, Cambridge and Roxbury. While Muddy River was still part of Boston, most of its inhabitants attended church in Roxbury, and in 1672 they footed one-quarter of the bill for that town's new meetinghouse. In 1686, over the objection of Boston's government, the province gave Muddy River the quasi-independent status of a hamlet, and in 1705 this became the town of Brookline. The cornerstone of the Puritan commonwealth, the meetinghouse, took nine more years to complete, and the town's first minister was not settled until 1719.[6]

The new town grew slowly, mirroring the sluggish population increase of Boston during most of the eighteenth century.[7] On the eve of the American Revolution only about 350 residents lived in Brookline. Four out of five households in 1770 operated farms, and many of the rest, including households headed by blacksmiths and other rural craftsmen, also worked small plots of land and kept livestock. Boston consumers provided a ready market for the town's corn, apples, cider, vegetables, and hay, making Brookline's farmers among the most prosperous in New England. The men at the heads of Brookline's forty-four farming households dominated all facets of town life, from politics to religion. The other sixty-three adult males, as well as all females, were clearly subordinate. As elsewhere in New England, until a man became head of his own household he was unlikely to marry, be elected to town office, obtain a militia commission, or sit in a prominent pew in church. While awaiting his own farm he lived in someone else's household—usually but not always his parents'—and contributed his labor. In addition to their own sons and daughters, some households included unrelated young, single, propertyless men who drifted in and out from other towns.[8]

In this society most farmers viewed economic success more as a means of maintaining household autonomy than as an end in itself. Historians have argued that early Massachusetts farmers pursued not so much wealth as they did a *competency,* "a degree of comfortable independence."[9] Nearly all Brookline farms yielded a surplus, and Yankee farmers were never averse to turning a profit. But the subsequent history of Brookline agriculture suggests that the relative prosperity of the town's farmers owed more to rich soils, a growing season longer than that in inland towns, and the proximity of Boston than to entrepreneurial zeal. For labor most farmers had largely themselves and their sons; in 1770 the tax list showed only thirty-seven propertyless men who were not sons or nephews of one of the town's forty-four farmers. Farmers grew a broad mixture of crops, nearly all of which could be consumed as well as sold.[10]

Eighteenth-century Brookline was dominated by a well-defined political and social elite. Three families—the Whites, the Gardners, and the Winchesters—had taken charge of Muddy River in the 1650s and never let up. Over the next century members of these kinship groups often intermarried and continued to hold important town offices, govern the church, occupy the best pews in the meetinghouse, command the militia, and own the finest farms. Brookline's gentry, in turn, were linked to the provincial elite: patronage came from Boston in the form of commissions as justices of the peace, while Whites, Gardners, and Winchesters sent their sons to Harvard.[11] In one crucial respect, however, Brookline's elite differed from their counterparts in Virginia, England, or elsewhere: at least in outward appearances, little set them aside from the average farmer. Their farms may have been slightly larger, but members of Brookline's gentry had to work their own lands themselves, just as other farmers did. Their property was valued higher than others and their homes were more gracious, but the difference from the average farm was not significant.[12]

Positioned as it was on Boston's rim, Brookline could not escape involvement in the American Revolution. The town appointed a Committee of Correspondence in the aftermath of the Boston Tea Party, and on April 19, 1775, sent a militia company to support the colonists at Lexington. During the bloody British retreat to Boston on that fateful day, Brookline's Capt. Isaac Gardner, Esq., justice of the peace, town clerk, and former moderator and selectman, joined a band of militia who "imprudently posted themselves behind some dry casks . . . near to the road, unsuspicious of the enemy's flank-guard, which came behind them and killed every one of them dead on the spot."[13] Gardner was the first Harvard graduate to die in the Revolution.[14]

Support for the revolutionary cause in Brookline was nearly universal, with only three known Tories.[15] During the siege of Boston that followed, Brookline hosted two gun batteries and two companies of troops. The soldiers probably brought on the outbreaks of smallpox and dysentery in 1775 and 1776 that elevated the town's death rate to its highest level ever.[16] Even after the British evacuated Boston in March 1776 and the theater of combat shifted southward, the war did not go away. For years to come Brookline faced runaway inflation, insatiable recruitment quotas, and constant uncertainty.[17]

The closing of the Boston market in 1775 forced Brookline farmers to alter longstanding ways and seek new outlets for their surplus produce. With everything in flux, taking greater risks could not be avoided. High produce prices, combined with the town's location near Boston, presented ready opportunity for profit. The Continental Army itself provided an important market for meat, vegetables, and fodder. Brookline farmers responded by bringing 22 percent more land under cultivation. Eastern Massachusetts farmers pursued wartime opportunities with such relish that the urban poor and less-favored interior farmers accused them of heartless profiteering.[18]

The arrival of peace in 1783 turned agricultural expansion into a boom. A census taken that year showed a population of 364, only slightly larger than the 338 inhabitants counted in 1764. Seven years later the first federal census in 1790 found Brookline with 484 residents, a gain of 33 percent. The population grew faster than the number of housing units, making the average household slightly larger. At the same time, wealth was becoming more unevenly distributed. The upper tenth of taxpayers enlarged their share of assessed wealth from 47 percent in 1770 to 52 percent in 1787, while the number of men without property increased from 42 to 55 percent of all adult males. There seems little doubt that Brookline's farmers were hiring additional hands to supplement family labor.[19]

Although it offered opportunities for gain, deeper involvement in the market economy was not without peril. Many eastern Massachusetts farmers funded their ventures by incurring debt, which could prove ruinous if produce prices fell. In 1786 Daniel White, owner of one of Brookline's largest farms and the town tax collector, fell behind in his accounts and saw the town seize some of his lands. When his uncle, Capt. Benjamin White, Harvard graduate and member of the Governor's Council, died four years later, his heavily mortgaged estate was declared insolvent.[20] By the 1790s the changes that had begun during the

Revolution continued transforming Brookline into a different community from what it had been in 1770.

By 1821 Brookline's 48 farms were growing 11,433 bushels of grain (94 percent of it maize), compared to 4,763 in 1771. The average farmer in 1771 had produced only 91 bushels; fifty years later his successor averaged 213. Cider production increased from 751 to 1,041 barrels, and more hay was grown too.[21] Brookline farmers produced more by bringing greater amounts of land under the plow, the number of cultivated acres more than doubling between 1771 and 1821, as trees gave way to fields across Massachusetts.[22] Hired labor made this change possible. In 1820 the census showed 215 men engaged in agriculture—more than twice the entire adult male population of Brookline in 1770. Since the number of farms remained constant, at about fifty, most of these men must have been farm laborers, with nearly four per farm. Meanwhile, the number of men without property increased from 44 in 1770 to 102 in 1812 and 177 in 1826, by which time they represented fully two-thirds of the adult male population. Most of these men were young and unmarried and spent only a few seasons in Brookline before departing.[23]

Brookline farmers were now well attuned to the marketplace, and after 1820 they radically altered their practices to maximize profits. In 1770 farm families had limited their risks by supplementing grain production with a wide variety of crops that could be consumed as well as sold at the market in Boston. As early as 1817, however, it was being noted that with Brookline's good soils, "Indian corn and other grains might be cultivated to advantage. But from the vicinity of the town to Boston market it is mostly improved for the cultivation of esculent vegetables which cannot conveniently be transported from a much greater distance."[24] Given the large amount of grain still grown in 1821, this likely exaggerated the importance of vegetable cultivation. Still, by 1840 grain output had fallen to 4,385 bushels, while the agricultural workforce increased from 215 in 1820 to 325. Vegetables now accounted for three-fifths of the value of the town's agricultural output. Some farmers concentrated on producing milk, with the number of cattle more than doubling between 1821 and 1840.[25]

Market gardening (truck farming) demanded skills and dedication beyond those of traditional New England agriculture. Closely managing a wage labor force and buying large amounts of fertilizer were only the beginning. Farmers had to master specialized techniques like the "Boston hotbox"—long, low planks supporting glass sheets to cover the growing plants, heated on cool nights by fermenting manure—which gave farmers an edge by artificially extending the growing season. Market gardeners had to time production carefully to meet both the competition from other growers and the demands of the Boston market, with little margin for error. Moreover, the potential profitability of intensive agriculture boosted land values, which further increased pressures to abandon less remunerative traditional practices.[26]

Brookline farmers appear to have entered this new world of market-oriented agriculture willingly. Although the opening of the Erie Canal in 1825 and the development of the rail network in the 1830s exposed all Massachusetts farmers to competition from western grain, the market for New England corn (maize) did not precipitously decline. Corn prices in Massachusetts fluctuated considerably but moved only gradually downward in the 1820s and 1830s; even by 1840 the price was only 13 percent below what it had been in 1821. In nearby Concord, corn production also declined in the 1820s and 1830s, although to a much lesser extent than in Brookline, before rising to an all-time high in 1855. There was nothing to stop Brookline farmers from continuing to plant fields of corn or other grains. The shift away from grain production in Brookline to more lucrative vegetables, hay, and milk seems a conscious effort to maximize profits, even if it involved greater effort and risk.[27]

One sure sign of the growing importance of market-oriented agriculture was an increased interest in transportation, particularly the condition of town roads. Brookline had long tolerated poorly maintained local roads, but the commercialization of agriculture increased dissatisfaction with the condition of town ways. In 1832 the town formed a committee to investigate their state and suggest improvements. Four farmers and a merchant were named to the body (although the merchant did not sign the final report). The time had come, the committee concluded, for the town to pay "a more vigorous attention to" better roads. Full participation in the market economy demanded access:

> We believe that money judiciously applied in making good roads and keeping them in good repair would be very amply repaid at any expence it would cost, more especially in this Town, as the Farmer here requires so much more use of them than those remote from the City—Here we have daily intercourse with the City, the receipt of the produce of our farms to be carried to the market is in many cases as much greater than that from the farms at a distance as one hundred to one, and the weight of the manure necessary to be transported over the roads

> for our farming operations is still more, and added to those whose necessary constant intercourse with the city with light carriages are considerations to show the great advantage that would accrue to us as an agricultural community to keep our roads in good repair at all times.

For those still unconvinced, the committee added, "Should any of the Inhabitants be desirous of selling their estates, what can they add to allure the attention of purchasers better than" superior roads?[28]

To no one's surprise the committee found town roads "not near as good as they ought to be," the result of the inadequacies of the ancient district system of highway surveyors responsible for their maintenance. It had long been the custom that each district maintained its own roads, with most men working off their "road tax" with their own labor. The committee recommended that the town require the road tax to be paid in cash only, under the control of commissioners who would hire labor to get the job done. The town meeting rejected this change but did adopt the committee's recommendation that the prevailing rate of crediting a ten-hour day for $1.50 in tax liability be reduced to $1.00, bringing it in line with the market wage and thus reducing the incentive to work out one's tax in lieu of payment.[29]

Owners of farm land who were not inclined to engage in intensive market agriculture could sell their property and leave altogether. A ready market had developed for prime Brookline acreage, both from other farmers and seekers of country estates. One by one, the scions of Brookline's old colonial elite families—the Whites, Gardners, and Winchesters—departed. By 1837, not one Gardner or Winchester remained, and the Whites were greatly reduced. Brookline-born Whites became plantation owners in Georgia and Mississippi; a Gardner turned up as a newspaper editor in Newark, New Jersey; and at least one Winchester removed to Ontario, Canada. This in turn opened the way for new farmers from outside the community. But since Brookline land was expensive and the other capital required for truck gardening was steep, only a few succeeded. Some outsiders married daughters of Brookline farmers: Timothy Corey of Weston in 1767; David Coolidge of Watertown in 1814; and Moses Jones of Watertown, New Hampshire, in 1822, took this route. Others, like Charles Stearns of Waltham (who arrived around 1804) and George Babcock (who first appeared around 1830), leased land for several years before accumulating enough money to buy farms of their own.[30]

Country Seats and Cultivating Gentlemen

Brookline's association with wealthy outsiders had begun as early as the 1660s when John Hull (1624–83), Boston merchant, goldsmith, master of the mint, land speculator, and treasurer of the Massachusetts Bay Colony, first acquired land in the eastern part of Muddy River. By the time of his death in 1683 he had assembled a three-hundred-acre farm there. The Hull farm passed to his son-in-law, the famous diarist Judge Samuel Sewall (1652–1730) of Boston. Neither Hull nor Sewall ever lived on the farm, and the first dwelling on the parcel was not constructed until 1703, when the judge's son, Samuel, Jr. (1678–1751), took up residence there while retaining a Boston mansion. Although a part-time resident, Samuel Sewall, Jr., was immediately acknowledged as one of the new town's leading citizens, serving as selectman, town clerk, treasurer, and moderator. His lands and offices eventually passed to his son, Henry Sewall (1720–71).[31]

By the middle of the eighteenth century, well-heeled Bostonians were acquiring the same taste for pastoral living as their counterparts in London.[32] Carriages made it possible for the wealthy to savor the pleasures of both town and country. Many towns within a few hours' drive of Boston became the seats of one or more gentlemen's estates, where the fortunate could stroll through formal gardens while admiring the vistas.[33] In 1740 Nathaniel Gardner, a Boston merchant, retired from trade and erected Brookline's first true mansion. Although he had made his fortune in Boston, Gardner was born and raised in Brookline. The grandson of Thomas Gardner, the progenitor of Brookline's prominent Gardner family, Nathaniel built his house on Gardner land near the center of town. A year or two later his first cousin Dr. Zabdiel Boylston (1679–1766), the famous Boston physician and another Brookline native, put up a second mansion near Gardner's, also on land inherited from his Gardner grandfather. Boylston became Brookline's first gentlemen farmer, taking particular pride in breeding fine horses.[34]

When Nathaniel Gardner died unmarried around 1745, none of his twenty-two heirs were prepared to take over the property. Maintaining a country estate was beyond the means of even the most prosperous Brookline farmer. The mansion was therefore sold to an eminent Boston lawyer, Jeremiah Gridley (1702–67). Militia colonel, grandmaster of the American Masons, and frequent government counsel, Gridley trained a generation of Boston attorneys, including John Adams and James Otis. Just before his death Gridley was appointed attorney general of Massachusetts. Although continuing his career in Boston, Gridley spent increasing time at his Brookline estate. His high social standing was acknowledged by the townspeople, who repeatedly chose him to represent them in the legislature, preside over town meetings, and sit on the Board of Selectmen.[35]

After Boylston died in 1766, his house and lands were bought by Boston dry-goods merchant William Hyslop (1714–96), a native of Scotland. As with Gridley, the town recognized his high social status by asking him to serve on several committees and chose him to preside at a town meeting. Soon after Jeremiah Gridley's death in 1767 his estate passed to Henry Hulton (1732–91), who had the misfortune to arrive from England bearing an appointment as king's commissioner of customs for the port of Boston just as the Stamp Act made royal officials especially unpopular. He was understandably anxious to put some distance between himself and the mobs of Boston. Hulton improved Gridley's estate in the latest English fashion, including the construction of one of New England's first greenhouses. Unlike Gridley and Hyslop, however, Hulton never held office in Brookline, and at the onset of the Revolution he and his family permanently returned to England.[36]

The Gardner-Gridley-Hulton and Boylston-Hyslop estates became the nucleus around which upper-class Brookline coalesced. Wartime opportunities and the departure of many wealthy Boston and Cambridge Loyalists brought an influx of ambitious men from the secondary port cities of Essex County into Boston. The most successful sought country estates in the rural towns surrounding Boston. Wealthy merchants, retired sea captains, and Federalist politicians found Brookline's picturesque landscape and proximity to the city a powerful draw. By 1798 six prominent Bostonians already held 12 percent of Brookline's acreage, accounting for 17 percent of the value of all real estate.[37]

Fashion decreed that aspiring gentlemen should have both country estates and urban townhouses, so most of these proto-suburbanites retained their Boston addresses and occupied their estates only from April to October. Freed of fixed schedules—business often took but a few hours each day—gentlemen and merchants could well afford the expense in time and money demanded of those with urban interests who sought to live in the country. Federalist U.S. senator George Cabot did attempt to occupy his Brookline estate throughout the year, but long periods of snowbound isolation cooled his initial enthusiasm for country living.

Ten country winters proved enough for the socially active senator, who sold his Brookline property and returned to Boston permanently in 1803.[38]

During the first decades of the nineteenth century, upper-class Bostonians established three nearly contiguous zones of affluence in central Brookline (fig. 1.1). The first was clustered around the old meetinghouse where Gridley and Hyslop had lived. The second took shape a half mile to the south. When Senator Cabot returned to Boston, his ninety-acre estate was subdivided and conveyed to a coterie of the city's elite, including Stephen Higginson, Jr.; Thomas Coffin Amory, Jr.; and Thomas Handasyd Perkins. The Cabot estate formed a splendid setting to erect fine houses (fig. 1.2). Nowhere else was there said to be "rock scenery in the town so picturesque as this, with the wild mosses and ferns growing from the crevices, and crowned with the woods . . . covered with luxuriant vines." Adding to its attractiveness was proximity to the Jamaica Plain section of Roxbury, already a well-established haunt of Boston's aristocracy.[39]

A third fashionable neighborhood appeared a half mile west of the town center. Here Boston merchant king Thomas Handasyd Perkins; his partner, Stephen Higginson, Sr.; and Federalist U.S. senator Jonathan Mason all purchased large tracts. Perkins, who had been raised in Boston, first experienced country living in 1797 when his family sought refuge from a yellow-fever epidemic in Roxbury. Two years later he bought a sixty-one-acre property in Brookline and built an impressive mansion. This "very model of a gentleman's country estate," with its "extensive gardens" and "elaborate greenhouses and exotic plants," became a major attraction. Its visitors included President James Monroe, the Marquis de Lafayette, and John James Audubon.[40]

During the nineteenth century these three neighborhoods expanded into one contiguous band of wealth and high social status. From Walnut Street on the edge of Brookline Village to Heath Street and Chestnut Hill, this district—a realm of trees, rolling lawns, multi-acre lots, narrow winding lanes, and elegant mansions that belied the nearby city—formed the core of upper-class Brookline well into the late twentieth century.[41] Aside from membership in the local church, most of the wealthy estate owners had little contact with other Brookline residents. Their social circle included few local farmers or tradesmen. The primary business and social interests of these aristocrats lay in Boston, the site of their winter homes. As in other nearby towns, some of the estate owners ran their lands as model farms, championing expensive agricultural improvements that set them

FIGURE 1.2. Green Hill, the old Gardner Estate, Warren Street, April 2016. Built by sea captain Nathaniel Ingersoll in 1806 on part of the old estate of Senator George Cabot, this Warren Street mansion belonged to Boston's Gardners for more than a century. Isabella Stewart Gardner lived here for many years. It remains one of Brookline's best-known houses, one of the few to retain an imposing lot.

even more apart from the typical Brookline farmer.[42] Their sons and daughters did not take marital partners from the townspeople of Brookline, even from scions of the old elite clans, such as the Whites, Gardners, and Winchesters, that had long dominated the political and social life of the town. Unlike their prerevolutionary predecessors, they avoided serving in town offices.[43]

The estates themselves, however, greatly affected Brookline's future course of development. In 1826 fourteen wealthy Bostonians alone held title to nearly one-fifth of the total value of the town's real estate.[44] The three nearly contiguous neighborhoods of estates (along with a fourth that developed after 1820 in the eastern part of the town) established a reputation for elegance and refinement that put the stamp of fashion on the entire community. By 1828 a gazetteer was calling attention to Brookline's "beautiful country seats . . . which add much to its beauty and respectability."[45]

The Rise of Brookline Village

Although the owners of the great estates cast long shadows, it was the stream of incoming artisans, tradesmen, farmers, and farm workers who led the town into the new market-oriented society of the nineteenth century. Only a handful of craftsmen or shopkeepers lived in Brookline before 1775, but by the time war returned in 1812, their numbers had gradually grown to include a stone mason, two carpenters, a saddler, a tailor, a hatter, two shoemakers, a carriage maker, a blacksmith, a wheelwright, two tanners, two grocery storekeepers, and a tavern keeper. By 1820, 42 men (16 percent of the total male workforce) worked outside of agriculture; by 1840, there were 107 (25 percent of workers).[46]

The vigorous expansion of Boston's economy after 1790 spurred economic growth in surrounding towns as well. After stagnating for nearly half a century, the population of the town of Boston—it would not become an incorporated city until 1822—nearly doubled between 1790 and 1810. Thousands of new jobs were created as ships bound to and from ports the world over crowded the wharfs. For the first time bridges linked the peninsula-bound capital to the mainland, providing the incentive to construct improved highways. Toll roads fanned out of Boston to Salem, Providence, Newburyport, and Worcester. In 1804 a canal had been opened—only the second in New England—from Charlestown to the Merrimack River. By 1825 Boston was the center of a vast network of roads and waterways reaching far into the hinterland of New England. Stages departed daily on dozens of routes bound for points as distant as New York City. Even more important were the great volume of farm products flowing into the city and the return stream of manufactured goods.[47]

The construction of the Worcester Turnpike through Brookline from 1806 to 1807 was a visible sign of the new economic order. All existing town ways followed the natural contours of the land, their builders having preferred gentler grades over more direct but steeper routes. At considerable expense the new turnpike triumphed over topographical barriers, slicing through hills to produce a road both straight and yet reasonably sloped. But unlike previous public roads open for all to travel, this privatized way could only be used by those who paid the toll. Boston capital built the turnpike for the benefit of the city and towns to the west along the road's path, not for the sake of Brookline. This became the first of many such ventures that would increasingly incur resentment from a large portion of the town's inhabitants.[48]

For some, however, the increased flow of traffic spelled opportunity. All along the perimeter of Boston, from Charlestown to Dorchester, economic activity quickened after the Revolution as new enterprises appeared to supply products for Boston customers. Leather, soap, bricks, rope, ice, glass, and meat formed the cornerstone of what historian Henry C. Binford has called the gatekeeping, or fringe, economy of Boston's suburbs. In Brookline, tanneries were established in the 1790s to take advantage of a favorable site near the Brighton cattle market, which supplied raw materials. The tanneries in turn fed saddlers and makers of boots and shoes. Wagons, sleighs, cabinets, and yarn came out of Brookline shops. For several years in the 1830s a shipyard operated on the Charles River, producing ten vessels, including a 337-ton bark.[49]

Nothing better illustrated the new market economy than the rise of Brookline Village. As was the case in most rural New England towns, prerevolutionary Brookline showed no concentrations of population, even at the nominal town center, the meetinghouse. Elsewhere in New England, villages began to take shape around meetinghouses in the 1790s, but this was not the case in Brookline. Well into the nineteenth century the church and the adjacent brick schoolhouse had few neighbors.[50] A mile to the east, however, a new town center was emerging. Early in the eighteenth century, John Ellis built the Punch Bowl Tavern down at the point where the roads from Cambridge, Watertown, and Sherborn converged before crossing into Roxbury and onto Boston. Originally a conventional two-story, hip-roofed structure, the tavern evolved into a remarkable aggregation of ramshackle buildings, each bought cheaply in Boston and grafted on to the existing units. The tavern is said to have thrived, serving weary drivers of heavy wagons hauling produce into Boston. For a time it was a popular rendezvous, attracting patrons even from the city.[51]

By the time the old tavern was torn down in 1833, it was surrounded by a well-established village. Artisans and shopkeepers appear to have begun locating here as early as the 1780s. The opening of the turnpike in 1807 (which began a short distance down the Sherborn Road) and the road to the newly constructed Milldam at Sewall's Point (now Brookline Avenue) in 1821, along with droves of livestock going to and from the Brighton stockyards, ensured a steady stream of potential customers for the village's tradesmen. By the early 1840s some forty houses, workshops, and stores lined lower Washington Street, with several other houses nearby. Still more buildings lay across the town line in Roxbury.[52]

As elsewhere in southern New England, this commercial village increasingly took on the role of a town center.[53] Here, in 1788 Brookline's first fire company was organized. When the Baptists organized Brookline's second church in 1828, they located it in the village, as did the Congregationalists in 1844. The first Brookline post office opened here in the 1820s, and it was from the village that stagecoaches departed for Boston. In 1844 Brookline annexed the portion of the village that lay across the line in Roxbury, further accenting its importance as the town's hub. The following year, the village became the civic as well as commercial center when the new town hall was sited there. Only twenty years earlier Brookline had built its first town hall, adjacent to the meetinghouse. When population growth and rising expectations rendered this obsolete, a town committee recommended locating its replacement in the town's new commercial center, and the town meeting had little difficulty agreeing to this.[54]

While few of the men who worked in the shops and stores along Washington Street had been born in Brookline, some nevertheless rose to prominence within the community. In 1790 John Robinson, twenty-seven years old, left his native Dorchester—where his family had resided for more than a century—to start a tannery in Brookline. With his partner and brother-in-law, Enos Withington, Robinson bought land on Washington Street a mile up the road from the Punch Bowl Tavern. The tannery flourished, and Robinson's standing in his new hometown rose. In 1797 he was named one of the town's two church deacons, just as fellow Dorchesterite John Pierce took the pulpit. Eight years later Robinson was elected selectman, the first of the twenty-eight terms he would serve in that office. Subsequently he served as moderator at every town meeting between 1819 and 1838 and was elected state representative every year save two between 1819 and 1833.[55] Although Robinson's success was exceptional, other tradesmen also became prominent members of the community, displacing the farmers who had heretofore governed. A year after his first election to the Board of Selectmen in 1806, Robinson was joined on the five-man board by a newcomer to town, stagecoach operator Eliphalet Spurr. In 1810 the board was reduced from five members to three, with businessmen Robinson and Spurr now a majority. By 1817 the board comprised a tanner, a carpenter, and a storekeeper. Farmers did not return to the board until 1825 and would never again constitute a majority.[56]

Enlightenment

Aside from local government, early Brookline had few social institutions. Until 1810 the town had but one church, the local outpost of the state-sponsored Congregational Standing Order, ministered since 1797 by the reverend John Pierce (1773–1849). The First Parish, as the church is now known, had gained membership under Pierce's tenure and boasted a new meetinghouse erected in 1805. Until 1833, when church and state were separated in Massachusetts, the First Parish was supported by local taxpayers. In the 1820s the Standing Order split into two competing movements, which formed rival evangelical Congregational and liberal Unitarian denominations. Pierce held his parish together; keeping his theology vague and palatable, he slid the church into the Unitarian camp so gracefully that it is not possible to date the transition with any precision.[57]

Pierce helped keep his church prosperous by taking pains to minister to the fashionable sort who were building their mansions around his church, especially the women (Pierce reported that women made up 65 percent of his communicants in 1797 and 76 percent by 1837).[58] Genteel Bostonians of both sexes found his liberal theology reassuring and his refined manners comforting. He was a frequent guest at Thomas Handasyd Perkins's estate, and the colonel would take his pastor into Boston to show off his newest mansion or out to Nahant for some rest by the sea. When the town built Pierce a new meetinghouse in 1806, the estate owners dug into their ample pockets: Stephen Higginson donated an expensive English bell, John Lucas contributed four hundred dollars toward construction and purchased "an Elegant clock," and Thomas Walley presented the church with "an Elegant New Bible."[59]

Although John Pierce appealed to wealthy, urban merchants and prosperous local farmers, only a few village tradesmen or farm laborers bothered to attend his services. Some resented his open veneration of his more fashionable parishioners. In 1810, according to Pierce, "a plain and illiterate farmer" named Elijah Corey publicly broke with the church, accusing the minister of favoring "the gentry" over men like himself. Corey invited Pierce and other local worthies to his house and then, according to Pierce, there came "a most disgraceful scene in his criminating all, with whom he contended, and passionately justifying his own extraordinary conduct. I rejoiced, that such an opportunity was afforded to let our principal people discern the true character of the man. . . . He betrayed a temper and conduct allied to the malice and revenge of infernal spirits."[60]

Corey was not the first to break with Brookline's Standing Order church, but he became the earliest to establish a rival congregation. Corey began holding prayer meetings in his home, which led to further withdrawals from the town church. An informal Baptist church was organized, with its membership drawn almost exclusively from Corey's relatives and neighbors. Itinerant preachers (one of the favorites being Thomas Paul from the African Baptist Church in Boston) led services conducted in private homes. By 1818 the irregular church had eighteen communicants, and Corey's "ambition [was] gratified by being made deacon."[61]

But by the time the Baptists built their own church building in Brookline Village in 1828, Pierce's opinion of them had changed radically. He now reasoned that while the new church might deprive his own parish of "a large portion of the domesticks, hired men & tenants," still "it may thus be the means of exerting a salutary influence upon many, who would be wholly out of the reach" of his own church. Even more important, it might keep revivalist preachers from inflaming "some of the more illiterate" of his parish. The Baptists, who had patched up their differences with him, now seemed moderate. The threat of a feverishly evangelical Congregational church being established in Brookline made Pierce realize "that I liked the Baptists better than the exclusive sect of Congregationalists." By 1837 he could proclaim, "How uniform, how undisturbed, how intimate the union between the . . . Baptist Society here and our own! . . . We have pleasantly walked together, where we could agree; and where we could not see, eye to eye, we have agreed to differ."[62]

When Brookline's evangelical Congregationalists finally established their own church in 1844, not far from the Baptist church in the village, it turned out to be a respectable, moderate, middle-class body not unlike the Baptists.[63] By this time, however, churches had lost the unique place they once had held. Before the Revolution the church was virtually the only organization most rural towns knew, aside from town government. Now, as in nearly every Massachusetts community, Brookline's citizens were gathering into numerous cultural, religious, fraternal, educational, and political organizations.[64]

For the earliest, the volunteer fire company organized in 1788 at the Punch Bowl Tavern, the town government agreed in 1795 to cover half of its expenses. Fires were rare, fortunately, since the company was more a congenial social club than an effective defense against conflagrations. The company met at the tavern, where elaborate annual banquets became a tradition. Village artisans and tradesmen, along with some nearby farmers, made up the bulk of the membership.[65] A private academy, the Brookline Classical School, was chartered in 1823 with the help of Reverend Pierce, who had once taught school himself. Throughout the fifteen years the school existed, an average of thirty to forty male students each year received instruction beyond the rudiments provided by the public schools. A number of women operated private schools for girls. Pierce also assisted in the establishment of a private nonprofit lending library.[66]

In 1832 newcomer Isaac Thayer brought the Lyceum movement to Brookline, the first major secular cultural activity in the town. The Lyceum provided a forum for lectures and debates that livened many a winter's night for the townspeople: "Quiet farmers who scarcely read anything before but the Bible and the almanac were roused into new mental life." Topics ranged from philosophy to phrenology, providing as much entertainment as intellectual stimulation. In 1841 the Brookline chapter of the movement incorporated and raised a Lyceum building on part of the site of the old Punch Bowl Tavern, complete with meeting rooms for still more organizations. By this time speakers of national repute, such as Ralph Waldo Emerson, were appearing to further disseminate the emerging market-oriented American popular culture.[67]

A similar urge for self-improvement produced the Brookline Temperance Society. Established under the watchful eye of John Pierce in 1831, this attempt to curtail inebriation was succeeded in 1842 by a local chapter of the more militant Washington Total Abstinence Society. Some 171 individuals were said to have taken the pledge at the organization's first meeting, and the Brookline Washingtonians soon claimed nearly 600 members.[68] Less successful was Quaker Samuel Philbrick's attempt to establish a local chapter of an abolition society in 1837. Despite aid from such luminaries as the Grimké sisters, John Greenleaf Whittier, and Wendell Phillips, he failed to attract more than a few members. Pierce was not amused when Philbrick disrupted services by allowing a black girl to sit with his family instead of using the "nigger pew" in the back of the church, as required for all persons of color. The abolitionists were denied the use of town hall for a meeting ostensibly because of the threat of mob violence. Reform had its limits.[69]

The changes that were transforming Brookline in the first five decades of the nineteenth century—the commercialization of agriculture, urbanization, and the development of a thoroughly market-driven economy—were experienced throughout much of the republic.[70] Only the proximity of a great and growing city set Brookline apart from hundreds of other developing rural communities throughout the northeastern United States. After 1840, with the arrival of newcomers and new transportation technologies accelerating the pace of change, it would become increasingly obvious that Brookline had crossed a threshold that would henceforth distinguish it from most other American communities. Brookline was becoming suburban.

CHAPTER 2

Commuters and Immigrants

✦

The increase of business having made inroads upon private dwellings, together with the influx of foreign population, have induced many to remove to remote parts of the city, or to neighboring towns.

—*Boston Directory,* 1849

The rapid increase of this school during the winter term, by the addition of a considerable number of large boys, mostly foreigners, and often ignorant of even the first rudiments of education, has for some years operated as a serious drawback upon the progress of the whole school.

—Brookline School Committee, *Annual Report,* 1849

DURING THE 1840s Brookline's population nearly doubled, and the change this represented was even more qualitative than it was quantitative. In this decade two groups of newcomers—commuters and immigrants—transformed Brookline from a prosperous agricultural town (including a rural village) into a different sort of community. The appearance of both groups was a consequence of the enormous transformative power of nascent industrial capitalism, reshaping the landscape and redefining the law in its own image. Despite sporadic resistance, the traditional economy of rural America was in retreat, with wage and salaried labor displacing independent artisan households, while farmers were increasingly at the mercy of distant markets and financial institutions. Railroads linked together the entire American North, and throughout southern New England factories flourished in cities, old rural towns, and new industrial villages.[1]

This robust economic expansion was reflected in the population growth of eastern Massachusetts. Between 1840 and 1860 Boston's population increased from 93,383 to 177,840, while that of its inner suburbs climbed from 40,400 to 126,722. The hub city of New England thrived as a port and briefly was the nation's rail center with direct connections to all New England industrial cities. Although the great New England textile factories were located elsewhere, Boston was not without its own industries. Shipping, financing, wholesaling, and manufacturing meant jobs and opportunity. The prospect of high urban wages or commercial employment lured thousands into the city each year from rural Massachusetts, Maine, and New Hampshire. More came to Boston from abroad. Recovery from the depression of 1837 was in full swing by 1843, and Boston, along with the nation, enjoyed an unprecedented boom until halted by another downturn in 1857.[2]

Among the most important consequences of this urban expansion was the growth of a prosperous middle class. In 1840 Boston had some four thousand families whose male head worked in white-collar jobs in stores or offices, accounting for nearly 30 percent of all households. Most of the men and women in these households came from small New England towns, often having been raised on farms and sharing a common Protestant culture.[3] In rural New England, where the household had been the basic unit of production, all family members, save the youngest, participated in the raising of livestock and produce as well as chores such as cooking, cleaning, and maintaining the property. Tasks were allocated by age and sex, to be sure, and the legal status of women and children made them subordinate to adult males, but all worked together, eating and sleeping under the same roof. Urban middle-class households were different. Men, women, and children now moved in distinct spheres, with men working away from home, children spending significant amounts of time in school or at play, and women charged with the sole responsibility for managing the household and yard.[4]

On the whole the urban middle class welcomed the move from country to city. Few would have willingly exchanged their carpeted floors, whale oil lamps, papered walls, looking glasses, paintings, stoves for cooking and heat, libraries, musical instruments, and rooms full of comfortable and stylish furniture for the crudely furnished farmhouses, bare floors, unpainted walls, drafty open fireplaces, candles, unheated sleeping lofts, and modest chests, chairs, and tables that many of them had left behind. Of course, older rural houses could—and eventually would—be upgraded, but this was hard to do without the higher incomes obtainable in cities.[5] Women in particular appreciated the denser networks of friendship and cultural and religious opportunities available in the city, as well as the pleasures of urban shopping.[6]

Despite its obvious advantages, urban life also posed risks. Americans worried about the physical and moral dangers of living in cities such as disease, crime, noise, pollution, crowded streets, and cheap amusements. Thomas Jefferson was not the only one who regarded cities "as pestilential to the morals, the health, and the liberties of man." Even the most ardent champions of urban living recognized that something had been lost in leaving the farm and village behind.[7] Rural life may have been harsh, but it provided a disciplined, moral environment in which to raise Christian children. As the years passed the farms and small villages that many urbanites had left took on a nostalgic glow, the artificiality of the crowded city contrasting with the remembered wholesome pleasures of childhood amid snug firesides, trees, farms, rolling hills, and pastures.[8] Would their own children, they wondered, be able to say the same someday about their urban upbringing?

Commuters

As the urban middle class in Boston expanded, the search for appropriate housing was becoming more difficult. Most middle-class families seem to have embraced the ideal in which the masculine sphere of the workplace should be separated from the feminine sphere of the household, which required them to raise their children in neighborhoods free from commercial activity. In England and around New York City residential suburbs had begun to appear in which men traveled each day to jobs in the city while their wives and children remained behind in nearby small towns.[9]

Boston's commercial district was expanding into residential neighborhoods, reducing the amount of housing at the very time when the city was attracting record numbers of migrants.[10] Now forced to live further from their places of employment, middle-class men faced longer journeys to work. Since most early commuters relied on their feet to take them to and from work, few wanted to live very far from their daily destinations. Only those with ample time and stamina or the means to keep a private carriage could consider moving to the rural towns beyond the crowded streets of central Boston. Even walking was not always free, since bridges leaving Boston charged tolls for pedestrians as late as 1858.

Long-distance commuting was largely the prerogative of the rich, though most of Boston's wealthy preferred to live on fashionable streets close to the center of town, except during summers.[11]

But before long-distance commuting could become practical, middle-class Bostonians would need both improved means of affordable transportation and new places to raise their families. As late as 1825, however, no city anywhere in the world had a system of mass passenger transportation, and the communities surrounding Boston had limited housing available. The market economy soon supplied both. Boston took the first steps toward establishing mass transportation in the mid-1820s when local promoters introduced regular stage service between Boston and some its inner suburbs, with coaches running every other hour. In 1834 other entrepreneurs brought to Boston the first major mass-transit innovation, the omnibus. Initially introduced in France, the omnibus was an enlarged stagecoach drawn by a pair of horses capable of hauling a dozen or more passengers at a time. Lengthwise bench seats and access through a rear door facilitated quick entrances and exits. Omnibuses operated on fixed routes and made numerous stops, at fares lower than those charged by the stages. By 1840 passengers could ride omnibus lines out of Boston to all adjacent towns.[12]

Although an improvement over the service provided by stage coaches, the lumbering omnibuses were slow and subject to delay as they wound their way through narrow city streets and out to unevenly maintained suburban highways. A logical alternative was the network of rail lines that fanned out of Boston. When Boston's first three railroads were built to Lowell, Worcester, and Providence in the early 1830s, little thought was given to local freight and even less to short-distance passenger service. Railroad promoters assumed nearly all of their revenue would come from persons and goods traveling the lengths of the lines. Fares as high as 3½ to 5 cents a mile—at a time when many workers were lucky to earn a dollar a day—and inconvenient schedules discouraged regular use until the 1840s. The railroads then bowed to popular pressures, lowering fares and agreeing to sell season tickets at a further discount. Train schedules were revamped to provide more convenient service in and out of Boston.[13]

Stimulated by fares reduced "to approximately the price of an omnibus ride *within* the city of Boston," long-distance commuting gained in popularity. Previously practical only for the wealthy, living in a home located miles from work was now possible for moderately successful businessmen, professionals, and even some of the better paid clerical workers. Thousands took advantage of the opportunity to leave the city. By 1848 one-fifth of Boston's businessmen were said to be living in the suburbs of Cambridge, Charlestown, Roxbury, and beyond. Three years later a traffic count showed nearly thirty thousand persons arriving in Boston by rail each day (including long-distance and through travelers). Suburban land developers and house builders responded to market demand by erecting houses clustered around nearly every one of the railroad stations that were spaced each mile or so along lines out of the city, as far as ten miles from Boston.[14]

Even after more than half a century of steady growth, Brookline in 1840 remained rural. With a population of less than 1,400, agriculture still employed three-quarters of the male workforce. The lack of convenient access to the city and the shortage of appropriate housing had long discouraged middle-class Boston families from moving there. The only public transportation was two daily round trip omnibuses operating between Brighton and Boston via Brookline, and house lots or finished large houses seldom went up for sale. Ten years later the population had climbed to 2,516, and a decade later stood at 5,164.[15] By 1850 at least 111 individuals with business addresses in Boston commuted from their Brookline homes. Commuters were at the head of at least 79 households, while another 15 households had one or more members who commuted.[16] Albeit small in absolute numbers, this represented a significant proportion of the town. Commuters formed 14 percent of the male labor force, but commuter-headed households accounted for 19 percent of all Brookline households. Moreover, households headed by commuters were larger than average, so that the 633 persons who lived in them constituted a quarter of the town's population.

In the 1840s and 1850s market forces had responded to consumer demand, overcoming the barriers hitherto imposed by lack of transportation and shortages of housing. Omnibus service provided by private operators increased from two to seven daily round trips to Boston between 1839 and 1845, and three years later there were ten. In 1848 the fare had fallen from 25 cents in 1839 to 18¾ cents a ride or eight tickets for a dollar.[17] Brookline's first railroad, the Boston & Worcester, cut across the northern part of the town just south of the Charles River. The first locomotive-powered train to operate in New England passed through the town on its way to Newton in 1834, and the line was completed to Worcester the following year. The railroad introduced Boston-to-Newton commuter service in 1843 as "an inducement to many whose daily avocations connect them with the city, to establish their residences" in the latter town. But no Boston & Worcester trains stopped in Brookline. A station at Cottage Farm, in the isolated northern part of the town, far from busy Brookline Village, was not opened until after 1845.[18]

In 1847 a group of Brookline residents urged the Boston & Worcester to construct a branch line to serve Brookline Village. The railroad surveyed a route from the village along the Muddy River to Sewall's Point (today's Kenmore Square), where it joined the main line. The proposed route was only a mile and a half in length and crossed no public roads. "There is, at present, a large amount of travel to the village in private carriages and omnibuses," the railroad management told its stockholders, "and this will doubtless increase rapidly, with the growth of population, and the increase of traveling facilities." The Brookline branch opened on April 10, 1848, with seven daily round trip trains scheduled to and from Boston.[19] The railroad's optimistic expectations were realized, the Brookline Village line being one of the few branches of the Boston & Worcester to show an operating profit in the 1850s. An additional station was added on the branch at Longwood three-quarters of a mile from the village. By 1858 the railroad sold tickets for 259,000 rides between Boston and Brookline via the branch, while another 6,700 used Cottage Farm station. In 1867, 423,000 passengers were carried over the Brookline branch, and another 25,000 boarded or departed at Cottage Farm.[20]

Brookline obtained another rail line in 1852 when the Charles River Branch Railroad extended the Brookline branch westward from its village terminus through central Brookline to Newton and Needham. In 1863 the line reached Woonsocket, Rhode Island. The Boston & Worcester continued to provide local service to the village between Brookline Village and Boston, while the Charles River Railroad served more distant points, using trackage rights over the Boston & Worcester to reach Boston. Freight accounted for most of the traffic over the Charles River Railroad, most notably the gravel trains that operated around the clock between a pit in Needham and the Back Bay between 1858 and 1863. Two stations were built along the line west of the village depot, the first at Cypress Street and the second at Brighton Street (now Chestnut Hill Avenue).[21]

The increasing popularity of commuting in the 1850s led to yet another mass-transit innovation, the street railway. Streetcars operated in the public ways like the omnibus but with an important advantage. Rails enabled the same twin-horse team that hauled an omnibus to pull a considerably larger vehicle, capable of carrying sixty or more riders at a time. Tracks offered less resistance than primitive pavements and superior guidance and stability for large vehicles. Streetcars had appeared in New York in the 1830s, but the Boston region's first street railroad, from Harvard Square, Cambridge, to downtown Boston, did not begin operating until 1853. A sharp increase in steam railroad fares in the mid-1850s helped popularize the cheaper street cars. By 1860 street railway companies were operating more than fifty-seven miles of routes in Boston and its nearby suburbs and carrying 14 million passengers a year.[22] In 1859 the Metropolitan Railway extended its Roxbury horse car line to Brookline Village. Although the street railway offered more frequent service than did the steam railroad—cars left for Boston every half hour during the day—the ride was long and slow, the cars frequently crowded, and the fare relatively high. When the line first opened, the cost of a ride from Brookline Village to Roxbury Crossing was five cents, seven cents to Roxbury Center, and ten cents for a trip to downtown Boston. Most Brookline commuters to Boston took the train.[23]

As late as 1840 only a few houses were available for sale in Brookline at any given time, but with rising demand from middle-class Bostonians and the promise of improved transportation, a new industry now appeared to provide the housing would-be suburbanites wanted. The real-estate development business arose with surprising speed in the 1840s. Even in the first quarter of the nineteenth century only a handful of Bostonians had made their livings selling or developing real estate. Most land transactions took place among relatives or close acquaintances without brokers, and there were few professionals available to subdivide larger properties and market lots to builders and future homeowners. All this began to change after 1830 as the number of Boston-based real-estate agents and brokers, auctioneers, and surveyors sharply increased, and interest in Brookline properties grew.[24]

The land development process got underway in 1843 with the laying out of Brookline's first subdivision, Linden Place, on high lands overlooking Brookline Village, by Boston jeweler and future mayor Thomas Aspinwall Davis (1798–1845). Using ancestral farm lands, partly inherited, Davis hired a fashionable surveyor to lay out the town's earliest curvilinear street and divide the property into lots, then commissioned an auctioneer to market and sell them off to prospective owners and speculative builders. For a pioneering venture the whole process was remarkably sophisticated and quite successful.[25] Beginning in 1843 several commuter subdivisions—none of them as tastefully developed as Linden Place—were laid out off Harvard Street, which itself was lined with new homes. Land developers created new building lots for builders, speculators or future occupants, who would then hire their own builders. With the opening of the branch railroad in

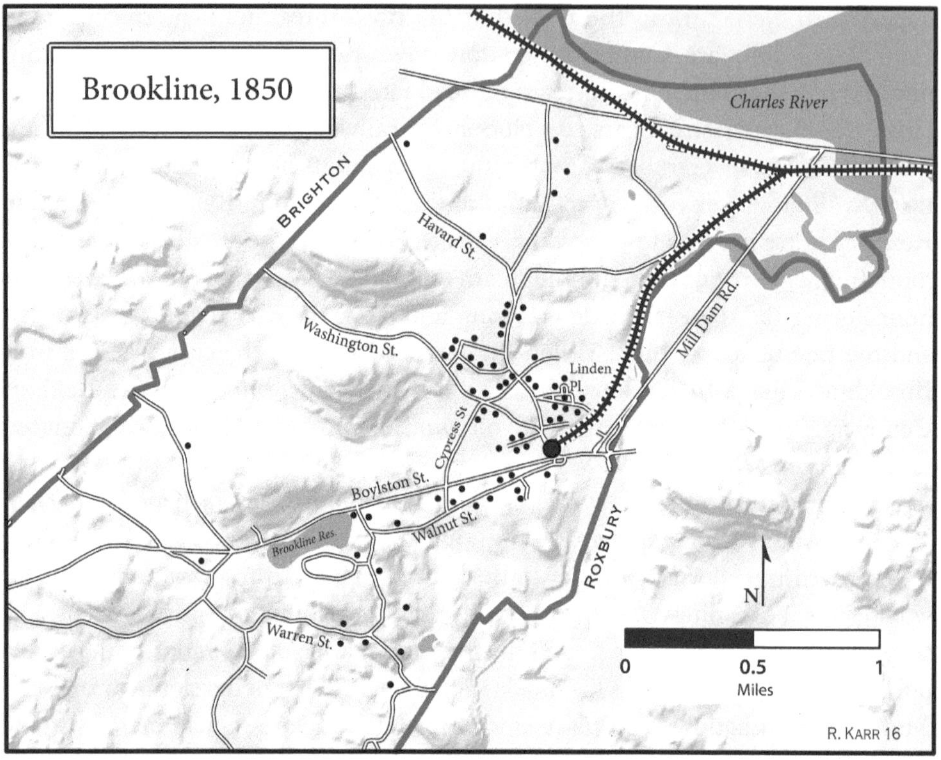

FIGURE 2.1. Map of Brookline, 1850, showing households with commuting heads.

1848, these houses were within convenient walking distance of the depot, making them attractive to middle-class commuters (fig. 2.1).

Yankees to the core, almost three-quarters of the pioneer commuters who headed households in 1850 had been born in Massachusetts, and nearly all of the rest came from New Hampshire or Maine.[26] Their ages ranged from twenty-one to sixty-five, with half between thirty and forty-four years old. Commerce provided the means for suburban living. No fewer than thirty-nine of the seventy-nine household heads described themselves as some type of merchant on the census. The next two most frequent occupations were seven lawyers and five brokers. Altogether, three out of four commuting household heads were merchants, lawyers, brokers, manufacturers, or corporate officers. Most of the rest were shopkeepers, clerks, or government officials.

A handful of wealthy Boston merchants had been living in Brookline for more than half a century, but most of the new commuters lacked the fortunes enjoyed by their predecessors. Using an 1851 town tax list it is possible to determine the assessed real and personal property of all but eight commuting household heads of 1850. The median assessment was $9,000; 68 percent had less than $15,000. Their incomes may have been high, but lacking independent means, the new commuters had to pay close attention to their Boston businesses in order to support their new lifestyles. Regular, even daily commuting was required. Unlike the truly wealthy, they had to content themselves with a home on a lot rather than a country estate, much less the luxury of a maintaining a second home in the city.

Nevertheless, a few commuters were in fact rich men. Among the commuting household heads in 1850 were such grandees as James Amory, William H. Gardiner, John Lowell Gardner, Ignatius Sargent, and William Fletcher Weld, who ranked near the top of Boston's mercantile elite. Although they maintained Boston offices, the wealthy could escape the rigors of daily rail commuting and the walk or ride between the depot and work. Whenever they left their Brookline estates for the city, their coachmen drove them to their counting-house doors. Once business was concluded, they were free to linger in their Boston townhouses for as long as they chose. Such opulence, however, was beyond the reach of most early Brookline commuters.[27]

From the surviving evidence it is difficult to be sure what motivated the first commuters to leave the city and submit themselves to the regime of the extended daily commute. In later times, when suburban living had become routine, young upper-middle-class families might desert the city almost as a matter of course, but in the 1840s suburbanites still formed a small minority of Boston businessmen and professionals.[28] The commuters themselves doubtless would have had difficulty sorting out all the factors behind such an important decision. The prospect of a home in a semi-rural neighborhood, far from the crowded streets of Boston, certainly lured some parents seeking to raise children sheltered from the disagreeable sphere of commerce. Although bearing fewer children than their mothers' or grandmothers' generations, the wives of Brookline commuters had not abandoned motherhood. All but 3 of the 79 households included children of various ages of the male head, with an average of 3.1 children per household; 42 percent contained 4 or more children.[29]

To be sure, in the 1840s some parts of Boston were becoming less attractive to middle-class families. Although still relatively compact, Boston's business district was expanding westward, spilling over into once-fashionable venues like Pearl

Street. The rapid increase of poor Irish Catholic immigrants, particularly after the famine of 1845, expanded their soon overcrowded neighborhoods. To what extent did urban change affect the decision to leave the city? Half of Brookline's commuting household heads of 1850 can be traced back to Boston addresses in 1840. Many do seem to have lived in neighborhoods that were changing in the 1840s. Central Boston was increasingly home only to the rich and the poor, as the middle classes relocated to the South End, South Boston, or the suburbs.[30]

Nearly all Brookline commuters worked in offices or shops in Boston's congested central business district. Many if not most presumably walked from their new homes to the depot in Brookline Village to ride the Brookline branch railroad into downtown. The Boston & Worcester Railroad's Boston terminal was more than half a mile from the business district, which meant a second walk as long as the entire commute many of them had made from their old houses in 1840. More than two-thirds of the commuters lived within a half-mile radius of Brookline Village station (fig. 2.1). The median assessed wealth of the majority of commuters living within a half mile of the railroad station in Brookline Village was $8,000; for those living further away, $34,000. Away from the village, well-heeled commuters could still rusticate on country estates.[31]

If not rich, most pioneer commuters lived comfortably in their new homes. Nearly every commuting household had live-in servants to assist in its management. The average commuter household included eight persons, about 30 percent more members than in the typical Brookline household.[32] Although commuters had slightly more children living in their homes than did those who worked in town, live-in domestics accounted for most of the difference in size.[33] The first commuters seemed to like what they found in Brookline. Two decades later, 40 percent of the 1850 male commuting heads of households still lived there and another 5 percent left a widow remaining in town.[34] A number of the earliest commuters eventually came to play prominent roles in their new community. Six became selectmen. Others served as deacons or prominent lay members of the Unitarian, Baptist, Congregational, and Episcopal churches; library trustees; state representatives; or trustees of the Brookline Savings Bank.[35]

Exiles

Although the pioneer commuters of the 1840s differed in some respects from other town residents, they nevertheless shared a common culture. As late as 1844 nearly every inhabitant of Brookline was descended from prerevolutionary Yankee stock and was at least nominally Protestant. Six years later in 1850, more than six hundred natives of Ireland, nearly all of them Roman Catholic, lived in Brookline, forming 24 percent of the population.[36] For many years Boston had been receiving small numbers of immigrants from the Emerald Isle, but the famine that followed the destruction of the potato crop in 1845 turned a stream into a torrent. Hundreds of thousands of desperate peasants and farm laborers and their families joined a massive diaspora that scattered Irish men and women across the English-speaking world. Boston became a major destination because packet ships provided direct service between there and Liverpool, the primary embarkation point for Irish refugees. With their limited funds exhausted by the passage to America and lacking lucrative skills, many Irish had no choice but to try to make a living close to where they landed.[37]

The handful of Irish immigrants who had found their way to Brookline sporadically since colonial days had not remained long. The first significant group of Irish arrived in town in 1845, but large-scale immigration did not begin until 1847. Jobs brought the Irish to Brookline. Two large construction projects in 1847 and 1848, the Brookline branch railroad and the reservoir and associated water lines constructed by the city of Boston, required hundreds of strong backs willing to work for low wages. More than three-quarters of Brookline's Irish-born men in 1850 listed their occupation as laborer, working the fields of truck farms, building new subdivision roads, digging foundations for new houses and stores, shoveling snow and ice, and performing any other available chores. Much of the demand for day labor was seasonal, and the poorest Irish families faced a grim struggle for survival. Young Irish women could find employment as domestic servants in the households of commuters as well as with other prosperous families.[38]

Most of Brookline's 608 Irish-born residents in 1850 lived in households with a non-Irish head, usually as servants or farmhands who lived with their employers. Eighty-nine households in 1850 were headed by a native of Ireland (22 percent of all Brookline households), and those formed a sharp contrast with the seventy-nine households headed by male commuters. Irish households were much smaller, partly because they contained fewer children and mostly because two-thirds of Irish homes did not include boarders or live-in servants. Irish-born household heads were younger than their commuting counterparts, and 67 percent of them worked as day laborers. Not a single Irish household head in 1850 held a white-collar job. Only 8 percent of the Irish heads owned real estate (none worth more than $2,500), compared to 75 percent of the commuting heads.[39]

Whether from prejudice, poverty, or by the desire to hive together, Irish households were mostly confined to a few crowded streets in Brookline Village. (The primary exception was families of servants who lived on or near the estates that employed them.) The sudden explosion in the town's Irish population in the late 1840s led to overcrowding as contractors and landlords rushed to build and convert existing structures in the village into tenements. Brookline's first Irish neighborhood, the Marsh, took shape on poorly drained lands cut off from the rest of Brookline by the tracks of the new branch railroad that took the commuters to their jobs in the city.

The almost simultaneous arrival in the 1840s of Yankee middle-class commuters and poverty-stricken Catholic Irish produced the most rapid change the town had known since its initial settlement. By 1850, 41 percent of Brookline's population lived in households headed either by a commuter or a person born in Ireland.[40] Growth continued into the 1850s, with the population doubling again by the time of Abraham Lincoln's election and not slowing significantly until the outbreak of war in 1861, which temporarily delayed further suburban development.

The Suburban Prospect

The arrival of these newcomers in the 1840s certainly altered Brookline but by no means had the town become a modern suburb. Fifty years later a majority of the town's inhabitants would come to share a common vision of what the town had become and what it should be, a distinctive, attractive, well-governed community poised between country and city, combining the best traits of each. But in 1850 no such consensus existed. The dominant Yankee Protestant majority, including both the newly arrived commuters and the more established residents, itself held differing expectations, while the Irish Catholic immigrants struggled to carve out their own role in the community while maintaining their own culture.

At the onset of commuting, Brookline's institutions and services, both public and private, were still those of a prosperous rural town. Led by the commuters, however, some town residents came to demand that these be raised to urban standards. By the 1830s educational reformers in Massachusetts and elsewhere such as Horace Mann were calling for a new system of local schools that would produce the disciplined, literate, and mathematically knowledgeable workforce citizens and consumers needed in a capitalist society. At first, however, most rural towns, even wealthy places like Brookline, resisted the call to reform. As late as 1839, the school committee (with John Pierce as a member) was unable to suggest any improvements to the town's schools: "The general course which has been pursued the past year," it concluded, "is well suited to the wants of this Town." Two years later a committee was appointed to consider a establishing a high school, but nothing seems to have come of it.[41] In 1840, as it had for many years, Brookline's educational system comprised four district schools, with male teachers usually supervising the winter sessions attended by older children, while female teachers presided over the summer schools that catered to the younger. Students seeking education beyond the elementary level had to go elsewhere. Nearly 250 children attended the four schools, which were overcrowded and not in the best of repair. Irregular attendance and frequent teacher turnover added to the difficulties.[42]

In 1842 six citizens petitioned the town for the creation of a public high school, contending that "the provisions hitherto made for the education of the youth of this town, is inadequate to the wants and necessities of the rising generation." The newcomers—none of the six had been born in Brookline—were all prosperous members of the commercial and professional classes (by occupation there were two merchants, a trader, an auctioneer, a physician, and a commercial farmer).[43] This time the school committee concurred. "There seems to be an increased interest among us in relation to the cause of education," the committee noted in its next annual report. Parents were now asking "what can be done and what ought to be done in order to give their children such mental training as will fit them for respectability and usefulness in future life. They perceive that in respect to knowledge, demands are made in every department of business of those who are now coming upon the stage of active life, which were not made in former times, and, without a thorough education, the rising generation will not be able to meet their demands." The school committee was committed to reform: "The public schools in this town ought not be inferior to those of any other town in the Commonwealth, and we ought not to be satisfied without evidence that we are every year elevating their character and improving their condition."[44]

To implement this ambitious goal, the school committee in 1843—the year of the first commuter subdivision—launched a broad reform program of the sort advocated by the leading educational theorists of the day. First, male teachers were replaced by women in all district schools, which in turn were restricted to children under ten years old. This saved money, since female teachers were paid much less than their male counterparts.[45] Second, a central school for older children was established under the direction of a single male teacher. The following year, the committee warned the town that reform had just begun: "New plans must be adopted, to meet the wants of society in its onward march. There is no one of us who supposes that the . . . common school education . . . of our childhood, will meet the demands of our children. . . . As society progresses in literature and general knowledge, nothing is more evident than that changes must be effected in the system of common school instruction."[46]

In 1846 the school committee set entrance requirements for the central school, which was now being widely referred to as the high school, and at the same time established two new intermediate schools for pupils over ten years old who were not yet ready for the central school. In just three years Brookline's public education system had been transformed from a loosely administered conglomeration of four semi-independent rural district schools to an increasingly centralized system of three primary schools, two intermediate schools, and one high school. In 1847, at one of his final public speeches, John Pierce boasted that "Brookline, the last year, raised the largest proportional sum for scholars between four and sixteen years of age, of any of the 309 towns in this Commonwealth."[47] Enthusiastic support for (supposedly) high-quality public education had now become the first footing of a truly suburban ethic.

In 1848 Boston opened its first municipal water supply, bringing water from the Cochituate Reservoir in Framingham to the city via an aqueduct across Brookline, including the construction of a reservoir near Boylston Street.[48] The fact that none of this water was for the use of the town vexed many commuters, who were well aware that other urban improvements such as gas, streetlights, sewerage, sidewalks, and paved streets were likewise denied to town residents. Commuters who daily encountered these conveniences while in the city saw no reason why they should be denied them at home. Increasingly, commuters proved willing to support expansion of municipal services, even if this meant higher taxes and fees. Surprisingly, their non-commuting neighbors came to agree, and in time this attitude would prevail.

PART 2

INVENTING SUBURBIA 1850–1885

✧

During the second half of the nineteenth century Brookline completed its transformation from a rural village into a fully realized middle- and upper-class suburb of Boston. Although elements of its rural past continued, residents and outsiders alike now regarded it as a community distinctive from both the countryside beyond and the city proper. Several traits set it apart: a systemized process of land development, which converted raw farmland into suburban house lots; a highly stratified class system characterized by pockets of great wealth, upper-middle-class commuters, and working-class tenement-dwellers, sharply divided by religion and ethnicity, and segregated from each other; and the evolution of a suburban consciousness distinct from both city and rural areas.

Nothing like this had previously existed in the United States, and indeed, nothing quite like it exists today. Thanks to zoning and an aesthetic steeped in the preservation of rustic views, modern elite suburbs rarely expand at all (at least in well-established metropolitan areas), and when they do, they invariably exclude poor minority groups altogether. During this period Brookline's population more than tripled, and yet this rapid growth spawned remarkably little controversy. To be sure, Brookline rejected annexation by Boston, but this was not primarily intended to halt growth in hopes of preserving the town's rural ambiance. The affluent dominated Brookline politically and economically, although periodically they were forced to recognize and accommodate the poor Irish Catholics in their community.

By 1885 Brookline had developed a popular suburban ethic that stressed the maintenance of a strong local government capable of providing a high level of municipal services, together with the expectation of amenities from the private sector, so that its citizens (at least those who could afford them) would lack nothing that residents of the finest Boston neighborhoods enjoyed. On the other hand, there was as yet no consensus, even within the privileged classes, over what constituted the appropriate level and form of development in the town and whether what survived of the town's rural ambiance was worth preserving—or even capable of being saved.

CHAPTER 3

The Great Divide

✦

God Almightie in his most holy and wise providence hath soe disposed of the Condicion of mankinde, as in all times some must be rich some poore, some highe and eminent in power and dignitie; others meane and in subieccion.

—John Winthrop, "A Modell of Christian Charity," 1630

Brookline, unlike any other town in America, has, substantially, no middle class. We have the opulent class who occupy the country houses, on the one hand, and on the other, the laboring class and editors.

—*Brookline Chronicle,* January 4, 1879

NINETEENTH-CENTURY SUBURBS like Brookline were as much renowned for the wealth of their inhabitants as for their scenic beauty. "A large part this delightful town," a gazetteer in 1874 informed readers curious about Brookline, was said to be "covered with elegant mansions, with ample grounds and gardens, walks, and avenues, decorated with ornamental trees, shrubbery, and flowers, and occupied by gentlemen engaged in professional or mercantile business in" Boston.[1] Although some parts of Brookline matched this description, the reality was that few of its inhabitants were fortunate enough to own great estates. Still, hundreds of the town's families could be found in handsome, if not palatial, houses, living in considerable comfort. At the same time, however, a nearly equal number of suburban residents subsisted in squalor, barely able to make ends meet. Midcentury Brookline was a deeply divided community. Prosperous servant-employing Protestant Yankee households, headed by men who worked at business or professional jobs, formed a stark contrast to the poverty-haunted Irish Catholics, most of whom worked as laborers and domestics. Initially thrown together by the workings of national and international markets, the relations between these groups largely defined the social dimension of the railroad suburb.

"To Be Rich Would Be My Delight"

When Harvard student Amos Adams Lawrence pondered his future in the fall of 1834, he envisioned himself "a merchant, not a plodding, narrow-minded one pent up in a city, with my mind always in my counting-room, but (if such a thing were possible) I would be at the same time a literary man in some measure and a farmer." Having given some thought as to how the seemingly disparate careers of commerce and agriculture might be combined, he proposed living "in the country a few miles from town (excepting when devoted to business, which would be forenoons), and there I would read and work on my farm." Even for a Harvard man, the prospects of achieving this vision might have seemed remote were it not for the fact that Lawrence belonged to one of Boston's premier families, charter members of what would later be called the Boston Associates, those interconnected clans that owned much of the region's industrial and commercial wealth. Lawrence, Massachusetts, would soon bear the family name in honor of Amos's father and uncle. "My advantages for becoming rich," he noted bluntly, "are great: if I have mercantile tact enough to carry on the immense though safe machine which my father and uncle have put into operation, it will turn out gold to me as fast as I could wish: and to be rich would be my delight."[2]

Mercantile tact the young man possessed in abundance, and truly delightful sums soon accumulated in his coffers. Marrying well—his father-in-law, William Appleton, was another Boston Associate—and maximizing family connections, Lawrence's business ventures rarely faltered. Commission merchant, corporate director, mill owner, and land developer, he rapidly rose within the highest circles of Boston's mercantile elite. His involvement in philanthropic causes and both state and national politics made him a well-known public figure (he even ran unsuccessfully for governor of Massachusetts and helped found the Constitutional Union Party, which sought a compromise over slavery that might preserve the union short of war). In Kansas grateful antislavery settlers acknowledged his financial and political support of their venture by naming their primary settlement in his honor.[3]

Amos Lawrence with his wife, Sarah, and their growing family lived in Boston until 1851, when they joined the suburban trek to Brookline. At the beginning of the nineteenth century the northernmost part of Brookline, which lay closest to Boston, was cut off from that city by the vast waters and mud flats of the Back Bay. The land there, three hundred acres in all, had been held for more than a century by the Sewall family. In 1815 financial reverses forced Edward K. Wolcott, Hannah Sewall Wolcott's alcoholic husband, to sell the property. The buyer, one Uriah Cotting, was the primary promoter behind a scheme to dam the Back Bay and harness tidal power. Along the top of the dam a toll road would run connecting Brookline directly with Boston for the first time, obviating the long, roundabout route to the city through Roxbury and over the Boston Neck. Cotting reasoned that with the completion of the road, land in northern Brookline would become extremely valuable, and he anticipated a large profit from his Brookline acquisition. Unfortunately, Cotting died in 1819 before the dam could be completed. Three of his associates, Ebenezer Francis, David Sears, and Israel Thorndike, bought the Sewall tract from his estate and divided it among themselves.[4]

When the project opened in 1821, however, it disappointed its sponsors. The tidal power capture never worked properly, the toll on the road discouraged mass travel, and enough developable land was available closer to Boston to satisfy real-estate demand. The anticipated Brookline real-estate boom never materialized. Two of the owners, Sears and Francis, did eventually build mansions on their properties. When Amos A. Lawrence and his brother, William, learned in 1850 that Ebenezer Francis's lands were on the market, they seized the opportunity to buy his eighty-two-acre estate, Cottage Farm, for the princely sum of $94,000 (subject to a $79,000 mortgage). As if to show they had not entirely lost their heads on such an extravagant purchase, the brothers prudently laid out streets and subdivided the property into numerous yet large lots, which they leisurely sold over the next few decades, generally to relatives, friends, and retainers.[5]

If not quite the working farm Lawrence had once envisioned occupying, Cottage Farm was certainly "in the country a few miles from town." In place of Francis's modest wooden cottage, Lawrence commissioned architect George M. Dexter to design a splendid mansion, "a beautiful English house of Roxbury pudding-stone, with large open fireplaces and a great hall, really unique in its time. In front was an open lawn, behind a large grove of oaks." Amos and Sarah Lawrence moved their family of then four children into their new home in the fall of 1851, and over the years it served as their primary, if hardly their only residence (they acquired a summer home at Nahant and another "farm" in Chestnut

Hill). In the early years at Cottage Farm the Lawrences kept "cows, hens, horses, puppies, etc.," in addition to their large household, Amos riding into Boston every work day in his "large English coach with C springs, a great brocaded coachman's box, massive lamps heavily mounted with silver, and with platform and straps at the back for the footman." Not long after the Lawrences' arrival, the Boston & Worcester Railroad conveniently opened a station at Cottage Farm, providing them with still another route to the city.[6]

In the summer of 1870 Cottage Farm was still surrounded by seventeen acres of Lawrence's own land, with most of the adjacent lots as yet unbuilt. The Lawrence household included Amos, now fifty-five years old; his wife, Sarah, forty-nine; and their daughters Susan, seventeen; Hettie, fourteen; and Hannah, eleven (four older children having left home) as well as several live-in domestic servants. Twenty-nine-year-old Dutch-born William Barker, the Lawrence coachman, lived on the estate with his twenty-six-year-old Nova Scotian wife, Ann. Completing the household were three unmarried female servants, all from the maritime provinces: Catherine Mackenzie, thirty-five, from Nova Scotia; Elizabeth Caldwell, twenty-five, of New Brunswick; and Mary McLeod, thirty, of Cape Breton. That summer Lawrence told the census-takers that he estimated both his personal and real estates to be each worth half a million dollars.[7]

The Lawrences continued to live at Cottage Farm until Amos's death in 1886 and Sarah's five years later. Of their two sons, Amory continued his father's business ventures in a casual manner and enjoying the life befitting a gentlemen of leisure, while William, a clergyman, became the long-serving Episcopal bishop of Massachusetts. Both kept their primary residences in Boston, although they owned many other properties. Their five sisters married into the Amory, Brooks, Loring, Cunningham, and Hemenway families, all well-established Boston clans with ample means of their own. The Lawrence farm in Chestnut Hill eventually became the campus of Boston College, while the original Cottage Farm estate was subdivided into prime residential lots. Today, though set on a small lot and turned on its axis, Cottage Farm remains an impressive house; in 1994 Boston University paid one million dollars for the building, which now houses that university's president.[8]

Across the Tracks

If John O'Hare was aware of Cottage Farm, he surely gave it little thought as he awoke each day in search of work. In 1870 O'Hare lived with his family little more than a mile from Cottage Farm on Pearl Place. Instead of the bucolic view that Amos Lawrence enjoyed from his bedroom window, O'Hare could see nothing more than closely packed wooden houses from his. Pearl Place, a short, dead-end, unpaved street, consisted of a dozen or more wooden buildings in which lived nearly fifty households, every one of them of Irish descent. Pearl Place was part of Brookline's poorest neighborhoods, with nearly four of every five men working as laborers and virtually all the rest at blue-collar jobs.[9]

Like most of his neighbors, John O'Hare was a laborer. Born in Ireland around 1815, most likely on a farm, he crossed the Atlantic probably sometime in the 1840s. On March 3, 1851, he wed Mary Lavery at a Catholic church in Boston. At the time both were living in Roxbury. Mary had also been born in Ireland, around 1826, which made her a decade younger than her husband. At the time of his wedding John listed his occupation as a teamster, but for the remainder of his life he would be listed as a laborer. By 1855 John and Mary had moved to Brookline, for that year their first child, Patrick, was born there. A daughter, Mary, followed in 1861. These would be their only recorded offspring. In the spring of 1870 the O'Hare household on Pearl Place consisted of John, then around fifty-six years old; Mary, perhaps forty-five; Patrick, now fifteen; and Mary, eight. Patrick was listed by the census as still attending school, although undoubtedly he worked for wages whenever he could. The household differed from most of its neighbors, however, in that it included John O'Hare's eighty-seven-year-old mother-in-law, Catherine Lavery. But in other respects the O'Hare family resembled the other households on Pearl Place, most notably in lacking real estate or personal assets. Their apartment was rented, and they owned little beyond their clothing and meager furniture.[10]

The spheres of privileged Yankee Protestants and destitute Irish Catholics were not entirely separate. Although Amos Lawrence did not employ live-in Irish-born servants in 1870, most of his neighbors did, and even he must have employed Irish day laborers and domestics from time to time. Lawrence made no effort to isolate his children from the Irish who attended the public schools with them, and he apparently did nothing to discourage the friendship his son William struck up with the son of an Irish day laborer in the 1850s. The paths of

Amos Lawrence and John O'Hare may have even crossed briefly in 1877, when Lawrence donated one hundred boxes of strawberries to the laborers working on the town's new sewer system.[11]

For working men like O'Hare, retirement was not an option. He died of heart disease while still living in Brookline in 1884, at age seventy, his body doubtless worn out from a lifetime of grueling physical labor. His wife had preceded him to the grave two years earlier, aged only sixty. Of their two children, Patrick would marry in 1886, by then already past thirty. At the time he was still living in Brookline, working as a teamster. The 1900 census found him and his wife living childless on Pond Street; by that time he worked as a night watchman. Of his sister, Mary, no record could be found after 1870.[12]

The Entrepreneur

In 1860 Francis ("Frank") Adams White and his wife, Caroline, lived in a mansion set on a well-manicured five-acre estate on the far fringe of Brookline Village, surrounded by the sprawling estates of wealthy Bostonians. Yet it would be a mistake to assume that White was a gentleman of leisure to be found yachting off Nahant or that his spouse presided over a fashionable salon. On the contrary: he worked long hours at a trade that required considerable physical skill as well as business acumen. Francis White was a fortunate beneficiary of what historian E. J. Hobsbawm has termed "the sudden, vast, and apparently boundless expansion of the world capitalist economy," which coincided with Brookline's suburbanization after 1845.[13] He was born at the right time, in 1824, and at the right place, in rural Boylston, Massachusetts, the youngest child of an ambitious farmer and storekeeper who had married a minister's daughter. White's father was a native of Roxbury, grandson of Brookline selectman Moses White, and thus an offspring of the town's most distinguished family (Francis Adams White was fourth cousin once removed to President John Quincy Adams and double third cousin to Linden Place developer and Boston mayor Thomas Aspinwall Davis). All of Francis White's six older brothers had become merchants, manufacturers, or professionals, and one of his two sisters had married a Congregational minister.[14]

After a public and private school education, at age seventeen White went to work in his older brother's tannery back in Roxbury. Tanning leather demanded strenuous physical labor throughout the slow, painstaking process of converting raw animal skins into finished sides suitable for shoes, boots, saddles, and harnesses. White mastered the business, and when his brother, then aged forty-five, retired from active involvement in the business ten years later in 1851, Frank took over the operation. Financial assistance from this brother (who continued as a silent partner), and probably from others, enabled him to acquire the business, which he merged with a larger competitor, Frederic Guild, to form Guild, White & Company. The two young men became effective partners and close friends.[15]

Over the next two decades Guild ran the company's store and office in downtown Boston while White supervised the Roxbury tanning yard. Shoes, boots, and other leather products formed a rapidly growing segment of Massachusetts's booming industrial economy, and Guild, White & Company competed in global markets. The tanning operation was located along the tracks of the Boston & Providence Railroad, which provided ready access both to the national rail network and to a convenient stream that offered ample water for use in tanning leather as well as for no-cost disposal of hazardous chemical wastes (thus externalizing this expense). In the yard White directed seventy employees in the laborious process of washing and removing hair from rawhides, rinsing, soaking in tanning vats of bark and water, and cutting. This could be exhausting work—even with the use of steam-powered machinery and nineteen horses—and there is every evidence Frank White was a hands-on manager. His wife reported a time when he returned home "with a large bruise on his head" made "by an iron bar in the hands of one of his workmen—accidentally."[16] He made frequent rail trips to New York, presumably to acquire raw materials—imported South American cowhides (which were sometimes preferred over the local skins available from the Brighton and Cambridge stockyards), hemlock or other tanning bark, sulfuric acid (two of his brothers ran a New Jersey chemical plant), dyes, and other items.[17]

The business amply rewarded Frank and his partners. In 1860 the firm reported sales of $300,000, which made it the fifth largest manufacturer in Roxbury, more than double what its two predecessor tanning firms had grossed in 1850. Subtracting reported wage and raw material expenses left $87,400, a sum seemingly more than adequate to cover taxes, loans, and other expenses and still leave the partners with a tidy profit. The workers, despite their long hours of toil, were not so fortunate: annual wages only averaged $343, down 25 percent since 1850, despite strong gains in labor productivity.[18]

In 1858 Frank and Caroline White and their two-year-old son left their rented house in Roxbury for a rambling, romantic-style Brookline mansion, which featured a distinctive Mansard-roofed tower. It had been built in the 1840s for a nephew of merchant prince Thomas Handasyd Perkins.[19] "*It is a beautiful place,*" the new co-owner confided to her diary, "with about five acres of land—and will, I doubt not—make a *very beautiful home* for us—but the price—almost frightens me—eighteen thousand one hundred and eighty dollars—then there are repairs to make and finishing." This was indeed an enormous sum at a time when the costs of construction did not yet include plumbing, electricity, central heat, or other improvements, and workers were lucky to make ten dollars a week. (More than a century later, the median price of a new American home was still less than what White paid; in 2016, Zillow.com valued the house, 222 Warren Street—on a lot reduced by half—at more than $6 million.)[20] Moreover, the Whites paid cash.[21] That a thirty-two-year-old tanner could come up with such a sum suggests the enormous profits the nineteenth-century American economy could generate for successful capitalists.[22]

Their estate, which they named Cliffside, was located at the corner of Warren and Cottage Streets, in one of Brookline's most fashionable neighborhoods (Senator Cabot's old mansion is across the street). Landscaper Andrew Jackson Downing singled out this part of Brookline as being "a kind of landscape garden" of which there "is nothing in America, of the sort, so inexpressibly charming as the lanes which lead from one cottage, or villa, to another. . . . The open gates, with tempting vistas and glimpses under the pendant boughs, give it quite an Arcadian air of rural freedom and enjoyment. These lanes are clothed with a profusion of trees and wild shrubbery, often almost to the carriage tracks."[23] To assist in running their household in the early 1860s, the Whites typically kept two domestic servants, young Irish or English girls, as well as a young Irish male who worked as a driver, farm laborer, and general handyman. With no public transportation available, Cliffside's location more than a mile from the rail depot in the center of Brookline Village would have been most inconvenient had the Whites not owned several horses, carriages, and wagons.[24]

Frank and Caroline White would live at Cliffside until their deaths in the twentieth century, raising four children, and typically sharing the house with frequent visitors from their extensive network of kin and friends. Frank's business continued to prosper: the 1860 federal census shows him owning $8,000 of personal property; by 1870 this had jumped to $100,000. During all this time White continued to work hard, reporting an impressive income of over $15,000 in 1866, which enabled him to retire from the rapidly changing leather business in 1871 at age forty-seven.[25] Their four children became comfortably upper middle class, if not socially prominent: a mechanical engineer, a Boston lawyer, the treasurer of a manufacturing company, and the wife of one of the nation's leading landscape architects. Two of their sons attended Harvard, while the third graduated from the Worcester Polytechnic Institute.[26]

The Facilitator

No matter how capable, capitalists could not function without the aid of skilled professionals who provided services, both personal and for their businesses, and were paid salaries or received fees rather than shared in profits. A lawyer, physician, civil engineer, architect, college professor, or clergyman could enjoy a comfortable living, though fortunes rarely could be amassed quickly, and men customarily worked until death or well into old age. The career of Brookline lawyer Theophilus P. Chandler was not atypical. He was born in 1806 in the remote town of New Gloucester, district of Maine, twenty-two miles inland from Portland and a dozen south of Lewiston. His paternal grandfather had left his native Duxbury, Massachusetts, as a young man, arriving in Maine by oxcart with his new wife in 1764, and went on to clear the land, raise a large family, keep a tavern, be elected state representative, and send a son to college in distant Rhode Island. Theophilus's father, Peleg Chandler, a graduate of Rhode Island College (now Brown University), married the daughter of the man who had commanded the town's soldiers in the Revolution, farmed, studied the law, and sent a son to Bowdoin College. New Gloucester was one of those rural hives of enterprise historian David Jaffee calls "cosmopolitan communities": notwithstanding its size and location, this Maine town of 1,600 in 1824 boasted five stores, five taverns, a social library, a Masonic lodge, three lawyers, three physicians, a cabinet-maker, a brass founder, two tailors, and two chair makers. The town had sent eleven students off to college and produced one major general, three brigadier generals, and three colonels.[27]

By 1827, however, New Gloucester was too small to contain the mounting ambitions of Peleg Chandler, and that year he relocated his entire household to Bangor, Maine, where his younger son, Theophilus, began the study of law with his father instead of attending college like his brother. Once his studies were completed, Theophilus joined his father—now a judge—in practicing law in Bangor, although at some point in the 1830s the young lawyer found himself engaged in business with a rising Delaware clan named Du Pont. While in Delaware he wooed and won the orphaned daughter of a once-prominent Philadelphia merchant who had lost both his fortune and life while still young. Elizabeth Schlatter, taken in by the Du Ponts after her parents' deaths, became Chandler's wife in 1837. She was twenty-eight years old, two years his junior. Shortly before their marriage he left Bangor for Boston, quickly becoming an increasingly prominent member of the Suffolk Bar (along with his two brothers). His legal and networking skills helped him to become the president of the Northern Railroad of New York in 1849.[28]

In the spring of 1848, at the very time that the Boston & Worcester Railroad was opening its Brookline branch, Theophilus and Elizabeth Chandler moved to the town. Prior to this the Chandlers had been living at 4 Chestnut Street on Beacon Hill in Boston, a substantial brick townhouse on a fashionable street of relatively new brick townhouses, mostly built after the War of 1812. Why they left Boston can only be guessed. Perhaps they found their townhouse cramped, with five children and a couple of servants; perhaps he missed the fields of New Gloucester; perhaps they felt the city an inappropriate place to raise children. Whatever they gained in moving to Brookline, it came at the expense of convenience—the Boston & Worcester's downtown railroad station was located farther from Theophilus's office on Court Street than his house on Chestnut Street.[29]

In Brookline the Chandlers bought two adjacent lots on Washington Street in a new subdivision, Harvard Place. Included was a four-year-old substantial wooden house. Combining the two parcels gave the Chandlers a single lot 240 feet wide and 200 feet deep, a little over an acre. They had close neighbors: to the east was the new Brookline Evangelical Congregational Church; to the west, a two-story wooden colonial-style house built in 1765. Their new home had cost the Chandler's $8,000. Theophilus Chandler's legal and business income was high, but he lacked a fortune. The subdivision's developer, Samuel Craft, gave Chandler a five-year, $8,000 mortgage with no money down. The terms were not the usual, interest-only, with a balloon payment at the end; in addition to 6 percent interest paid annually, Chandler was required to pay $1,000 after one year, and another $1,000 after the second, with the remaining $6,000 due in five years (Chandler took the entire five years to pay off the loan).[30]

In 1850 the Chandlers, now forty-three and forty-one, were living on Washington Street with their six children; Theophilus's sister, Anna Ropes, born in Maine, age forty-one, with her children, Edward, thirteen, and Alicia, eight; and three presumably domestic servants: Chloe Ochelee, fifty, a Virginian-born black woman, and Catherine and Bridget Byrnes, sixteen and twenty, the former born in Massachusetts, the latter in Ireland. On the census form that year Theophilus estimated the value of his real-estate holdings at $10,000, suggesting that he owned little real property beyond his home. Three years later the Chandlers bought the old house next door for another $7,425, this time without a mortgage, and removed it to a lot around the corner, apparently to provide themselves with a larger lot. The sale left the Chandlers with a parcel twice as large as before, with nearly five hundred feet of frontage on Washington Street and more than two acres of land. They eventually dug a pond on part of their new property, built a large stable, and laid out winding paths across what had become a mini-estate.[31]

Over the following decades the Chandlers continued to prosper, sending their four sons to Harvard. Like the Whites, the Chandlers lived into their eighties: Theophilus died in 1886, Elizabeth in 1892. As with so many Boston bourgeois households, their eldest, Charles, only twenty-four years old, was killed in Virginia in 1864 while serving as a lieutenant colonel in the Union Army. Two of their remaining sons became Boston lawyers, and the third a prominent Philadelphia architect. In 1860 Chandler's former law partner, John A. Andrew, was elected governor of Massachusetts as a Republican, which positioned him to help Chandler obtain the post of U.S. assistant treasurer for Boston in 1863. All this time Chandler maintained a Boston business address, which meant daily commuting from his Brookline residence, either by walking the half mile to the Brookline depot, taking the train to Boston, and then walking (or taking the horsecars) another three-quarters of a mile to his law office on Devonshire Street or at the Custom House, or riding to work in his own carriage.[32]

Although Theophilus and Sarah Chandler enjoyed a style of life similar to Francis and Caroline White's, there were significant differences. The Whites' five-acre estate was surrounded by the spacious grounds of some of Brookline's most picturesque properties; the Chandlers still-substantial house was on a smaller lot located on busy Washington Street in Brookline Village. Francis White had bought his way into suburbia at a young age, paying cash (as he typically did); Theophilus Chandler came a decade older, buying on credit a lower-priced place. Finally, as a successful capitalist White was able to retire from business activities while still in his forties, spending the remainder of his life traveling the world and enjoying his estate. Chandler, like nearly all of his contemporaries, apparently never fully retired: he still maintained a Boston law office at least until 1885, a year before his death at age eighty.[33]

Bourgeois Brookline

It is tempting to reduce the social class structure of post–Civil War Brookline to a struggle between an overweening bourgeoisie and a downtrodden proletariat. Indeed, in many ways the 422 households that in 1870 employed live-in domestic servants constituted a coherent social class, even if many historians might be uncomfortable using the term *bourgeoisie* in an American context, where (outside of the antebellum South) no politically powerful landed gentry served as their foil.[34] Contemporaries agreed that hiring live-in help was an important milestone, which marked a family's entry into the upper rungs of the class structure.[35] Despite their differing levels of wealth and income, the Lawrence, White, and Chandler families had much in common, living in well-apportioned, well-staffed houses; traveling about in private carriages and even going abroad; and enjoying the cultural amenities of the nearby city. All three families sent sons to Harvard.

Most homes of Brookline bourgeois families were located within a mile or so of the Boston & Albany Railroad depot in Brookline Village, although scattered affluent households could be found throughout the town (fig. 3.1). Whether palatial or merely of ample size, the interiors of most bourgeois houses shared a common appearance. Once a visitor entered one of them, he or she expected to encounter a clear demarcation between the public rooms on the first floor and the rest of the house, the kitchen in the back and the private bedrooms and studies upstairs, to which nonfamily visitors seldom were welcomed.[36] Mostly built after 1840, bourgeois houses typically featured a prominent staircase, often of carved, dark-stained hardwoods, for the exclusive use of family members and overnight guests. In order to minimize contact with their betters, servants had to use their own narrower stairs at the rear of the house. Downstairs, furniture, art, and other furnishings tended to be crowded into parlors, libraries, and other rooms, which were mostly decorated in the latest European-inspired revival styles embraced by all levels of the bourgeoisie. Antique American relics had not yet emerged from the attic.[37]

Bourgeois families supported and paid for the broad range of political and social services for which Brookline was becoming noted. Indeed, to those less-fortunate

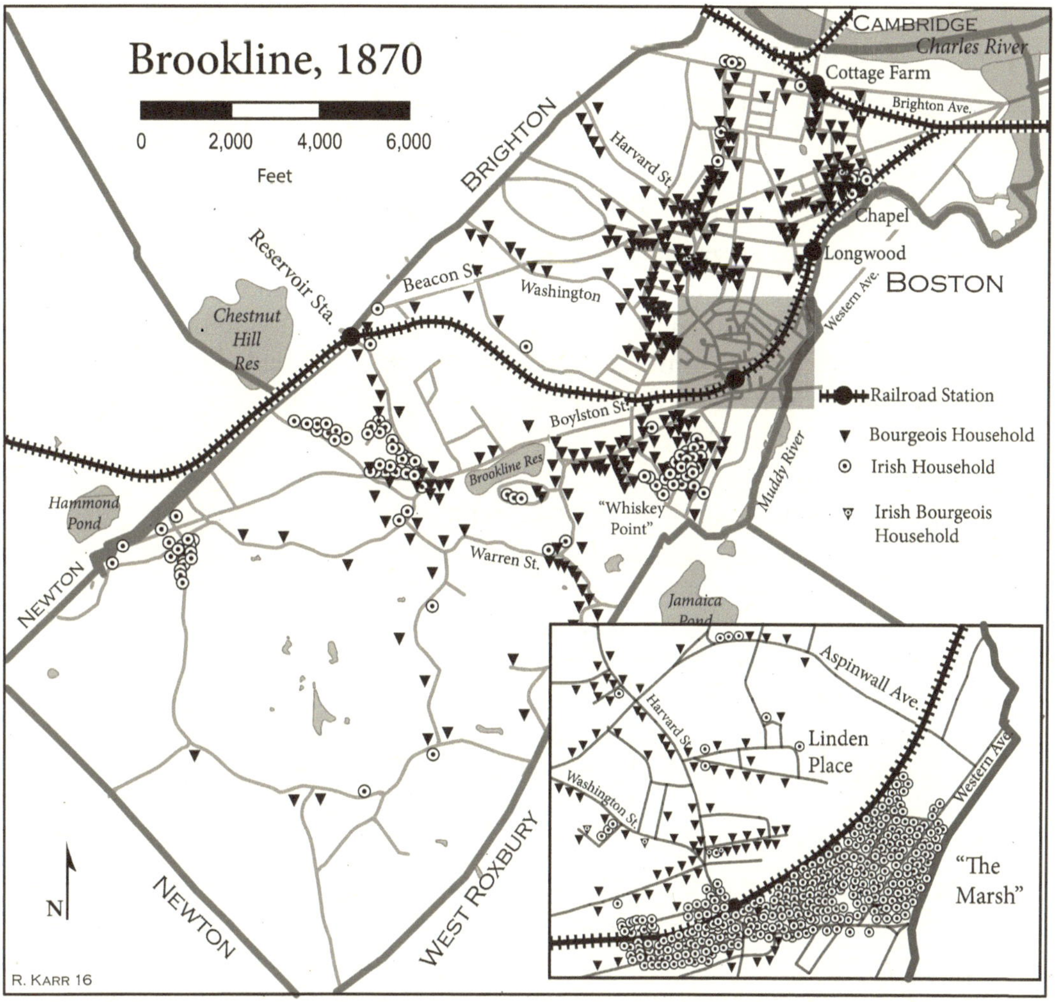

FIGURE 3.1. Map of Brookline, 1870, showing residences of bourgeois (servant-employing) households and households with an Irish-born head.

families they must have seemed a largely coherent bloc, and they often functioned as such when confronting the Irish Catholic working class. Still, there were differences within this group, of which individuals within the bourgeoisie were all too aware. Most obvious was the vast range in household income, as well as the varying means of obtaining it. Thus, although Theophilus Chandler's Washington Street mansion and estate made a fine impression on visitors, the social distance between the Chandlers and the Lawrences was considerable.

Theophilus Chandler and Amos A. Lawrence had arrived in Brookline around the same time, but the Lawrence brothers had paid more than ten times as much for their nearly ninety-acre estate—without a house. In 1865 the Chandler household consisted of the couple, three of their minor children, and two Irish-born female domestics, on their two-acre estate in Brookline Village.[38] Lawrence's stone mansion sat on seventeen acres and employed a coachman and his wife, plus three female domestics. More importantly, Chandler had no choice but to continue to work to maintain his lifestyle, whereas Lawrence's vast fortune—over $1 million—freed him from any such necessity. And although Francis White owned a fine property and eventually was able to retire, he did not own a Boston townhouse, a summer place, or a yacht.

In 1879 nearly nine out of ten Brookline households with resident servants listed a male head, and most households included one or more men who worked as businessmen or professionals. (Of the fifty-three female-headed bourgeois households, only four women reported occupations other than keeping house.) To be able to employ servants required a house, owned or rented, with sufficient capacity to house them, as well as enough money to pay their wages and board. In the Civil War era and afterward this necessitated a household income of several thousand dollars. At a time when married women who aspired to bourgeois status could not work outside the home, there were only a few ways to obtain reliably large earnings. Ideally, one derived one's income from rents, interest, or dividends, either inherited, married, or accumulated. To be independently wealthy meant owning an amount of property capable of generating income sufficient to provide a comfortable living without the need to work. In the 1860s or 1870s a good income was perhaps $4,000 or $5,000; on this a family could afford to maintain a ten-room house with a pair of servants. At the prevailing rates of return, at least $100,000 in assets would have been needed to generate a comfortable amount, but since not all assets (such as noncommercial real estate) generate income, a realistic conservative limit for wealth might be at least $150,000.[39] Using the property valuations from the 1870 federal census (which, being provided by the subjects themselves, doubtless understate these holdings), there were eighty-eight households such as the Whites with holdings of $100,000 or more, and another sixty-six with holdings between $50,000 and $99,999. The truly rich, thus, probably represented about a quarter of all Brookline bourgeois households, perhaps a hundred households in all.

These hundred or so truly wealthy households included a handful of members of prestigious and interrelated Boston clans that later observers would term Proper Bostonians, Boston Associates, or Brahmins. Among these were a score or more households representing the Lawrence, Bowditch, Sargent, Dwight, Gardner (unrelated to the colonial Brookline family of the same name), Amory, Lowell, Lee, Lyman, and Cabot families. Their Brookline holdings, in most cases acquired more than a half century earlier, accounted for no less than 573 acres, about one-seventh of the entire town. Together, the assessed value of their real estate, including buildings, came to 18 percent of the town's total real valuation. The wealth and power of these families derived from their industrial and commercial holdings throughout New England. They had built and still owned the mills of Lowell, Lawrence, and Manchester; the banks that financed them; and the railroads that served them.[40] These prestigious families, a mere 2 or 3 percent of Brookline's households, exerted an oversized influence on the town.[41]

The heads of the remaining three hundred or so nonwealthy bourgeois households worked as merchants, manufacturers, managers, professionals like Theophilus Chandler, proprietors of both Boston and Brookline businesses such as Francis White, and commercial farmers. Their high incomes allowed them to maintain bourgeois households, as long as they maintained their jobs, practices, or businesses. These bourgeois households supplied the town with nearly all of its political leaders, developed its real estate, and ran its stores, churches, schools, farms, and factories.

Bourgeois households without fortunes to support them knew insecurity. Behind many a successful facade lurked a secret fear of failure. Bourgeois families knew that disaster might strike at any time. Epidemic diseases, such as diphtheria, whooping cough, and scarlet fever, periodically carried off scores of children, not all from poor households. Crime, especially burglary and arson, threatened cherished possessions.[42] The security of most bourgeois families rested on the success of the family business. Economic slumps raised the specter of bankruptcy and lost social status. "Frank came home with a sad story of Hard Times," Caroline White wrote in her diary on September 30, 1857, of "new failures every day." Sudden catastrophes, such as fires, could wipe out the gains of years of striving in a single night. The great Boston fire of November 7, 1872, caused losses for at least thirty-nine Brookline residents, many of whom were caught underinsured. For some, the setback was permanent: leather dealer Isaac Sears had just built a "beautiful house" in Longwood "when the [Boston] fire came and swept away his fortune," forcing him to sell his home. Although he lived another quarter of a century he never recovered his standing.[43] The truly wealthy, whose fortunes typically consisted of diversified investments, rarely knew such fears.

Aside from the minority who had inherited wealth, most bourgeois men worked hard to obtain the money needed to support their family's style of life. More than two-thirds of Brookline's bourgeois heads of households ran businesses. In 1870 the most successful worked as merchants, manufacturers, bankers, brokers, or corporate officers. Mercantile, banking, and manufacturing incomes exceeded those of all other occupations. In 1866 an enterprising compiler published a list of the largest incomes reported on federal income tax returns, then considered public information. It was revealed that fifty-seven Brookline residents reported taxable incomes in excess of $10,000, with twenty-six of these exceeding $20,000. At $46,338, Amos A. Lawrence's income was one of the highest, though by no means the largest. That honor went to commission merchant Edward S. Floyd, who was said to have taken in no less than $87,109 in 1866 (plus at least another untaxed $1,200). Merchants William Fletcher Weld and his kinsman William G. Weld each reported $79,400. Incomes like these represented more money than a typical day laborer would see in a long lifetime. Of the fifty-seven high-income Brookline residents, no fewer than forty-four were merchants, bankers, or executives. Only two were professionals (a lawyer and a minister), and another three were Boston retailers (two jewelers and a dry-goods dealer). None of the over-$10,000 set held lower white- or blue-collar jobs. Despite the high value of Brookline land, none was a farmer.[44]

Out of a total of 1,182 Brookline households in 1870, 191 were headed by merchants or executives (16 percent). With an average of nearly eight persons, these were the town's largest households, partly because of the number of live-in servants but also because they had more children at home (including adult children) than any other occupational group. Not surprisingly, they were the richest, with a mean reported household wealth of more than $100,000. The resident domestic servants in the Lawrence and White households were typical of this group: 91 percent of merchant and executive households had live-in help. More than a third of these households had three or more servants.[45] The vast majority of the heads of mercantile households—70 percent—had been born in Massachusetts, and nearly all the rest elsewhere in New England (21 percent). Only eleven had been born abroad, three of these in Ireland. In all, 40 percent of bourgeois households were headed by a man working as a merchant, manufacturer, or executive; another 16 percent were proprietors (chiefly of shops in downtown Boston),

5 percent skilled (mostly contractors or small manufacturers), and 6 percent commercial farmers. Nearly all of these men owned part or all of the businesses at which they worked, and most of their income presumably came from profits and investments. Another 15 percent of bourgeois household heads did not work at all (gentlemen, retirees, or widows) or at an occupation that could not be classified, and most of them similarly depended on investment or rental income.

Some bourgeois households, however, did not generate most of their income from profits, rents, or investments. Nine percent of household heads practiced professions, while another six percent held jobs with clerical titles, such as secretary or cashier.[46] These men worked for salaries or professional fees. Lawyers, doctors, ministers, civil engineers, lower-level executives, and college professors combined incomes from fees, salaries, and investments to live a bourgeois lifestyle. Law and medicine were the best-paid professions. In 1866 the published federal income tax returns of eight Brookline lawyers showed taxable incomes (less exemptions and deductions) ranging from $400 to $38,785 (although only three had incomes above $3,000). The seven physicians listed had incomes from $100 to $6,471, with four above $4,000.[47] But even the ministry, traditionally the poorest compensated profession, was well-rewarded in Brookline. In 1872 the Harvard Congregational Church (which the Whites attended) offered a minister a $4,000 salary (he refused the post), and four years later the Baptists paid their new minister $3,000. All told there were only 45 professionally headed households in Brookline in 1870 (4 percent), more than four out of five of which enjoyed the services of live-in servants. Their average size was slightly smaller than those of the merchants, and their mean property holding was half as large, but as with the merchants nearly all of the heads (89 percent) were New England–born (only one had been born abroad).

Did these professional and salaried households differ from the majority of bourgeois families who lived off profits, investment income, and rents? Some observers, most notably Marxist sociologists or economists, would limit the term *bourgeoisie* to the owners of the means of production. They would argue that professionals held a status distinctly subordinate to the bourgeoisie proper.[48] Non-Marxist sociologists in the tradition of Max Weber have viewed American society as being divided into various strata of individuals and families who share common styles of life. Weber himself divided the uppermost strata into two groups, the coupon-clipping rentiers and the hands-on entrepreneurs, which is reflected in the differences between the Lawrences and the Whites.[49] At least for some purposes of analysis the classic sociological divisions of the upper strata associated with Lloyd Warner and his followers could be seen in nineteenth-century Brookline: that is, an upper upper class of inherited wealth, a lower upper class of new money, and an upper middle class of professionals and working businessmen, of which the Lawrences, Whites, and Chandlers, respectively, were broadly representative.[50] Throughout the rest of this book, I use both sets of terms: *bourgeoisie* to designate the households with live-in domestic servants as a whole, and *upper class* and *upper middle class* to differentiate—among servant-employing households—between the independently wealthy and those who could maintain a high income only through active engagement in a business or a profession, which often involved daily commuting to a Boston office or store as well as keeping individual clients or customers satisfied.

Indeed, commuting was a way of life for the bourgeoisie. In 1870 nearly two-thirds of the male heads of bourgeois families listed offices, stores, or other commercial addresses in central Boston, which most of them had to visit each working day.[51] Some may have used their own private carriages to reach their workplaces, but most would have taken one of the two railroad lines or even the slower, lumbering, horse-drawn streetcars through Roxbury Crossing when they missed a train. Both of the rail lines terminated at the Boston & Albany Railroad's depot on Kneeland Street, near the present-day South Station, at most a half-mile walk from the office and retail district of downtown Boston.

An Irish Proletariat?

Despite the prominence of the town's upper strata, it would be a mistake to label nineteenth-century Brookline a bourgeois community without considering the town's resident Irish Catholic working class. For even after nearly a quarter of century from their initial appearance in Brookline, the Irish remained largely mired in the lower realm of the social order. Of the 476 Irish-born household heads in 1870, no more than 13 held white-collar jobs. Most of the rest were day laborers, servants, or at best semi-skilled workers; only 57 (12 percent) claimed a skilled occupation. Even here the difference between Irishman and Yankee was telling. The eighty-three households headed by Yankee-born skilled workers reported a mean of $5,955 worth of property; the Irish-born, only $1,246.[52] Two-thirds of Irish-headed households reported owning no real or personal property at all, compared to less than a tenth of those born in Massachusetts. Less than a quarter of Irish households owned real estate, typically only a modest dwelling.

If not synonymous, Irishmen and laborers were closely associated in Brookline: in 1870, 62 percent of all Irish-born adult males worked as laborers, and 72 percent of the town's laborers had been born in Ireland. The largest component of the town's workforce, Brookline's 564 laborers, took work wherever they could find it, hauling lumber to construction sites, digging trenches for pipes and foundations for buildings, grading streets, and shoveling snow. Without their ready labor, Brookline's more fortunate classes could never have enjoyed their suburban sojourn. Paid by the day—ten hours of work yielded only $1.75 (and by the end of the 1870s, $1.00 to $1.25)—a day laborer was lucky to pull in $400 a year, far below the minimum to support a growing family. The availability of work was never guaranteed, since the weather and market conditions were always in play. Laborers' families survived through a combination of wages (from both adults and children), taking boarders into their already crowded households, raising chickens and goats, washing laundry, illegally selling alcohol, and, in bad times, receiving charity or resorting to begging or even theft.[53]

Nearly 16 percent of Irish-born household heads were female. Whether single, widowed, or married with an absent husband, these women faced an especially daunting task, particularly when younger children were present. In Brookline there were few ways for a woman keeping house to support her family financially, aside from taking in boarders or laundry. Her best hope was to send her older children into the workforce as young as possible, making it difficult for them to attend school.[54]

In 1870 much of the town's Irish population, which made up no less than 41 percent of the town, was confined to a few crowded neighborhoods near Brookline Village (fig. 3.1). Pearl Place and the district immediate adjacent to the west and south to Brookline Avenue formed "the Marsh," the heart of Irish Brookline. When Irish immigrants first arrived in town in the 1840s, the low-lying lands south of Brookline Village had been carved into lots and covered with cheap houses and tenements and, later, the gas works. The arrival of the railroad in 1848 cut this area off from the higher ground to the north. The other side of the tracks was an unpleasant and unhealthy place to raise a family. As early as 1861 conditions there were reportedly "very bad," and one writer in 1870 described the Marsh as being inhabited by "poor and desolate widows, and also laborers, in miserable hovels." Typhoid, scarlet fever, and other ailments plagued the inhabitants, allegedly because of the poor drainage of the land, which routinely filled cellars with standing water. The stench was reportedly almost beyond bearing. Residents were accused of living in filth, with "hens and goats . . . allowed free access to the houses, and until the recent notification from the chief of police, the goats roamed around the yards and streets at will. Besides these breeders of filth, rubbish is thrown into the yards and streets and left to rot and decay."[55] Conditions in other Irish districts, such as Hart's Content (later Whiskey Point), were only marginally better.

Although disdained by most Yankee Protestants, the Roman Catholic faith provided the moral, intellectual, and organizational foundation of early Irish Brookline. Public mass was first said in Brookline at the Lyceum Hall in 1852, and Bishop John B. Fitzpatrick of Boston proclaimed the establishment of St. Mary of the Assumption Parish, taking in the towns of Brookline and Brighton. The three structures that followed reflected the growth of Catholic Brookline. A wooden church was opened on Andem Place, near the rail depot, at the end of 1853. A fire in 1855 destroyed most of this building, which was soon rebuilt significantly larger. In 1886, after five years of construction, a more imposing brick church was built on an adjacent site at the corner of Harvard Street and Linden Place.[56]

The various pastors and curates of St. Mary's (all but one of Irish extraction) did their best to both minister to and represent their parishioners to the Yankee community. This came at a time when Irish-born clergy were taking charge of a reinvigorated American church, infused by the arrival of millions of Irish, German, and Canadian Catholic immigrants, a clergy determined to impose on "Catholics of various different backgrounds in the United States . . . a single, coherent and powerful faith, not simply by preserving the faith of immigrants, but in most cases by educating them on basic doctrines and enforcing regular worship for the first time."[57]

This meant that in confrontations with Yankee authority, Irish economic and political weakness was countered with a clergy (and increasingly with political leaders as well) who could speak for a broad segment of the Irish Catholic community. The Irish certainly needed this, for notwithstanding the strength of their religion, they were at a severe disadvantage when confronting the concentrated economic and social power of the Yankee elite. Although town institutions nominally served the entire community, the Irish had little confidence that these were being run for their benefit. As late as 1885 no Irishman—or even a Roman Catholic—had ever been elected to a major town office. From 1845 to 1885 some thirty-nine men held the office of selectmen, the town's highest political office. All but three were natives of New England (of native-born parents), though only six had been born in the town itself (five of them sons or grandsons of Brookline selectmen). Three were foreign-born, but two of these had American parents. All thirteen of the selectmen who served between 1865 and 1875 were from the bourgeoisie.[58]

The Missing Middle Class

Contemporary observers were struck by Brookline's lack of a prominent intermediate class between the bourgeoisie and the working poor. The vast number of households headed by small neighborhood shopkeepers, salesmen, and clerical workers, so prominent in other Boston suburbs such as Dorchester, Roxbury, and Somerville—who together accounted for perhaps 35 to 45 percent of the households of greater Boston in the 1870s—were largely absent from Brookline.[59] Taken together, the mostly Yankee Protestant servant-owning families—the bourgeoisie—and those headed by the Irish-born accounted for 73 percent of all Brookline households in 1870. Of the rest only 8 percent of the heads held white-collar or farming jobs. Another 11 percent of the heads of households without servants (mostly women) reported either no job or one difficult to classify, so at best this middle group accounted for no more than 15 percent of Brookline households and perhaps as little as a tenth.

In the absence of an intermediate class, the town developed few institutions to bridge the gap between rich and poor. In the years after the Civil War the town did develop an impressive list of diverse social organizations. The number of private social groups rose in tandem with the population, increasing from three churches, two political parties, and a half-dozen other such entities in 1845 to seven churches, three fraternal organizations, three social clubs, three fire companies, a temperance group, a charity, and two political parties by 1870. By 1887 there were eight churches, eleven chapters of national fraternal organizations, eighteen social and cultural clubs, two temperance bodies, a charity, and five political parties or clubs. Yet because the membership of these organizations was largely confined to particular classes or ethnic groups, they did little to bridge the town's ethnic, religious, and economic divisions.[60]

In the end, the absence of a significant lower middle class in Brookline underscored the sharp division between a prosperous Yankee Protestant bourgeoisie and a largely impoverished Irish Catholic working class. As will be seen, bourgeois Brookline itself was not without its own internal divisions, but none of them could rival the intensity of the rift between the Yankees and the Irish. Indeed, the relationship between the two groups could be felt in nearly every aspect of the social, political, cultural, and economic life of the emerging suburb.

CHAPTER 4

Building Blocks

✦

[Brookline] is no longer a Country Town, but rather the suburb of a great and growing city. . . . It seems as though the time is near when farms . . . will gradually be cut up into building lots and become the homes of a large population.

—*Brookline Transcript,* March 30, 1872

THE STARKLY divided social landscape of suburban Brookline was reflected in the town's newly altered physical environment. During the first four decades after 1840, Brookline's population soared from less than 1,500 to more than 9,000 inhabitants by 1885. This growth entailed the erection of well over a thousand units of new housing placed along dozens of recently built streets as well as infrastructural improvements that guaranteed its denizens access to a host of services that rivaled those available in cities (fig. 4.1). A combination of private enterprise and public policy created the suburb: market forces built the new dwellings and laid out the streets but government oversaw the process and provided many of the enhancements. Unlike in more recent times, when privately constructed new housing is almost exclusively built for higher-income households, in nineteenth-century America new housing was available for a wide range of incomes, from palatial estates built for the very rich to modest tenements and cottages rented to the households of unskilled laborers.[1]

Subdivisions

The process of converting fields and large estates into streets and building lots evolved quickly in the 1840s. Linden Place, Brookline's first subdivision in 1843, served as the prototype and model for much that followed. Its developer, Thomas

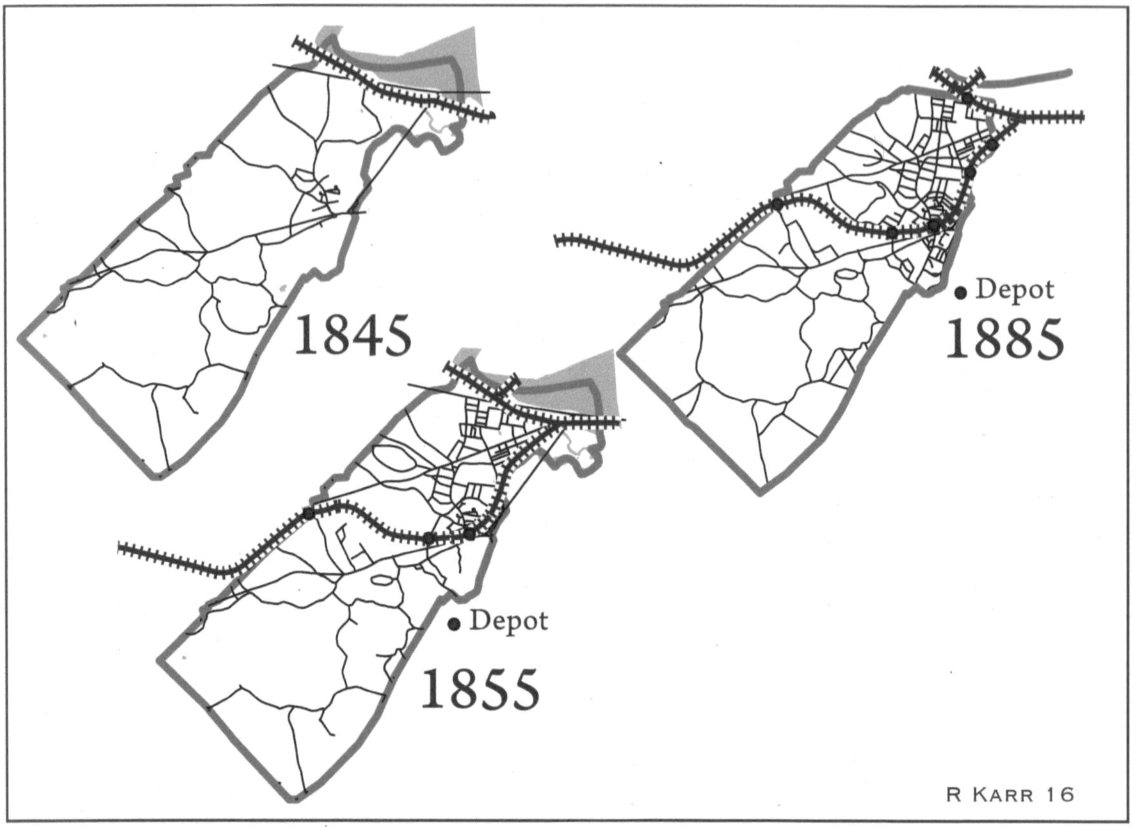

FIGURE 4.1. The growth of Brookline's street network, 1845–85.

Aspinwall Davis, had reassembled, through inheritance and purchase from relatives, a twenty-acre parcel of farmland once owned by his ancestors. Davis hired Alexander Wadsworth, one of the state's pioneer suburban surveyors and landscape architects, to draw up the plans. The site had been carefully chosen, on high ground on Harvard Street immediately to the north of Brookline Village. Wadsworth laid out a single curvilinear street that doubled back on itself forming an elongated loop, with a park in the center. The lots, even by twentieth-century suburban standards, were generous, ranging from 17,730 to 146,200 square feet (0.4 to 3.4 acres). Although relatively narrow (100 to 115 feet), some lots were extremely deep (fig. 4.2).[2]

The marketing campaign that accompanied the project was surprisingly sophisticated, considering that no real-estate development industry had existed up to this point. Targeted squarely at the more prosperous members of the middle class, the promotion of Linden Place touted the opportunity to live in a romantically scenic countryside and enjoy the prestige of living near wealthy neighbors, all within sight of Boston. Bostonians who opened their copies of the *Evening Transcript* on May 22, 1843, saw an article announcing Linden Place,

> in the pleasant town of Brookline. It consists of some 20 acres which have been arranged into building lots by the good taste and judgment of Alexander Wadsworth. It is delightfully located and combines every requisite for an

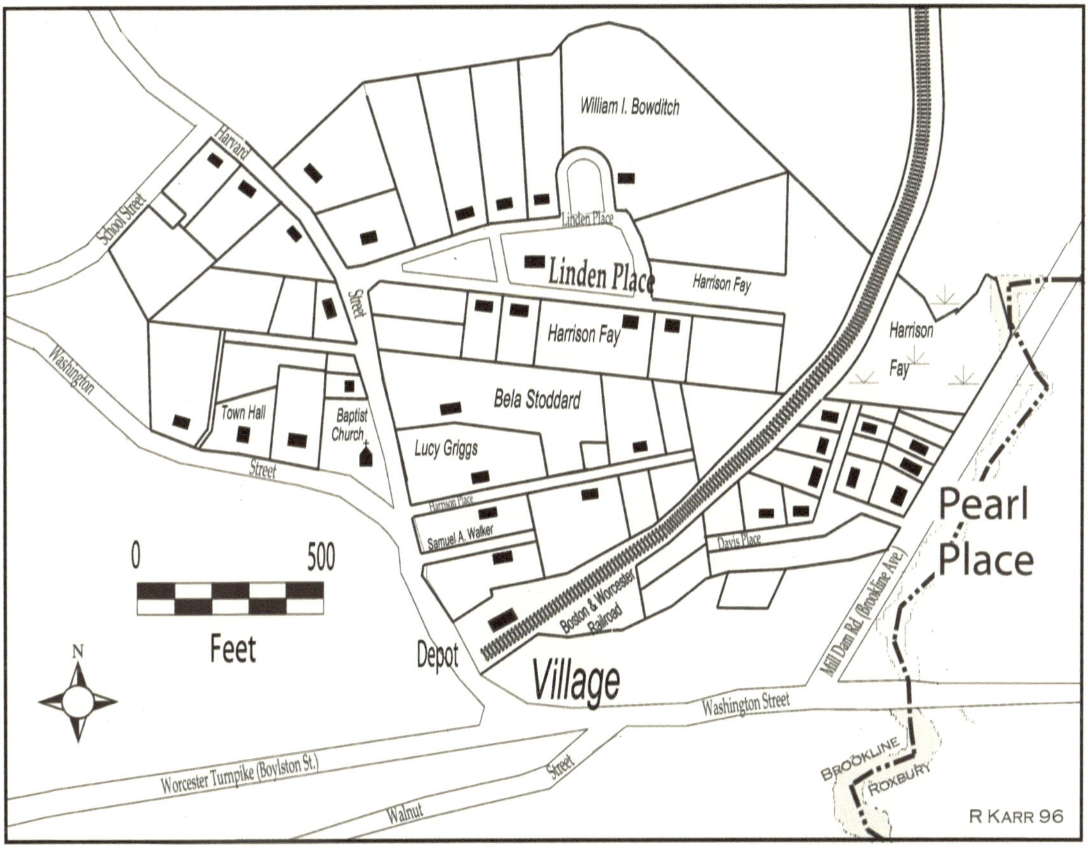

FIGURE 4.2. Linden Place and Pearl Place, 1850. Developed by Brookline native and Boston mayor Thomas Aspinwall Davis and platted by Alexander Wadsworth in 1843, Linden Place was Brookline's earliest subdivision. Pearl Place, already a less desirable building site due to poor drainage, was cut off from the wealthier, more elevated commuter streets to the north by the Boston & Worcester Railroad's Brookline branch line in 1848.

> agreeable country residence—grove, hill, and undulating plateau. Nothing could exceed the variegated beauty of the surrounding scenery. Our fair city with her suburbs forms a splendid crescent on one side, while the green hills of the distant country complete the circle. Everything around it is touched and civilized by the refining hand of art, and of the numerous mansions and gardens in view, each one seems more attractive than another.

As important as this scenic splendor was the "rare opportunity" to buy a house lot in Brookline, which "has always been considered a charming place and has for years, it is well known, been the summer-residence of many of our most wealthy and distinguished citizens. But land here, being so highly valued by the owners, is scarcely offered for sale, and the present (this estate having recently come into the possession of a gentleman of this city) is, we are told, the first instance in which any considerable quantity of land has been laid out into building lots." An adjacent ad, which announced that the twenty-eight lots would be sold at auction the following day, noted that "the short distance from the city" would afford "the man of business an agreeable ride after the duties of the day" and provide "a pleasing exercise to the gentleman of leisure." For those lacking carriages, "omnibuses run at accommodating hours."[3] Obviously, it was not by coincidence that advertisement and an ostensible news story were placed together on the same page of the newspaper.

Davis's promotion quickly yielded results. At the initial auction, twenty-four of the twenty-seven available lots sold, many to just the sort of prosperous Boston businessmen the development had been designed to attract. Several bought more than one lot. Within a few years expensive houses had been erected by some of the owners. By 1848 Linden Place was being called one of the few truly noteworthy attractions in Brookline, "a delightful spot—much admired by all who have a taste for the beautiful." In 1851 it was one of the two wealthiest streets in Brookline Village. Of the sixteen male workers listed as living there in 1871, twelve were merchants, business executives, or professionals.[4]

Most of the new houses on Linden Place resembled houses going up elsewhere in Brookline and the rest of the urban northeastern United States at this time. Notwithstanding the promotion of romantic architectural styles by popular authors and more fashionable architects, such as Andrew Jackson Downing and Alexander Jackson Davis, these houses were built in the now venerable Greek Revival mode, the most popular architectural style for the town's churches and

FIGURE 4.3. One of the original houses built on Linden Place shortly after the subdivision was launched in 1843. At the time the Greek Revival style of this house was also being employed for such public buildings as churches, the town hall, and the Lyceum building. The generous yard and lawn that once surrounded the house gave way to colonial-revival-style apartment buildings in the twentieth century. Photograph 1994.

other public buildings in the 1840s (fig. 4.3). Reflecting the values of domesticity, bourgeois respectability, family living, and security, they were designed (whether from plan books or by the builders themselves, since architects were usually not involved) to function as a place for a household of children and servants to live, sleep, and perform domestic duties. Unlike presuburban Brookline, most household income in Linden Place was generated by activities of the adult male household members working away from home.[5]

Brookline's second subdivision, Harvard Place, which appeared only a few months after Linden Place, formed an interesting contrast to that development. On land he had inherited more than twenty years earlier, farmer Samuel Craft (1787–1856) laid out a sixty-lot subdivision at the intersection of Washington, School, and Harvard Streets. The location was only a half mile north of the center of Brookline Village, already served by an omnibus line and soon to be the terminal of a new Boston & Worcester Railroad branch line. Craft hired the same surveyor that Davis employed at Linden Place, but this time Alexander Wadsworth produced a conventional grid plan with straight streets (fig. 4.4). The lots resembled those of Linden Place, mostly one hundred feet wide and twice that depth, although the precise depth was determined by a stream that formed the rear boundaries of many of the lots.[6]

Craft aimed Harvard Place directly at the same urban upper-middle-class clientele targeted by Davis, and the marketing campaign echoed that of Linden Place. On May 15, 1844, the Boston auctioneer house of Whitwell, Seaver offered for sale "20 House Lots, situated on Harvard Place and Harvard Avenue (near Linden Place)," providing "a rare opportunity to procure a site for a country residence, in one of the most delightful villages in New England." Touting "the proximity of the city to churches and schools of the highest order," the notice emphasized that the site was encircled "by the most elegant country residences of our most opulent citizens." For those without private fortunes, "a liberal credit will be given, and money loaned on mortgage, if desired, to those who wish to build." Liberal terms indeed: the lots sold, with prices generally ranging from four to nine hundred dollars, depending on size and topography. Buyers typically put only 10 percent down, the rest subject to a five-year balloon mortgage (interest payments only), although a few worked out even better terms, in some cases with nothing down. Many of the lots were sold to house builders, who could either build on speculation or custom build for clients. For some, even a half-acre lot was too small, and some houses went up on two-hundred-foot wide double lots, (such as Theophilus Chandler, as we have seen). In other cases, equally large houses were built on standard lots. Indeed, some of the smallest lots were subdivided again to produce lots no larger than a fifth or sixth of an acre.[7]

Subdivisions became the basic building unit of suburban Brookline, the process that converted fields into streets and backyards. The procedure soon became standardized: after acquiring, through purchase or inheritance, a parcel of vacant land, a developer hired a surveyor to lay out streets and plat house lots, and at some point engaged a contractor to build the streets. Finally, the lots were sold either to speculative builders, land speculators, or families, who had homes built for their own use. Typically, the first step was the hardest. Most undeveloped Brookline real estate belonged to farmers who depended on the land for their livelihood. Since farmers, whether working or gentlemen, generally aimed to pass their lands

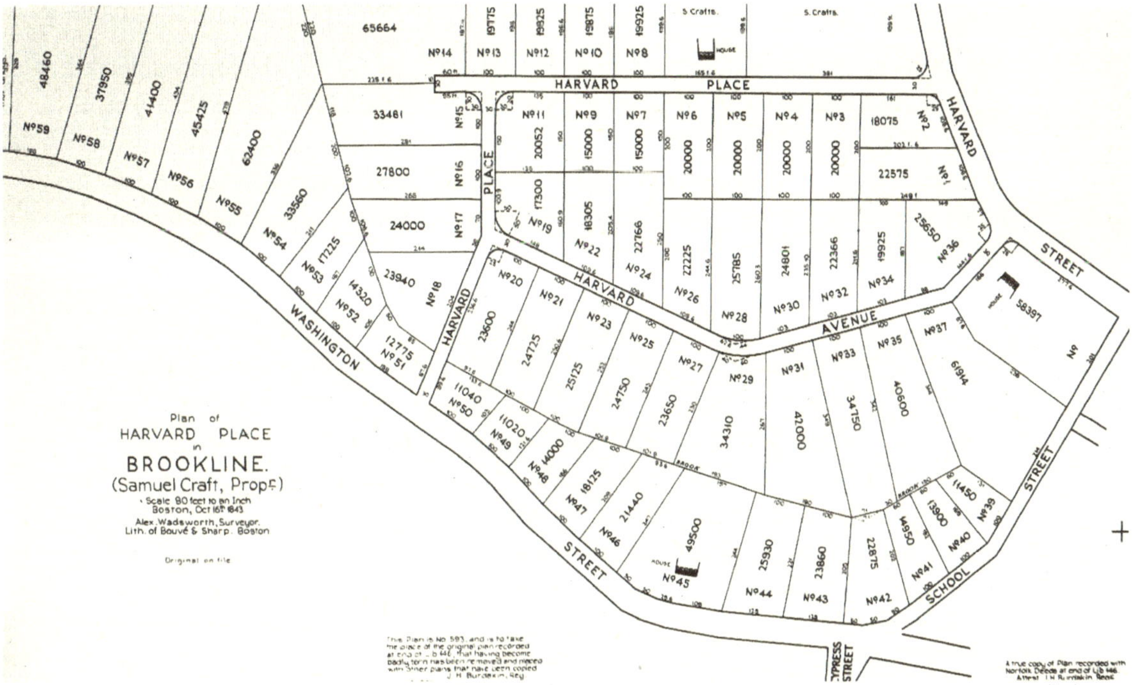

FIGURE 4.4. Laid out one year after Linden Place by the same surveyor, the Harvard Place subdivision (1844) used a modified grid pattern to maximize the available lots for sale. Washington, School, and Harvard Streets were existing streets that largely determined the layout, along with a stream that cut diagonally across the property, which the surveyor used to define rear lot boundaries. Norfolk County Deeds Planbook, 13:593.

onto their posterity, Brookline farms seldom came on the market for sale. Many of the most attractive potential building sites were found on the estates owned by prominent Boston families, who rarely wanted to sell. "It is quite safe to say," wrote Theodore Lyman, a Boston Brahmin who owned a large Brookline estate in 1880, "that nine-tenths of the inhabitants prefer to live comfortably on their places, and do not yearn to open a sixty-foot [wide] street through them, or cut them into houselots, or in any other way to 'improve' them."[8]

Taxation practices aided the preservation of great estates and farms. Large holdings of undeveloped lands deliberately received low tax assessments, far below market value, while smaller parcels and houses were taxed at a much higher rate. In northern Brookline tracts of land ranging from ten to forty acres were typically assessed at 1.5 to 3 cents per square foot in 1870. Assessments in the southern part of town were lower: F. E. Bacon's 117-acre estate on Clyde Street was rated at a mere 0.4 cents a foot. By contrast, of fifteen randomly selected plots of vacant land under an acre, all but one were assessed at more than 5 cents a foot, with most falling between 7 and 15 cents.[9]

Encouraging wealthy estate holders to retain their large acreage served to boost land prices throughout the town by limiting the supply of available building lots. In the mid-1870s land prices in Brookline Village exceeded a dollar a square foot: "Within four years estates have increased from 50 cents to $3 per foot in desirable locations, while in the extreme outskirts the increase has been equally large." Even a mile or more from the depot along Beacon Street, prices of fifty to seventy-five cents a square foot were said to be the norm for building lots. Good-quality houses with land were going for $10,000 to $25,000.[10]

When it finally took place, the subdivision process could assume a variety of forms. Most schemes were short streets laid out by a single small developer, often an active farmer, although large-scale projects also appeared. Larger schemes were promoted by commercial land companies, syndicates of real-estate investors that issued shares to raise capital. The first such body, the Brookline Land Company, appeared in 1860 when a group of individuals from Brookline, Boston, and Roxbury purchased an eighty-acre farm south of Brookline Village for $83,000. Two trustees and five directors governed the company, with thirty thousand shares of stock authorized. Later, these shares could be bought and sold on the Boston Stock Exchange. The company was slow to sell off its lands, and vacant lots remained until well into the 1880s.[11]

At the other end of the spectrum from land companies were developments where profit was a secondary goal. Another subdivision, Longwood, for example, took shape on the ancestral lands of the Sewall family in the far northern part of Brookline adjacent to the Back Bay and the Charles River. This three-hundred-acre parcel remained in that family until 1815, when it was acquired by Brahmin land speculators, eventually becoming the property of the Lawrence family and David Sears. During the 1840s Sears began the development of his Sewall lands. The ubiquitous Alexander Wadsworth was hired to lay out streets and parks. Thousands of trees were planted on the open farm lands, and Sears erected a few large houses for himself, his kin, and a some select friends and retainers. The Lawrence brothers followed suit a few years later on their adjacent lands.[12]

Unlike Linden Place, auctions were apparently never held for the lots in Longwood, as the new development was named, since neither Sears nor the Lawrences sought to maximize profits. Rather, as they continued to live there themselves, they seemed more interested in obtaining agreeable neighbors. In 1860 Sears erected his own church, and eight years later the Lawrences countered with one of their own. As late as 1874 Longwood residents largely remained relatives or close associates of the two families, with nearly all adult males professionals, gentlemen, businessmen, or their servants. Most of the houses, many of them large structures on lots the size of city blocks, had been constructed by Sears or the Lawrences themselves. Even in 1885, after nearly forty years of development, only three-score houses were to be found throughout Longwood, and the neighborhood was among the most desirable in Brookline (fig. 4.5).[13]

The rare for-profit subdivision aimed at truly upper-class buyers could experiment with fashionable design techniques such as curvilinear streets that followed the contours of the land. The gridiron formed by straight streets intersecting at right angles at regular intervals had been the standard for new urban development in Western Europe since the sixteenth century. In 1811 a grid of planned streets was imposed over nearly the entire island of Manhattan. For most Americans straight streets represented the discipline of civilization being imposed on an unruly wilderness. And the gridiron produced convenient, uniformly sized lots, which greatly aided developers in bringing their subdivisions to market. By the middle of the nineteenth century, however, some elite critics of a romantic bent found straight streets artificial, unnatural, and urban, part of an increasingly fashionable rejection of formality in gardening and landscaping in favor of the natural and the wild. Gridiron streets and uniform rectangular lots encouraged crowding and multifamily dwellings. As early as 1831 the nation's first garden cemetery, Mount Auburn in nearby Cambridge, featured curvilinear streets that hugged the site's rolling typography. The plan, drawn up in part by Alexander Wadsworth, was designed to maintain the site's natural appeal.[14]

Built on an attractive site overlooking the new Brookline Reservoir, the 1849 Fairmount subdivision featured a curving loop street that circled the hill. Although the hundred-foot-wide half-acre lots were similar to other commuter subdivisions, most of the lots were sold to a few wealthy buyers who combined them to form larger estates, so that by the 1870s little of the original lot configuration survived. As with Longwood (at least initially), Fairmount became a realm of trees and broad lawns. With their more generous consumption of expensive land, curvilinear streets and winding country lanes were only practical for high-end development, particularly since only the upper classes as yet showed preference for them.[15]

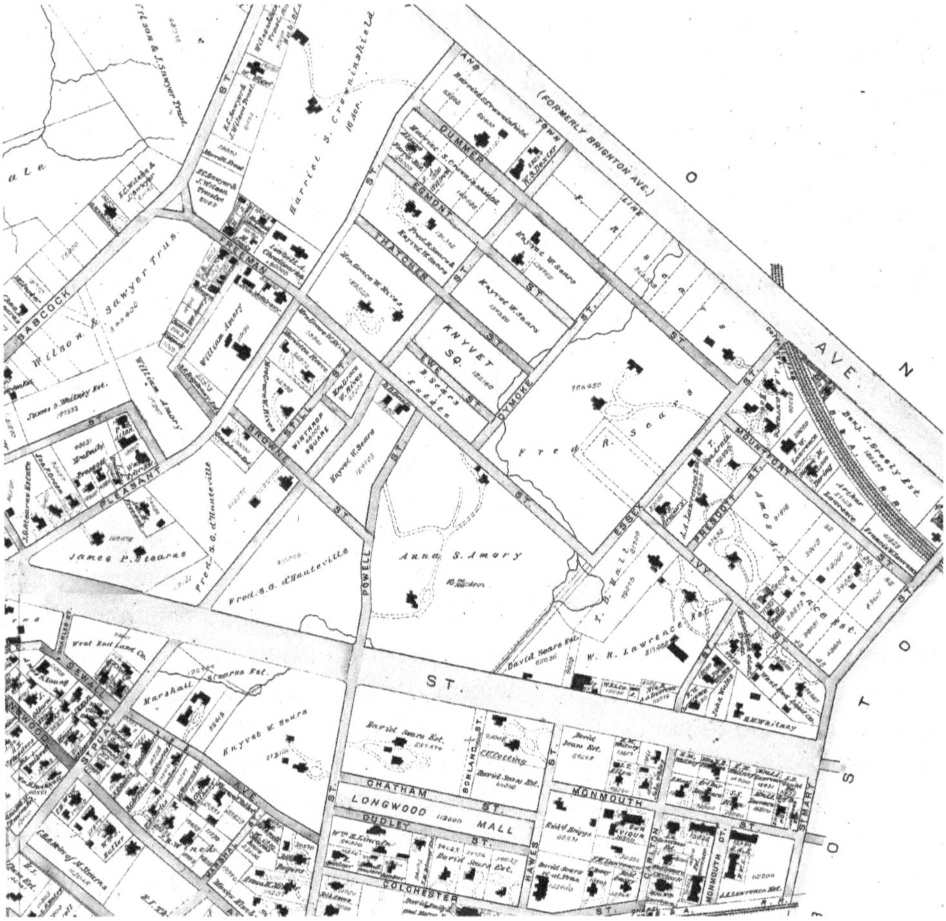

FIGURE 4.5. Map of the Longwood and Cottage Farm neighborhoods of Brookline, 1888. Beacon Street cuts through the area. E. Robinson, *Atlas of Norfolk County, Massachusetts* (New York: Robinson, 1888). Courtesy of the Brookline Historical Society.

Much the same market-driven process of subdivision also produced development intended for lower classes. Essentially a rural town in 1840, Brookline at first had no place to house the hundreds of poor Irish Catholic men, women, and children who arrived in the town beginning in the late 1840s seeking work. Just before this, in July 1845, two Brookline residents had acquired a swampy stretch of lowland to the east of Brookline Village along the road to the Mill Dam and hired a surveyor to lay out a street, Pearl Place. (Ironically, this tract was adjacent to the more elevated Linden Place and had in fact been part of the same farm.) The building of the Boston & Worcester Railroad in 1848 cut it off from Linden Place and the rest of the village to the north (fig. 4.2). The lots on Pearl Place were much smaller than middle-class subdivisions such as Linden Place or Harvard Place. The typical Pearl Place lot was a quarter of their size, fifty feet wide and a little more than a hundred feet deep. After a slow start, lots sold briskly after the arrival of the Irish. Soon the street became packed with wooden tenements, owned by both Yankee and Irish landlords, housing Irish households, and the street was extended westward. In 1851 the newly organized Brookline Gas Light Company found a site here to build its manufacturing plant, a place acceptable to its Yankee customers on the other side of the railroad tracks. The Marsh, as the neighborhood soon became known, had become the heart of Irish Brookline.[16]

As employment opportunities for laborers and domestic servants brought more Irish to Brookline, other low-rent neighborhoods appeared. Most notorious, if not the largest, was Hart's Content. When the Irish first arrived in numbers in the late 1840s, a local carpenter, Capt. Benjamin Bradley, built a settlement of cheap houses on his land on Boylston Street a mile west of the village. Bradley's Hill—or Grab Village, Dublin, or New Ireland, as it soon became known—housed a large population of destitute Irish immigrants. In 1852 Bradley sold the land and houses to one Samuel R. Hart of Boston, who continued the operation until 1870 when rising real-estate values led him to sell the now valuable land to developers. Hart then moved the entire settlement, comprising thirty buildings and two hundred inhabitants, off the hill and across Boylston Street into a marshy tract of land on Sewall Street (now Cypress). Hart's Content soon gained a reputation for permanent standing water in cellars, disease, and insufferable odors. Later enlarged by the arrival of a group from Pearl Place, it became known as Whiskey Point and, ultimately, the Point. This neighborhood survives today, with Hart Street commemorating its founder. Bradley's old 1840s buildings were finally replaced by triple-deckers (three-story homes, atypical for Brookline) at the end of the nineteenth century.[17]

Regardless of what income group a development was marketed to, developers faced risks and frustrations. The drawn-out attempt to develop Aspinwall Hill demonstrates some the difficulties involved. Located just south of the intersection of Beacon and Washington Streets in north central Brookline, this glacial drumlin had belonged to the Aspinwall clan since the end of the eighteenth century. The Aspinwalls had drawn up plans to subdivide their lands as early as

1857, but it was not until 1878 that William Aspinwall started laying out streets. The expenses of surveying and grading roads up that steep hill soon exhausted his personal funds, and in 1880 he transferred control of these and other family lands to the newly formed Aspinwall Land Company. The company hired noted landscape architect Frederick Law Olmsted to design a network of streets up the hill, his first of many Brookline commissions. Here they encountered a roadblock. Back in 1867 and 1870 the trustees of the recently founded Boston University had acquired two large tracts on the hill as a site for a seminary. It now became clear that development of the hill could not proceed without the cooperation of the university, since the latter owned a bewildering network of easements across the Aspinwall lands, and the tract's boundaries were such that any system of roads would have to encroach on university land. Fortunately for William Aspinwall, the university had dropped its plans to build a seminary in Brookline and was in fact looking to develop the land. But the university and Aspinwall had never been friendly neighbors, and the trustees did little to improve relations by appointing as their chief engineer and agent Ernest Bowditch, the son of Aspinwall's foremost adversary. It took years of bickering before the Olmsted plan was finally discarded and streets laid out in a manner acceptable to both parties. The sluggish pace of the project slowed the sale of lots, and the hill would not be built up until the 1890s.[18]

More than one development scheme ended in failure. Members of the Goddard family laid out Goddard Heights in South Brookline in 1873 on lands that clan had owned since the eighteenth century. Seventy-six rectilinear lots arranged along modified grid streets were surveyed, most lots ranging in size from five to ten thousand square feet. An auction held in June 1873 disposed of forty-one of the lots, at an average sale price of more than ten cents a foot, a good price. But for some reason the project never proceeded to the next stage, the construction of houses. Ten years later the lands remained vacant, and by 1888 they had reverted to the Goddard family. Either because of the deep business depression that began at this time or, more likely, due to the isolation of the development—the site was inconvenient to public transportation—Goddard Heights never materialized.[19]

Of the scores of subdivisions laid out in Brookline between 1843 and 1885, nearly all were aimed at either upper-middle-class commuters or blue-collar workers. Notably absent were the grid street and frontage small-lot mass developments marketed to lower-middle-class families that blanketed much of Dorchester and Roxbury in the decades after the Civil War. Still, even in Brookline, lot sizes were shrinking as land became more valuable. By the mid-1880s few new subdivisions—except in fashionable and remote Chestnut Hill—featured the generous half-acre lots with one-hundred-foot frontage that had been the norm in thc 1840s. Typical commuter lots now ranged from 7,000 to 12,000 square feet or so, with 50 to 75 feet of frontage, while the best-off Irish working families could now aspire to 3,600- to 5,500-square-foot lots 40 to 45 feet wide.[20]

Brookline's railroad commuters in particular had many housing options available to them. Those with the most to spend could obtain detached, substantial houses set on large lots well isolated from their neighbors, veritable mini-country estates. Increasingly, however, these were becoming harder to come by, especially within convenient distance to a railroad station, since existing estates were being subdivided into smaller lots. Still, whether by choice or necessity, even well-off commuters lived in an increasingly urban environment, typically in large, detached houses set on smaller lots squarely facing streets lined with houses of similar design and style. By 1885 there were several such upper-middle-class neighborhoods in or north of Brookline Village, only a few blocks from Brookline's busiest railroad station.[21] As was the case throughout the country, land developers who platted the streets and lots in Brookline rarely built the houses themselves, preferring to sell the lots either to individuals who hired their own builders or to builders who built on speculation.[22]

Although a number of prominent architects resided in Brookline, most notably Henry Hobson Richardson, and just about every Boston architect eventually designed a building there, the town could boast few architectural landmarks. Whether designed by builders or by architects, Brookline houses followed the architectural fashion of the day—Greek Revival and Italianate in the antebellum years (fig. 4.3), Second Empire in the 1860s and 1870s (fig. 4.6), and increasingly eclectic adaptions of the Stick Style and Queen Anne in the 1870s and 1880s. While the most expensive houses, which loudly proclaimed the prosperity and good taste of their fortunate owners, adhered the closest to the canons of style (fig. 4.7), even the modest tenements and cottages of blue-collar workers reflected, however faintly at times, vernacular versions of current architectural fashion.[23]

Brookline subdivisions were subject to minimal regulation aside from the discipline imposed by the real-estate market itself. Builders had learned that upper-middle-class buyers sought to live with those of similar or higher status, and that the easiest houses to sell were those resembling their neighbors in style

FIGURE 4.6. This unpretentious Second Empire–style house was built around 1862 for John Emory Horr (or Hoar), the Harvard-educated principal of Brookline High School. In 1880 he and his wife lived here with an adult son and two female domestic servants. It stood on Beacon Street at the corner of Centre Street, in what was once a quiet bourgeois neighborhood. With the widening of Beacon Street in the late 1880s it was shorn of its front yard, but it survived until being replaced by stores around the First World War. Brookline Photographic Collection, Public Library of Brookline, digitalcommonwealth.org. This work is licensed for use under a Creative Commons Attribution Non-Commercial No Derivatives License (CC BY-NC-ND).

and price. Most residents, especially those of the higher classes, were satisfied with the results. But at times the system threatened to break down. When a subdivision neared completion, speculators anxious to cash in on the last remaining lots were sometimes tempted to maximize the return on their investment by developing their now-valuable lands more intensively than the rest of the neighborhood, either by further subdividing the lots; erecting cheap, high-density tenements; or converting to commercial use. Municipal zoning and subdivision regulations, which would later rule out these choices, had not yet been introduced. It was this very process that was repeated time and again in streetcar suburbs such as Dorchester and Roxbury, as formerly upper-class neighborhoods were taken over by the lower middle and then the working classes.[24]

To reassure anxious upper-middle-class customers that their new neighborhoods were safe from undesirable change, suburban developers resorted to restricted covenants. These restrictions were written into deeds at the time of the original sale and were enforceable in court on the owners (including subsequent owners) by other landowners in the subdivision. Nearly every Brookline subdivision aimed at the upper end of the market employed these controls (significantly,

FIGURE 4.7. 112 High Street, 1884. With grounds laid out by Frederick Law Olmsted, this Cabot & Chandler–designed house represented the epitome of bourgeois taste for those not possessing palatial estates. Its owner, merchant Charles Storrow, was married to a Cabot. Photograph 2011.

Pearl Place contained no such restrictions). Deeds received by the buyers of lots in Linden Place in 1843 required all buildings be erected at least thirty feet from the street, and mandated that nothing be built except "dwelling houses and their appurtenances exclusive of all yards, shops, or other conveniences for mechanical or manufacturing purposes."[25] In Longwood, deeds from the Sears and Lawrence families commonly forbade commercial uses of the land for ten or twenty years, and some carried detailed restrictions on the type of buildings that could be built. One even prohibited buildings to be occupied "by any negro or native of Ireland," although Brookline covenants were rarely directed toward particular racial, ethnic, or religious groups, as was frequently the custom elsewhere.[26] Aspinwall Land Company lots carried restrictions running to 1921 requiring houses built to cost a minimum of $4,000 to $6,000, be set back at least twenty feet from the curb, and never be used for commercial purposes. Similar restrictions were imposed on lots sold by the Brookline Land Company and at the unsuccessful Goddard Heights.[27]

Infrastructure

Town government before 1885 may have avoided the close regulation of the building and development process that is typical of today's municipalities, but the town had long taken an active role in developing the physical and social infrastructure. Although the private sector constructed housing and laid out new streets, suburban development also relied on expanding government services. Brookline's governmental structure was an enlarged version of the system the town had employed since the town's founding in 1705, featuring an elected board of selectmen and other town officials exercising executive authority, and town meetings open to all eligible adult male voters responsible for legislation and monetary appropriations. The town, which once depended on voluntary boards and committees, now employed a full-time police force and hired numerous laborers for various projects. Rising land prices helped boost the town's assessed valuation on which the tax rate was levied: between 1850 and 1875 the town's valuation increased from $5.4 million to $27.9 million, enabling annual expenditures to swell from $11,000 to nearly $600,000, even though the tax rate only increased from $2.10 to $11.50 per thousand.[28] A public library had been in existence since 1857, and in 1871 the town acquired its first two public playgrounds.[29]

Despite the rancor that often accompanied town government, Brookline managed to implement an impressive array of improvements during this period. At least among the town's bourgeoisie a consensus had emerged on what amenities a proper suburb must offer. Foremost was a reliable supply of clean water. At a time when urban residents increasingly enjoyed fresh drinking water and flush toilets in their homes, inhabitants of Brookline saw no reason to settle for anything less. As late as 1874 Brookline still relied on numerous private wells to supply its 6,600 inhabitants with water. Boston, on the other hand, had since 1848 enjoyed city-supplied water piped in from the Cochituate Reservoir in Framingham and other external sources. Ironically, the aqueduct that conveyed this water exclusively to Boston passed directly through Brookline. As the quality of Brookline well water deteriorated and annexationists pointed to Boston's ready supply, the town's leaders were pressed to find their own water source. Various options, including Jamaica Pond and local springs, were considered before the town secured permission from the legislature to take water from the Charles River at Cow Bay, West Roxbury, a source Boston had rejected three decades earlier. Bonds for the project were issued in 1874, pipes laid, a pumping station on the Charles erected, and reservoirs constructed. Despite initial problems this system met the town's needs for the rest of the century.[30]

Closely tied to the problem of supplying water was the matter of its disposal. Most of the town's poorer inhabitants, primarily Catholic Irish, lived on poorly drained lowlands, such as the valley of the Muddy River near Brookline Village. These crowded neighborhoods, served by outhouses and cesspools, were menaced by traditional rural sanitation practices. Popular and scientific opinion blamed inadequate sewerage for allowing the accumulation of deadly "miasmas," which supposedly brought on periodic outbreaks of diseases like diphtheria and typhoid fever. Health and sanitation reformers succeeded in 1876 in launching an ambitious program of public sewers for the town, and despite protests by some taxpayers over the costs, by 1890 more than forty miles of town sewers were in place.[31]

Ever since the first arrivals of the commuters in the 1840s, public education had been a particular source of pride among the town's more fortunate inhabitants. Even some of the wealthy Boston grandees sent their children to the public schools, which were among the best funded anywhere. Between 1845 and 1880 the Brookline public school system had grown from 4 schools, 7 teachers, and 185 pupils to 10 schools, 36 teachers, and more than 1,000 pupils. By 1875 the town was spending $36.58 per pupil each year, nearly three times that of the average Massachusetts community.[32] School reform had proceeded at a steady clip. In the

1840s a three-tiered arrangement of primary, intermediate, and high schools was introduced, followed by graded schools in the 1850s, along with examinations to screen unqualified students out of the higher-level schools. In 1872 a superintendent of schools was appointed for the first time. He attempted to upgrade and standardize teaching practices, often encountering resistance from teachers. New central schools replaced one-room country schoolhouses.[33]

In 1850, at the onset of suburbanization, the Brookline School Committee noted, "in a town abounding as this does in beautiful and tasteful residences, where nature and art . . . combine to produce the most perfect and pleasing forms," it seemed incongruous that its schools not "be of a similar character, spacious, neat, cheerful, convenient . . . surrounded by ample grounds, and adorned with something of that shade and shrubbery which the child enjoys as much as the man, and which would render the spot attractive."[34] In short, the quality of the schools, both physical and academic, should echo the character and refinement of the town, especially of its bourgeois leaders. As will be seen, however, this maxim also applied to the schools provided for the town's Irish working class—the schools their children attended most certainly reflected the mean character of their neighborhoods.

Land developers, builders, and public works and services had made the suburb what it was in 1885. By then the suburb could boast fashionable neighborhoods, a municipal water works, improved drainage, good schools, a public library, and playgrounds. Behind the process of growth lay a political revolution, which saw a faction of the bourgeoisie (many of them commuters) and the Irish Catholic working class join in an uneasy alliance to govern the town. Ultimately, the workings of the capitalistic marketplace built suburbia, but here enterprise was guided by a visible hand.

CHAPTER 5

The New Landscape of Suburban Politics

✦

The administration of our town affairs beats anything done by the Tweed dynasty.

—Henry M. Whitney to William C. Whitney, April 21, 1875

As BROOKLINE grew in the middle years of the nineteenth century the town's political system underwent a major transformation. In 1850 Brookline's town government remained an expanded version of the institution that had governed the rural town a century earlier, relying on town meetings open to all (male) voters to legislate and appropriate, and a slate of mostly unpaid, annually elected officials to administer. Gradually, the town was converting from a system of volunteer government to one featuring paid town employees and rising annual appropriations: from $3,420 in 1837 to $11,595 in 1850.[1] Brookline residents, especially the dominant bourgeois class, could not yet agree whether or not this government was adequate for the town's present and future needs. For at least a few, the current level of government largely sufficed. These residents wanted to retain old-fashioned, limited, cheap government; they were willing to live with reduced amenities in exchange for rural charm and low rural taxes. In 1851 men with these views created the town of West Roxbury out of the rural part of the city of Roxbury, but in Brookline they remained a scattered, increasingly disgruntled minority.[2]

Most of Brookline's bourgeois inhabitants, especially the commuters, saw no reason why they should need to abandon urban conveniences to live in a suburb close to the city. To anyone who had formerly lived in Boston, especially those commuters who still worked there, it was obvious that Brookline's level of municipal services did not meet urban standards. The town had already shown that it was capable of providing public services equal or even superior to those of Boston: as we have seen, by 1850 the town's reformed school system was already being recognized for its high quality.

Schools were important, but how quickly the town could reach urban standards in other areas remained to be seen. Despite its rapid growth in the years before and after the Civil War, Brookline retained the same governmental structure. Year after year the town's leaders, backed by a majority of the voters, did their best to provide Brookline with popular services such as schools, water, sewers, firefighting, police, and libraries, even at the risk of higher taxes. The gamble paid off handsomely, as the town's growing reputation attracted more affluent residents. The town's immense wealth, reflected in soaring property values, enabled the actual tax *rate* per thousand dollars assessed to be kept much lower than the city's, despite expenditures that soared from $4,900 in 1840 to $216,000 in 1870.[3]

The Ring

The simultaneous arrival of hundreds of bourgeoisie and Irishmen in the late 1840s injected a new complexity into Brookline's politics. Over the next two decades the town was increasingly led by an informal association of upper-middle-class businessmen and professionals, dependent on both the votes of the Irish and the implicit support of the upper-class Brahmin landowners. Dubbed the Ring by their less successful opponents, its origins are obscure. Sometime in the 1850s or 1860s the town's political leadership appears to have struck a bargain with the town's Irish community: in exchange for their votes at town meeting and in local elections, municipal jobs would go to local contractors who would hire Brookline residents as laborers.

The so-called Ring's agenda was clear: the government would deliver a high level of municipal services for the bourgeoisie while encouraging high-value residential growth, especially in the vicinity of Brookline Village, in order to keep the tax rate low, especially on the great upper-class estates beyond the village. The arrival of the commuters had enlarged the ranks of those who supported the efforts to raise municipal services to urban levels, but the key to the success of this unlikely coalition was the town's Irish community. At first unable to participate in the political process, many Irish-born resident males became naturalized citizens and thus eligible to vote in town elections.[4] Unlike their counterparts in twentieth-century American suburbs, Brookline's wealthier inhabitants found it impractical to exclude the poor from their community. They discovered that they had little choice but to tolerate a population more diverse than they might have preferred. Before electric- and gasoline-powered appliances were developed, bourgeois households were labor-intensive; with men away at work and children in school, the employment of paid help seemed a necessity. The great influx of refugee Irish Catholics desperate for work of any kind provided an irresistible opportunity to obtain help at bargain wages, both in private households and on infrastructure projects. At a time in which the poor had no way to travel except by foot, a ready labor supply was needed close to home. But though they tolerated the Irish presence, the bourgeoisie determined the rules of the engagement—or at least tried to.

On the face of it, since their arrival in Brookline in the 1840s the Irish had been entirely excluded from political power. As late as 1875 no one of Irish Catholic extraction had ever been elected to a major town office. Clearly, they were junior partners in the Ring: newspaper accounts reported that during town meetings, Irish laborers were directed how to vote by town officials under threats of being denied town employment.[5] Nevertheless, the Irish benefited from the arrangement. When Irish men sought to work they knew that few jobs were available to them besides unskilled day labor. There were three primary sources of jobs in Brookline, all of them ultimately dependent on the Yankee middle and upper classes. Irish laborers could perform tasks such as shoveling snow, chopping firewood, or clearing brush at private households. In this age before bulldozers, they might also dig foundations for the many houses and other buildings being built in Brookline Village and elsewhere. Finally, they might be hired to dig ditches or construct sidewalks for the town government. All of these opportunities for employment would be enhanced by the Ring's agenda—more bourgeois residences and more municipal services required ever more labor.

Annexation Rebuffed

The Ring faced threats to its power both from other political forces in the community and from within its own ranks. Even among the affluent, not everyone agreed with the goals of the Ring. A frustrated minority of bourgeois taxpayers charged that the town overspent on schools and public works; others wanted the town to favor the development of their own lands, which were located away from the village.[6] "No proper legislation can be had," one disgusted critic complained in 1873, "because the laborers vote in the interest of the ring."[7] Two years later businessman Henry M. Whitney wrote to his brother in New York, "The administration of our town affairs beats anything done by the Tweed dynasty."[8]

These disgruntled opponents saw only one certain way to displace the Ring: annexation of the town to the city of Boston. They had reason to hope that the tide was turning their way. In 1867 the city of Boston had annexed the city of Roxbury, followed by the town of Dorchester two years later. In 1873 the city of Charlestown and the towns of Brighton and West Roxbury, which bordered Brookline, became part of the larger city.[9] With the absorption of the latter two municipalities, Boston now surrounded Brookline on three sides. Would not Brookline, the Ring's foes asked, be better off sharing the larger resources of the expanding city? As early as 1871 several residents petitioned the state legislature to annex Brookline to the city. In January 1872 a special Brookline town meeting voted 243 to 82 to oppose the measure and hire an attorney to fight it. In the spring a year later the legislature ignored the protests of the town government and passed a bill consolidating Brookline with Boston, provided that the voters of both town and city approved.[10]

The ensuing controversy rent the bourgeois community, revealing diverse visions of a suburban future. Supporters of annexation argued that a merger with Boston was logical, necessary, and inevitable. "As Boston continues her marvelous growth," wrote one annexationist, "we must grow too, not apart from her, but as part of her. Broad avenues, well-graded, lighted and drained, must supplant narrow country roads; and *pure* water, and *inexhaustible* at that, must flow into every home."[11] Annexationists contended that Brookline's destiny was being thwarted by its outmoded town government, controlled by a cabal hostile to growth and progress. Water, drainage, and sewerage remained inadequate because, according to one annexationist, "a few rich men prevent proper improvements being made." Land developers complained of the difficulty of obtaining town acceptance of subdivisions streets away from areas favored by the Ring.[12]

Opponents of annexation responded that Brookline's independence and identity were well worth preserving. Would Brookline, asked the editor of the fiercely anti-annexationist *Brookline Independent*, "sacrifice her freedom and independence, her glorious record of the past, and prospects of the future, her quiet and peaceful immunities, her proud consciousness of self-sustaining dignity, her world-wide fame for wealth and refinement, for beauty of natural scenery, and for the intelligence and order that pervades her community? Will she end all this to become the smallest, most insignificant, outlying suburban-ward of a commercial, money-worshiping metropolis? Is this an inheritance, a birthright to be bartered for a mess of pottage and a little water?"[13] Foes of annexation charged that the annexationists were a pack of land speculators and that the entire movement was "a mere land jobbing scheme."[14] Critics of annexation pointed out that most leading annexationists held real estate in northern Brookline—the part of the town closest to Boston—which would presumably appreciate sharply if the suburb joined the city.[15]

Some anti-annexationists appear to have been motivated by hostility toward urban growth itself, not simply city government. After annexation, one critic cried, "The beauty of the town would be destroyed by land speculators who would cut down the hills, remove the groves, and lay out streets everywhere like gridirons across the territory."[16] Others predicted that the rapid development that swept Roxbury and Dorchester after annexation would be repeated, with Brookline's "splendid trees," "romantic streets," and "velvet lawns" becoming "the dirty suburbs of a great city."[17] A former Brookline selectman argued that it was a mistake "to call the town of Brookline a city, as it was so rural in its character. . . . No suburb should be annexed until it becomes a city in character."[18]

Other differences are visible from an analysis of the newspapers, directories, property atlases, tax rolls, manuscripts, census schedules, and other sources that form a collective portrait of the pro- and anti-annexationist activists. Reviewing them, I was able to identify forty annexationists and seventy-four of their foes. These 114 individuals constituted the leadership and most active participants in the struggle. In other suburbs studied by historians, annexationists typically were newly arrived commuters demanding expensive urban services, while the opposition was led by old families, more settled commuters, and farmers.[19] But in Brookline annexationists were more likely than their opponents to be longtime town residents. At least 43 percent of the annexation activists had resided in Brookline for more than twenty years, compared with only 27 percent of their opponents. The annexationist camp included members of families present in Brookline for several generations. Only one of the leaders of annexation, Gen. James Whitney, was a relative newcomer, and even he had arrived in 1863. Also, among commercial farmers, seven out of nine backed annexation. Moreover, Boston Brahmins almost universally opposed annexation. Cabots, Lowells, Gardners, Amorys, and Sargents closed ranks in favor of Brookline's continued independence; only William I. Bowditch and his son Ernest among these proper Bostonian suburbanites wanted to join the city.

Both sides scored points in the ensuing debate. Opponents of annexation charged that the movement was a plot by land speculators heavily interested in the northern part of the town. Examination of the town property atlases for 1872 and 1874 at least partly confirms this charge. Annexation activists together owned some 250 acres in North Brookline between Beacon Street and the Charles River.[20] The leading annexationist, George Griggs, was a Boston lawyer from an old Brookline family who had inherited sixty-five acres in northern Brookline in the 1840s. In those days this part of town, despite its proximity to Boston, was isolated and sparsely settled. In 1850 Griggs had been the prime instigator behind the construction of Beacon Street, an extension of the street with the same name in Boston's Back Bay. Griggs had hoped that the street would open up his lands to development, but his plans were frustrated. Beacon Street remained a promise unfilled, a narrow country road rather than a thoroughfare to Boston. In 1873 many of Griggs's neighbors joined the annexation movement in the hope that Boston would recognize Beacon Street's potential.[21]

Annexationists, for their part, contended in vein that Brookline was in the grip of a ring hostile to progress. Unfortunately for them, they could not convince any of the groups affiliated with the Ring to abandon their support for it. The powerful Brahmin estate owners in southern Brookline were loath to give up a reasonably efficient government that held down taxes on their undeveloped lands. Local politicians and land developers wanted to maintain their favored positions. Most of Brookline's upper middle class (even including some developers) sought to guide and restrain the process of growth so as to retain the town's rural charm, bolster real-estate values, and encourage high-status development. Finally, Brookline's large population of Irish laborers saw their exclusive access to these jobs endangered should the town become another Boston ward, which would put them into competition with others allied with larger existing political organizations.

When Brookline's voters went to the polls in October 1873 the foes of annexation carried the day handily. Although Boston's electorate approved the merger, the citizens of Brookline voted it down 706 to 299.[22] Annexation failed because the annexationists were unable to persuade very many residents of Brookline that gains from a merger would outweigh losses. Their narrow base in a group with obvious special interests hurt the annexation cause. Their attacks on the Ring ignored the fact that most inhabitants were satisfied with the state of government in Brookline. To many the annexation supporters' accusations that the Ring was hostile to progress seemed absurd in light of the high level of services that the local government was already providing. Above all, most Brookline voters by 1873 had come to see themselves as permanently apart from the city, not inhabitants of a transitory urban fringe fated to be absorbed by Boston. Brookline's annexationists tried again in 1875, 1879, and 1880 before giving up the cause as hopeless.[23] The territorial expansion of Boston ground to a halt; with minor twentieth-century exceptions, the bounds of Boston have not changed since 1873. Brookline's example became the template for many a suburb near other eastern cities, whose boundaries would become frozen by suburban intransigence.[24]

Irish and Yankee

Within the Ring itself internal disputes threatened to tear the alliance apart. In order to keep upper-class Brahmin landowners happy, property taxes on their estates had to remain low and development schemes deflected away from their fashionable neighborhoods. Much more difficult was respecting Irish sensitivities. For their support, in addition to employment the Irish expected respect from town officials and the Yankee community. Given the history of religious and cultural conflict between Yankee Protestants and Irish Catholics, this was not always easy, especially since both groups refused to concede the other's moral and cultural superiority. Dependent as they were on their labor, the bourgeoisie resented the Irish for their poverty, their so-called rude behavior, and their superstitious Catholic religion. Irish culture was ridiculed in the town newspapers, which were clearly aimed at middle-class Yankee Protestant readers. Dialect stories featuring Pat, the hapless Irish laborer, and Bridget, the serving girl, were only the most blatant expressions of this sentiment. As elsewhere in America, addiction to strong whiskey, saloons, brawling, habitual uncleanliness, and universal ignorance were said to be the hallmarks of Irish life. Although anti-Catholicism declined in Brookline after the Civil War, the Irish religion still raised Protestant hackles. In return, Irish Catholics regarded Yankees as both heretics working to undermine the true faith and cold-hearted hypocrites who ignored their own moral failings and lack of Christian compassion. In 1875 the parish priest at St. Mary's Church forbade his parishioners from accepting aid from the Brookline Industrial Union—the town's leading private charity—because it entailed visits by Protestant ministers to Catholic homes. Many Protestants were outraged, including a speaker at the town meeting who urged rejection of a modest increase in town poor relief on that grounds that "if those people could not take proffered aid, which was so very objectionable, he hoped they would *starve* before the town came to the rescue."[25]

To most of the bourgeoisie, poverty stemmed from defective morality. The poor were often portrayed as able-bodied loafers unwilling to work. The good ladies of the Industrial Union believed that "intemperance and the improvidence arising from it" formed "the chief source of poverty in the town." The suffering that the poor experienced was largely self-imposed, a result, it was said, of their habitually filthy lifestyle. Attempts by low-wage workers to improve their lot through collective action, rather than individual initiative, were frowned upon. "Any individual who, by countenancing 'strikes' or cheapening honest and faithful labor, promotes ill-feeling between employees and employed," the *Brookline Transcript* editorialized in 1871, "is an enemy to his country and its institutions." When railroad workers struck throughout the country in 1877, the *Brookline Chronicle* called it a "reign of terror" that should be "remorselessly" repressed.[26]

And yet Brookline's bourgeoisie was forced to admit some sympathy for the plight of their poorer Irish neighbors. Loafers there might well be, but suffering of the poor in the latter half of the 1870s seemed to be caused by something greater than a sudden inexplicable lack of individual effort. "Of all the sad sights with which the hard times have made us familiar," the *Chronicle* observed in 1878, "the saddest is to see those who are willing to and eager to work, shut out from every opportunity."[27] Whatever the reasons for the condition of the poor, charity was the duty of the privileged. The newspaper at times displayed surprising empathy for the conditions faced by the poor. Catholicism gained in respectability among Protestants, and increasingly Catholic church-related social and cultural activities, such as fairs and picnics, appeared in the press, with emphasis on the decorum of the participants. When the local Catholic church organized its own sewing circle for the poor, following its rejection of aid from the Industrial Union, the *Chronicle* gave its blessing: "This is a sample of the practical charity which begins at home." As a gesture toward the Irish community, the Protestant ladies of the Industrial Union elected Margaret Driscoll, the wife of James Driscoll, one of Brookline's most prominent Irish Catholics, as a director in 1879.[28]

"A Thorough Education"

Nowhere were clashes of interests between Yankee and Irish more apparent than differing attitudes toward public education. As we have seen, Brookline's upper middle class saw Brookline's system of public schools as the jewel in the crown of its acclaimed municipal services. Ever since the first arrival of the commuters in the 1840s, public education had been a particular source of pride among the town's more fortunate inhabitants, who were willing to fund schools at a high level.

Yankee bourgeois parents viewed education as a means of assuring that their children would enjoy or surpass the advantages they themselves possessed and acquire the skills necessary to proceed onward to college, continue the family business, practice a profession, or seek good-paying employment. Lip service was sometimes paid to the transcendent benefits of learning: "The aim of all true education," the school committee proclaimed in 1847, "is to elevate the soul, to enlarge and strengthen the mind, to purify and warm the heart." But mostly, the justification was utilitarian: "A thorough education is the best of all capitals to commence life with. It secures to the child in after life, even though his station be humble, innumerable sources of happiness. It produces a feeling of self-reliance and manly independence, and prepares him to decide intelligently for himself the many important questions which must in after life present themselves for decision." (What benefits female students would receive, if any, were not stated.) The necessity of educational improvement seemed indisputable: "The rapid progress of the community in all the departments of practical life—in trade and commerce, manufactures, agriculture, and the mechanic arts, calls for a corresponding expansion in its system of education." And the results seemed impressive—of the fourteen 1880 graduates of Brookline High School, eight entered Harvard.[29]

The Yankee Protestants who ran Brookline's public schools—as late as 1870, not a single Irish man or woman ever served on the school committee or as principals, or even were hired as teachers—realized that the intellectual benefits of attending the public schools would largely accrue to the Yankee students. The schools would provide Irish students with the discipline they needed to work as laborers, servants, or factory workers. And with their superstitious religion, outrageous accents, and peasant ignorance it seemed the Irish needed plenty of correction if they were to overcome their backward ways.

In 1848 attendance at the North District school at the northern edge of

Brookline Village had surged, and by the end of the school year more than a third of the pupils were Irish. The school committee attributed "a very large proportion both of the absences, and of the tardiness" to these troublesome newcomers. At the Boys Intermediate School in the village, "the addition of a considerable number of large boys, mostly foreigners, and often ignorant of even the first rudiments of education, has for some years operated as a serious drawback upon the progress of the whole school." The school committee therefore "divided the school, placing the larger and more backward pupils by themselves, in a separate room" under a male teacher. The following year the committee excluded these dangerous students altogether by requiring entrance examinations for the intermediate schools.[30]

This did not solve the problem of how to handle children "too old for the primary schools" but "too ignorant" for the intermediate level. In 1851 the committee therefore established a special school, with most of its pupils drawn from the North District. The existing intermediate schools were renamed grammar schools, and the new school became the sole intermediate school, housed in "a very small room" in an office building. From there the school was relocated to equally tight quarters in town hall, and then to a temporary building on Western (Brookline) Avenue near the Marsh, where most of its pupils lived. In 1854 it was finally given a permanent site on nearby Pearl Place, in a new building that also housed a primary school. During the Civil War the Pearl Place schools were moved southward to a new location and renamed the Ward Schools. The district these schools served was carefully drawn to encompass only the section of Brookline Village south of the railroad, an area almost exclusively Irish.[31]

Conditions at the Pearl Place and Ward Schools were consistently the worst in the system. Overcrowding was endemic. In 1856 there were 43.5 pupils per teacher at the Pearl Place primary school, as compared to averages of 36.1, 25.6, 24.5, and 23.0 at the town's four other primary schools. By 1860 the ratio had fallen only slightly to 41.5 pupils at Pearl Place, compared to 26.6 at the town's six other primary schools.[32] In 1875 150 children at the Ward Schools were jammed into just three classrooms. The school committee blamed the pupils and their parents for the schools' shortcomings rather than their own niggardly financial support. The Pearl Place Grammar School, the committee reported,

> continues to be in as good condition as its peculiar circumstances will admit. The teacher, who is also truant-officer, never permits pupils to be absent from

> the school, without using his best exertions to ascertain and remove the cause; yet, in many instances, it is found that the services of the children are absolutely needed by the parents who are unable to obtain other assistance. In such cases we can only regret that it should be necessary to prevent children from getting that education which will fit them for attaining a better position in life than they can hope for without it.

Irregular attendance, "the crying evil . . . the bar to all progress toward universal education" had long vexed the committee. The attitudes of working-class parents toward the blessings of free public education seemed unfathomably perverse. "Ignorance is proverbially improvident," an exasperated committee lamented in 1870,

> yet one would think that if the parent who can hardly by the work of his hands earn food for the children growing up in idleness around him, could be made to understand, to feel, that by merely taking advantage of what is freely offered to him, by simply permitting his children to go to school, and seeing that they do as required he could put them on the same footing in regard to the wealthy. . . . Even the most ignorant and improvident would hardly neglect so little a thing, or would keep them from school for a day or an hour or on any light consideration.

Alas, the committee sighed, "such parents do not understand this."[33]

Frustrated, the school committee established an ungraded school to isolate chronic truants. This heavy-handed solution provoked immediate opposition, both from within the committee itself and from the Irish community (which, of course, was still unrepresented on the board). In 1872 four out of the nine members on the board took the unprecedented step of issuing a blistering minority report, calling the ungraded school "a cause of constant irritation to our foreign population. No explanation nor glosses can blind them to the fact that American children are not sent to the Ungraded School—nor obviate the inference that it is a degradation to be sent there." The unpopular experiment was ended the following year.[34]

The minority report—just as the annexation controversy was coming to a head—marked a turning point in Irish-Yankee relations. The dissenters had warned that it was "harmful to keep" the Irish community "in a state of chronic irritability." No longer would Irish sentiments be ignored by the committee. In

1875 the town elected its first Irish school committeeman, Michael Driscoll, a second-generation member of the town's most prominent Irish family. Five years later he was joined by Father Lawrence J. Morris, the pastor of St. Mary's. They endorsed a frontal assault on truancy, backed by truant officers, local bylaws, and new state legislation. When the great depression of the 1870s temporarily undercut these efforts, the committee in 1876 recognized that in poor households, "many of the pupils have been called upon to help eke out the scanty means of subsistence of the family, and this has been a very considerable cause of tardiness and absence at school. They have shoveled snow, picked coal, or done almost any work where they could earn a cent." With the economy improving, by 1880 attendance at the Ward Schools had become only marginally less regular than at other town schools.[35]

In theory Brookline's public schools offered the same opportunities to all students, but it was apparent that Irish pupils did not benefit the same as their Yankee counterparts. Partly, this was a matter of different expectations: Yankee children, especially those from bourgeois households, were being groomed for careers while the Irish children were largely taught discipline and respect for authority that would serve them in their future roles as manual workers and housewives. If, as expected, the Irish left school at an early age and few attended high school, most of the Yankee community regarded this as further evidence of the inherent inferiority or stubborn perversity of the poor, not a failing of the educational system or of the capitalist economic system itself.[36]

Domestic Politics

Despite their differences Irish men and women regularly interacted with Yankees. For Irish women and girls, the primary point of contact was typically domestic service. As elsewhere in the United States, middle- and upper-class families had become dependent on the services of live-in domestic servants. Rural Americans in the antebellum North had long employed men and women to help with farm chores, but these individuals typically functioned as part of an older preindustrial economy in which they formed part of the farmer's household, took their meals with the farmer's family, and were subject to household discipline. Both employers and employees rejected the term *servants* in favor of the more democratic *help*. Often kin to their employer, these women were normally of the same Protestant religion and Yankee ethnicity.[37] This older pattern could still be seen in rural

Massachusetts, where the 1875 state census recorded more women employed as housekeepers and house workers than domestic servants. But in the state's urban and suburban regions—three-fifths of the state's female domestic servants (as opposed to housekeepers or workers) lived in just a dozen municipalities—service was different. Although they lived on the premises, domestics were not regarded as members of the family but rather employed servants—even minions—whose lowly status was reflected by their cultural and social inferiority to their masters.[38]

By 1870 eight hundred women and sixty-two men served as domestic servants in Brookline. No less than 36 percent of Brookline households included live-in domestics. Yankees avoided domestic service—more than nine out of ten female domestics were born abroad or had foreign-born parents. As elsewhere in the northeastern United States the vast majority of Brookline's domestics (at least 76 percent) were of Celtic extraction; no fewer than 497 of them were born in the Emerald Isle, with the rest coming from New England, Great Britain, or Canada.[39] Non-Celtic servants included Yankees from rural New England, English-speaking natives of the Maritimes, a dozen African American women, and a smattering from Germany and other countries of continental Europe. These were young, single women, with nearly three-quarters of them in their twenties or thirties, and the median age only twenty-four.[40]

Only thirty-three of Brookline's eight hundred domestics were aged fifty or older, which suggests that most women left service by the time they entered middle age, in most cases to marry. For those who remained in service for a few years, Brookline employers paid wages sufficient for at least some servants to save money. In the 1870 census some 120 domestics reported owning property, with an average holding of $457. Unfortunately, sums like these were insufficient to support a spinster in her old age, and the poorhouse all too frequently loomed.[41]

In American bourgeois households it was well-established that the mistress ruled, hiring, firing, and supervising the family servants as she saw fit. Her authority over her servants was reinforced by the seemingly indisputable superiority of modern Protestantism to superstitious Catholicism, forward-thinking English culture to the backward Celtic, and bourgeois education and culture to working-class ignorance and crudity. Yet keeping servants proved to be a source of continuous frustration for housekeepers. "Oh!" Caroline White, wife of tanner Francis wrote in her diary, "these domestics make distraction in a family."[42] Even upper-class women who had been raised with (and often by) servants faced periodic domestic crises. "My housekeeper departed indignant," wealthy Brookline heiress Elizabeth Rogers Mason Cabot complained to her diary in 1872, "leaving me with no one in her place." Over the next two weeks she wrote, "The laundress has been in bed three days with face-ache, used up all the wood and nearly all the water in the house, and tore the clothes. The cook don't know how to boil a potato nor light a fire, and yesterday was sent to the hospital on account of a sore and varicose veins!"[43]

From her arrival in Brookline in 1858 Caroline White (who had been raised on servant-less farms) found herself confronting incompetent or rebellious domestics and facing a great deal of difficulty keeping her household fully staffed, even though she regularly employed only a cook and a parlor maid. Regularly, servants departed—either from her dismissing them or on their own accord. These departures could lead to ugly, emotionally grueling confrontations: on one occasion Caroline, then eight months pregnant, dismissed an unsatisfactory servant, offering

> her the wages due her for the time she had been here & informed her she could leave immediately—whereupon she most disdainfully turned on her heel & said she should not go till I paid her a week's wages—I told her she might take what I offered her or nothing, but told her *to go.* Just then Frank [her husband] came in the room, & I left him to fight the battle with her, of getting her out of the house. She refused point blank to budge and tried to intimidate him—by all sorts of threats but she had the wrong one to deal with if she thought she could frighten him—she *yelled* and *shrieked* and acted like a maniac—but finally started off without being forcibly ejected, though not without threats of being "heard from again," etc.[44]

Time after time Caroline White found herself going "to Boston . . . to find *good help* out of a mass of ignorance, falsehood & deceit. It is discouraging."[45]

In the end the same struggle between management and labor over control of the industrial process that was being waged on the floors of countless factories had been extended into the very household that was supposed to be a refuge from the commercial world.[46] Once hired, the mistress of the house closely supervised the help she employed. With every new servant came a period of "inducting the domestics into some of the details of the house work."[47] Although her servants generally cooked and cleaned alone, White did work alongside her servants while cooking, canning, and spring and fall house cleaning, and was not afraid of getting her hands dirty.[48] Standards must have varied from household to household but hers were strict. One of her domestics was "a good hearted girl I believe—but not neat enough." Another did "not please me much in any respect." Others "have not moved very briskly today." Caroline White was not impossible to please—"my new domestic promises exceedingly well—and my kitchen shows the effects of a *good cleanly servant*"—but she, like many bourgeois women, found it frustratingly difficult to retain the ones she preferred.[49]

For in their contest with management the workers here were not without leverage. Pushed too hard, there was nothing to prevent servants from leaving; other households always beckoned. As with slaves, servants could take advantage of their mistress's low opinion of their intelligence by feigning ignorance to avoid unwanted duties.[50] In the end, employers were forced to settle for something less than the around-the-clock service by always-willing hands they had hoped for. Still, many Brookline households had their pick of the best available servants, despite the relative isolation of many of its larger households. Brookline's high level of wealth offered better opportunities for domestics than elsewhere. Contemporaries agreed that the worst situation for a domestic was to be the sole servant in a household, on which any and all tasks might fall—cleaning, cooking, washing, polishing, answering doors, minding children, shopping, or any other chore to be done. But in Brookline in 1870 three-quarters of female live-in servants worked in households with two or more servants. In these households, servants had specific (and thus limited) tasks. Typically there would be a cook who supervised the kitchen and prepared the meals; a parlor/chamber maid, responsible for cleaning the body of the rest of the house and answering doors; and a nurse or governess to mind the children or care for the elderly.[51]

Behind the daily struggle between mistress and servant often lay the clash between Yankee Protestant and Irish Catholic cultures. Over and over again Mrs. White, a devout evangelical Protestant, proclaimed that the primary impediment to finding good servants was that most of them were Irish Catholics. Time and again she sought to hire "some good Protestant girls," but nearly always she found herself with Irish Catholics. She was, she confessed to her diary, "heartily sick of the Irish . . . sick of all the race."[52] But given the ready availability and willingness to work for "reasonable" wages, the Irish remained an irresistible bargain.

The Yankee women who employed live-in domestic servants made every effort to physically segregate their families from their Irish servants. Most middle-class suburban houses built after midcentury had separate back stairways so that servants could access their isolated living quarters without literally rubbing shoulders with their betters, and domestics took their meals by themselves in the kitchen, not in the family dining room.[53] But in the end these efforts failed, as servants became intertwined with the most intimate activities of middle-class home life, especially the raising of children. "With the separation of the home from the workplace and the consequent departure of the father for most of the day," notes historian Faye E. Dudden, "domestics provided important opportunities for adult contact and companionship for children."[54]

Community Standards

Often unintentionally, suburban reform movements heightened tensions between the Yankee Protestant bourgeoisie and the Irish Catholic community. Before the Civil War throughout the North the Irish had rejected both abolitionism and even antislavery Republicanism, whose leaders were largely Protestant bourgeoisie; nothing suggests that Brookline's Irish were any different.[55] No reform movement had deeper roots in Brookline than the temperance crusade. As we have seen, well before the Civil War Brookline had seen the establishment of a local chapter of the Washington Total Abstinence Society, affiliated with a national organization based in Baltimore. Hundreds of residents were said to have pledged personal abstinence from alcohol.[56]

After the arrival of the Irish the movement's emphasis changed from exhorting individual abstinence to outlawing public drinking. The decade of the Civil War seems to have seen the movement decline, only to be revived in 1877 with the establishment of a Brookline chapter of the Women's Christian Temperance Union (WCTU), appropriately a national organization based in Evanston, Illinois, a prominent Chicago railroad suburb.[57] Whereas the antebellum movement had been led by males, often clergymen, upper-middle-class women now set the agenda, which was to drive saloons and liquor dealers out of town. In theory alcohol could be sold in Brookline only under license from the selectmen. Few licenses were actually granted, but enforcement of the law was lax: the Irish shacks and tenements on and near the Marsh and at Whiskey Point housed countless "blind pigs," illegal rum shops. Prohibitionists demanded both the revocation of all existing licenses and the closing of the outlaw saloons. They faced an uphill battle, since the selectmen were increasingly unwilling to alienate the Irish community, whose votes helped keep them in office. Even when the selectmen were finally pressured into stepping up enforcement, the results proved disappointing. Despite frequent police raids—sixteen in July 1885 alone—liquor continued to flow. The existence of numerous licensed saloons in Roxbury Crossing, just over the Boston line and close by the Marsh, further undercut the effort to keep Brookline dry.[58]

Despite its best efforts the WCTU was unable to convince a majority of the town's (male) voters that it was necessary, feasible, or even desirable to keep the Irish from their drink. Prohibitionists might contend that "nine-tenths of the poverty of the town is created by the existence of these unlicensed rum shops," but many disagreed. "A law to be effective," wrote one correspondent to the *Brookline Chronicle,* "must have the support of the people. The prohibition law will never be thus supported, as common sense will teach us that it is neither just nor judicious to make somebody else than the drunkard himself responsible for his failing." In their hatred of liquor, the prohibitionists could see no difference between "*use* and *abuse.*"[59]

The only time the WCTU and their supporters made headway was when illicit saloons appeared beyond the Irish neighborhoods in the backyards of the respectable classes. In the summer of 1885 reports surfaced that the so-called Reservoir Hotel on Beacon Street "was beyond question a 'Road House' in the fullest and worst acceptance of the term." When neighbors and the land company trying to sell lots in the area complained, a series of police raids shut down the hotel and arrested the operator, who was fined and imprisoned. In November the hotel suddenly reopened with "a noisy and disreputable brawl, in which the worst characters, both male and female, from Boston and adjoining towns and cities took part." This time both the new operator and the owner were arrested. At the trial that followed, the operator, one Peter Sullivan, turned state's evidence and testified that the owner, Dr. James Simonds of Boston, had leased him the hotel in October, telling him that "it would be impossible to get a license to sell liquors there, but . . . he could take the house, keep light drinks for sale openly, and conceal 'hard stuff' in a neighboring house." The doctor plied him with more helpful hints, "one being the advisability of keeping a few women there." Simonds denied the charges, but the court convicted him and imposed an unusually stiff penalty of a thousand dollars, costs, and three months in prison.[60]

Meanwhile, a Watertown party had the audacity to request a liquor license from the selectmen to reopen the hotel once more. As would be expected, the opposition proved lively. A lawyer for the land company argued that the hotel was unneeded and unwanted, a threat to property values: "Brookline is one of the cleanest towns in the Commonwealth, and it should be kept clean." Twenty-one other property owners in the vicinity joined the land company in opposition. The trustees of Boston University, which owned land nearby, contended that the hotel would "render the neighborhood less respectable, and less desirable for the better class of residents." To no one's surprise, the selectmen rejected the application, and the hotel never reopened.[61]

CHAPTER 6

Suburbia Real and Imagined

✦

We were living in the country with the conveniences and luxuries of the city about us.

—William Dean Howells, *Suburban Sketches,* 1871

IN THE forty years that followed the arrival of the first wave of bourgeois commuters and Irish immigrants in the 1840s, Brookline completed its transition from rural town to residential suburb. Much of this growth had been directed by the workings of a newly developed land market, subject to sporadic and inconsistent governmental regulation. At the beginning of this process, Brookline residents had no clear vision of where this development would—or even should—be leading. Over the next decades competing suburban ethics emerged, based on rival aesthetics and differing visions of what the community ideally should look like. By the end of the nineteenth century an American bourgeois suburban ideal would develop, one that Brookline's experience would very much help to shape.

Toward a Suburban Aesthetic

The defeat of annexation was a major step toward defining a distinctly suburban vision. In Brookline, suburban now meant not merely a place temporarily perched between an expanding city and retreating country but one destined to remain politically independent of each. But the controversy also revealed different political fault lines. Annexationists made no bones about their desire to urbanize the town by linking it closer to Boston and expressed no more regret in giving up Brookline's rustic fields than its outmoded town meeting government. Somewhat surprisingly, however, even many of those opposed to annexation were ready, even anxious, to sacrifice rural charm for further development, particularly if the resulting houses were large and expensive.

As late as 1850 *suburban* was still being applied as a pejorative term to the traditional meeting ground of city and country, characterized by the unsightly hovels of the poor, soap works, tanneries, and cattle yards, and something of this negative connotation would persist for many years. Redefining the adjective was a contentious process in Brookline, given that its residents were heirs to several cultural traditions, not all of them easily compatible. Today the association between suburban living, the elite classes, and a preference for rural and natural scenery, trees, lawns, outdoor recreation, and the rustic life seems unremarkable, but in the middle of the nineteenth century this connection was still being forged. Medieval Europeans had been profoundly ambivalent about man's relationship to nature: woods were terrifying places full of dangerous animals and unruly men; the replacement of forests with cultivated lands represented an unabashed advance of civilization, and urban wealth was preferable to rural squalor. These attitudes persisted into the early modern period and were brought to the New World with the English colonists: "What could they see," Governor William Bradford had written in the 1640, "but a hideous and desolate wilderness, full of wild beasts and wild men—and what multitudes there might be of them they knew not."[1]

It was not until the eighteenth century that a new aesthetic emerged in England. There the relentless expansion of London into previously rural habitats, combined with the widespread burning of sooty coal, gave rise to a vigorous reaction. Poets once more sang the ancient virtues of Arcadia, reviving a tradition with roots in antiquity, promoting what Keith Thomas has called "the cult of the countryside." Reversing popular beliefs, the rustic scenery and their pastoral inhabitants were proclaimed morally and spiritually superior to the corruptions of the cities. That these musings were "an evasion of reality" that avoided the "harsh realities" of actually living in the countryside did little to stem the popularity of Arcadianism, or Pastoralism, which after all "did not even necessarily indicate a genuine desire to live in the country."[2]

Along with this shift toward a natural aesthetic came the growing popularity of weekend country retreats near London, and finally, the first true bourgeois suburbs, well-established by the outbreak of the American Revolution. By this time, as we have seen, Boston and other American cities were ringed by country estates on the English model. With the emergence of the Romantic literary and artistic movement at the end of the eighteenth century, cultivated persons in England or

New England enthusiastically proclaimed the scenic glories of nature and a nostalgic longing for rural living, even though necessity demanded that they spend most of their time in cities and towns.[3] Jeffersonian politicians sang the virtues of the sturdy yeoman, especially as their sons and daughters increasingly moved to cities.[4] This yearning for a lost rural past combined with ambivalent feelings about the cities reinforced a longstanding sentiment that families should try to avoid what Sam Bass Warner termed "artificial, incomplete, and temporal" cities altogether and return to the "simple, full, and timeless" country, where "the physical setting encouraged the family to live by some concept of harmony with the unending cycles and seasons of nature."[5]

Thus by the time popular landscape author Andrew Jackson Downing proclaimed in 1850 that the estates of Brookline were "a kind of landscape garden" of which "there is nothing in America, of the sort, so inexpressibly charming as the lanes which lead from one cottage, or villa, to another," the pastoral aesthetic was widely accepted among the American elite. Downing advocated cultivating for beauty, carefully integrating romantically inspired architecture with artful landscaping. Indeed, one of his inspirations was "the environs of Boston," which he singled out as being "more highly cultivated than those of any other city in North America. There are here whole rural neighborhoods of pretty cottages and villas, admirably cultivated, and, in many cases, tastefully laid out and planted." Looking ahead, he noted that "the character of even the finest of these places is, perhaps, somewhat suburban, as compared with those of the Hudson river, but we regard them as furnishing admirable hints for a class of residences likely to become more numerous than any other in the country—the tasteful suburban cottage."[6]

In the end, Downing's vision was wildly impractical. Like many subsequent observers, he had been mesmerized by Brookline's upper-class estates, largely ignoring the commuter district (and adjacent village) where most of the townspeople actually lived in the 1840s. "The owner of a small cottage residence may have almost every kind of beauty and enjoyment in his grounds that the largest estate will afford," he wrote, even if he has only "half a dozen acres." Although this might have seemed modest to Downing, few Brookline commuters could have afforded a house lot even half of that size within a convenient walk to the train depot. How many actual commuters tried to follow Downing's advice is impossible to say. Certainly many of them had neither the time nor the money to oversee the design and landscaping of their entire property, even a half-acre or acre lot, while others chose to use part of their properties for vegetable gardens or fruit trees.[7]

Not everyone in the new residential suburbs celebrated pastoralism or sought refuge in untamed wildness. Many of the new commuters brought with them an urbanist aesthetic that judged a community more by the quality of its buildings and municipal improvements, and the wealth and good taste of its inhabitants, than by the closeness of fields, cows, trees, and other markers of rusticity. Most middle-class Americans were instinctively boosters who applauded economic success and welcomed new construction. And although a large portion of Americans shared Thomas Jefferson's well-known antipathy toward cities, others celebrated urban growth as confirmation of the nation's progress.[8] Indeed, at least some urbanites found parts of the rural scenery that they actually encountered distasteful, marked as it was by indifferently maintained buildings, squalor, and unattractive industries. Many suburban residents could recall, not necessarily with affection, the cramped, drafty, and generally uncomfortable rural homes in which they had been raised. Replacement of old hovels, no matter how picturesque, with expensive new suburban houses, even along straight streets lined with relatively small house lots, was widely welcomed as advancing civilization.[9]

Thus by the end of the Civil War rival aesthetic ideals had emerged among Brookline's bourgeoisie: the rustic and the urban. The former insisted that authentic suburbs had to retain their rural character. They contended that Brookline's farms and fields set it apart from the city, and without them, the community would suffer an irreplaceable loss.[10] Brookline, one rustic champion wrote in 1872 in the heat of the annexation controversy, had "the real flavor of the country, not that mongrel character which is neither town nor country, and with the attractions of neither." Now that legacy was endangered by growth and development. Rustic critics complained of trees "ruthlessly annihilated," of widenings that changed "our beautiful streets into dusty, shadeless, glaring thoroughfares, unprotected even here and there from the vertical rays of the scorching summer sun." For some the worship of trees approached druidic proportions: "Let every tree be preserved, which can by any possibility be spared."[11]

For some advocates of the rustic, the town's better days had already passed. Town historian Harriet Woods in 1874 lamented "the building of crowded houses so close together that every vestige of rural beauty is sacrificed, and that the chief attractions, which have for years made our town proverbial for its charms, are rapidly disappearing before the march of greedy speculation." Another writer five years later noted that "Brookline is often called the Garden of Boston, so cultivated, shady, and floral, so rich in broad estates and tasteful in its residents." But that was in the past, for so-called progress had stretched "its mercenary hands over the country, leveling hills, filling valleys, destroying trees, blasting rocks, longing to transform all that is valuable in Nature to its own uninteresting level." Once Brookline Village was bordered by "green meadows . . . bright in early summer with golden cow slips, violets, and yarrow," but since the coming of the railroads and the Irish—"who never object to hiving together in close quarters"—the native vegetation had given way to "crowded tenements."[12]

Urbanists, on the other hand, embraced the urban attributes of Brookline, most notably its convenient access to Boston, the high level of modern conveniences available to its inhabitants, and above all the wealth and high social status of its leading residents. The editor of the *Brookline Chronicle* dismissed the pastoralists' "nonsensical whimpering and longing for a return to the 'cowslip and yellow yarrow' days of Brookline."[13] To the urbanists, suburban above all meant a location near (but not part of) the city, not necessarily one with bucolic vistas. Many were anxious to see the town grow and develop rather than rusticate. As in any nineteenth-century American town, there were boosters anxious to see Brookline evolve into an integral part of a greater metropolis. Brookline, the *Transcript* editorialized in 1872,

> is no longer a Country Town, but rather the suburb of a great and growing city. . . . Its interests and the interests of the City and adjacent suburban towns are more nearly identical than formerly. . . . In view of . . . the rapid change from country to suburban life, it seems as though the time is near at hand when farms . . . will gradually be cut up into building lots and become the homes of a large population, whose future wants should be duly considered.

Instead of resisting these developments, the *Transcript* counseled rational planning to avoid "a confused system of streets."[14] After all, the Back Bay, Boston's most fashionable new neighborhood, was being laid out with straight gridiron streets.

By and large Brookline's newspapers throughout the 1870s took the urbanist perspective. Editorials called for building more middle-income housing and new streets, the widening and straightening of existing ways, and the installation of utilities. Although describing Brookline as the "Garden Town of America," an account published in 1876 emphasized not the acres of fields and verdant hills but rather "the very air of neatness about our well-kept streets; the artistically laid out grounds and residences of our citizens, and the costly public buildings," which "bespeak to the visitor the abode of wealth and culture." The author hoped "to see this town a *live business place,* and more of the wealth expanded on home industries."[15]

Throughout the Boston region in the late nineteenth century most residents clearly fell into the urbanist camp. Historian Douglas Shand-Tucci has shown how a wide range of income groups, from blue-collar workers to successful professionals and businessmen, clearly preferred to live in homes set close together, massed in uniform patterns squarely facing the street, and set on small lots. These "were not in our sense of the term suburban houses at all," writes Shand-Tucci. "They were an attempt to revive in the vast new lands of the city the ideal town house—detached, and on its garden lot—that had been so characteristic of Boston until the scarcity of land had begun to obliterate the ideal in the 1820s."[16] During the 1870s and 1880s thousands of houses, including a few aimed at the very classes that dominated Brookline, sprang up in the so-called streetcar suburbs of Dorchester, West Roxbury, Somerville, Malden, and Cambridge surrounding the city. Whatever rural feeling survived in these new neighborhoods was provided by nearby parks and the lawns and backyard gardens of residents' own small yards. Even when ample funds were available, owners typically opted to spend the money on grander houses—or vacation properties—than on larger lots. Being in a convenient and socially prominent location trumped more remote locations with rolling lawns and rustic views.[17]

As realized by 1885 Brookline Village was gradually being built up along urbanist lines, with most of the straight streets lined with houses set back at the same distance from the curb. On their five- to fifteen-thousand-square-foot lots the houses presented a solid, substantial face to the street. Some of the houses were quite large, since they were built to accommodate several children and domestic servants, but there was little to suggest a rural locale.[18] Whatever temporary illusion of living in the country would have ended as soon as vacant lots disappeared and new streets were opened up in nearby fields.

One complaint sometimes heard was that the housing market offered few choices for those of middle incomes, the respectable lower middle classes so well represented in most streetcar suburbs. In 1870 the *Brookline Transcript* bemoaned "the scarcity of small dwelling houses for rent," which meant that "families are constantly arriving unable or indisposed to build, but willing to pay good rent for comfortable small homes, none of which are to be had."[19] According to the *Chronicle* in 1875, Brookline

> is growing very fast, and would grow much faster were it not for the lack of suitable dwellings for those who, though not able to pay the high rents asked for the costly houses, have tastes that will not permit them to live in tenement houses. We are not here speaking of the poorest working people . . . but of the salesman, the bookkeeper, the artisan, the teacher, the writer,—whatever he may be, the man of small means and cultivated preferences, who wants a home and not merely a lodging; who wants to own his home and be alone in it, as independence and true domestic happiness requires.[20]

Cynics undoubtedly read these words and muttered, "then let them move to Dorchester!" Again, the complaint here was the urbanist refrain that development was proceeding too slowly.

The disagreement between the rustic and urbanist aesthetics was muted in the later 1870s and early 1880s. Urbanists regarded the rustic attachment to open fields and rolling meadows as impractical as the town grew and prospered, and as yet there were no popular alternatives to streetcar-suburb streets, with their small lots and massed, street-facing houses. True, most Brookline residents continued to admire the great estates, with their mansions and sweeping lawns in the upper-class districts south of Boylston Street or in Longwood, but few saw them as a practical model for future growth in a modern suburb. Parks, such as the ones Frederick Law Olmsted was designing in New York and elsewhere, might offer some relief from urbanization, and indeed in 1871 the *Transcript* proclaimed, "This is an age of Parks." Brookline began its park system that year with the acquisition of two large playgrounds of four and five acres on the edge of Brookline Village. But after this promising start, rapidly rising land values, followed by the business depression of the mid-1870s, discouraged adding additional parks. "That public parks are in many respects desirable, that they conduce to the comfort and even health of the inhabitants, we do not deny," the *Chronicle* wrote in 1876. "But these advantages apply to crowded cities, not to suburban towns like Brookline," since "Brookline itself is a park."[21] How much longer that would persist if the town continued its rapid growth, the editor did not say.

Given the widespread acceptance of the urbanist view that further higher density growth was inevitable, if not positively desirable, the town exerted limited restraint over development. Town meetings frequently dealt with developmental issues, such as the acceptance of streets or where public improvements like sewers should be located, but these typically involved clashes of competing business interests rather than philosophical questions of what form development should take and what the town would look like in the future. The town's two most active political figures during this period, William Aspinwall and his archrival, attorney Alfred D. Chandler, were personally involved in land development. Aspinwall, as has been shown, directed the Aspinwall Land Company, while Chandler, the Harvard-educated son of Theophilus and Elizabeth Chandler, was the counsel and one of the managers of the Brookline Land Company that his father had helped establish. Annexation, which both opposed, was one of the few issues on which they saw eye to eye. The two clashed repeatedly at town meetings, each trying to get town backing for their pet schemes while denouncing the other man's projects as barefaced raids on the public treasury.[22]

Through their power to lay out new streets, the selectmen did exert some control over growth. Annexationists had charged that selectmen unnecessarily thwarted development by refusing to approve proposed streets. Behind this opposition was said to be "a few rich men" who blocked proposals to improve water, drainage, and sewerage. "I find great difficulty in getting streets laid out in town," complained farmer and land developer Willard A. Humphrey. "It took me three years to get one street laid out."[23] How much reality lay behind this annexationist rhetoric is hard to say, since the selectmen, although drawn exclusively from the bourgeoisie, otherwise represented a variety of backgrounds and income levels and showed no evidence of hostility to development per se.[24]

Searching for Suburbia

By the early 1880s a distinctly suburban ethic had emerged in Brookline, one that emphasized municipal independence and ready access to the city, with a high level of public and private services and the encouragement of developing neighborhoods of tasteful, costly homes. Similar views were emerging in other American suburbs at this time, where they had been promoted by developers, architects, writers, and journalists even before the Civil War. Many of these writers also endorsed a ruralist aesthetic that emphasized the delights of living in cultured communities surrounded by nature, even if this apparently remained something of a minority view in Brookline.[25]

Such ideals did not always accord with reality. No one has better captured the inherent contradictions between the new American middle-class suburban ideal and the suburb as actually experienced as novelist William Dean Howells, one of the earliest suburban chroniclers. He moved to Cambridge, Massachusetts, after the Civil War, seeking a distinctly suburban way of life. To his delight, he found his neighborhood poised on "a frontier between city and country." To be there on a splendid June day was to dwell in "a kind of Paradise. . . . We were living in the country with the conveniences and luxuries of the city about us." Peace and tranquility abounded: "It was very quiet; we called one another to the window if a large dog went by our door; and whole days passed without the movement of any wheels but the butcher's upon our street, which flourished in ragweed and buttercups and daisies, and in the autumn burned . . . with the pallid azure flame of the succory." Urban amenities mingled with bucolic scenes. Horse-drawn streetcars were conveniently close at hand, "while two minutes' walk would take us into a wood so wild and thick that no roof was visible through the trees. We learned, like innocent pastoral people of the golden age, to know the several voices of the cows pastured in the vacant lots."[26]

At times, however, Howells hinted of trouble in paradise: "We played a little at gardening, of course, and planted tomatoes, which the chickens seemed to like, for they ate them up as fast as they ripened." Blackberries had no sooner appeared then they fell prey to "gluttonous flocks of robins and orioles," while grapes were cut down by frost. More seriously, the quiet of the neighborhood was periodically broken by the "whistles of locomotives passing on the neighboring railroad. The trains shook the house as they thundered along, and at night were a kind of company." Suburbanites could not entirely escape the lower classes: "Now and then, also, the little ragged boys in charge of the cows . . . came and peered lustfully through the gate at our ripening pears."[27]

In the end the greatest peril turned out to be the delicate balance between country and city on which the entire suburban experience seemingly rested. Suburban life was transient: "All round us carpenters were at work building new houses; but so far from troubling us the strokes of their hammers fell softly upon the sense, like one's heart-beats upon one's own consciousness in the lapse from all fear of pain under the blessed charm of an anesthetic." Ultimately, development destroyed the suburban illusion of living in the country. By 1869 this once "ideal region" had "now become merely historical, a portion of the tragical poetry of the past. Many of the vacant lots . . . flourished up, during the four years we knew it, into fresh-painted wooden houses, and the time came to be when one might have looked in vain for the abandoned hoop-skirts which used to decorate the desirable building-sites. The lessening pasturage also reduced the herds which formerly fed in the vicinity." Moreover, the city had built a sidewalk, although on the other side of the street.[28] Even worse, as Howells confessed to a friend, the neighborhood "has lately become much less desirable than it was. The Irish have moved in." After only three years, Howells himself moved on to (literally) greener pastures, eventually settling on a larger suburban house in another Cambridge neighborhood before eventually abandoning suburbia altogether.[29]

The conflict between the suburban lifestyle sought by Howells and the metropolitan reality becomes apparent when one walks down his block today. Sacramento Street in Cambridge has clearly become a streetcar suburb, only one half-mile north of the congested traffic of Harvard Square. Looking out from what once was Howell's small front lawn, we see in both directions dozens of smaller, nineteenth-century houses set on modest lots squarely facing the narrow, straight urban street, flanked by curbs and sidewalks, interrupted by driveways that have long displaced what used to be grass. Whatever suburban features this urban neighborhood once possessed were lost long ago.[30]

The suburb that Howells had sought on Sacramento Street envisioned a place perfectly balanced between city and country, both in its location and its visible features. For Howells, the horse cars on nearby Massachusetts Avenue and the railroad station at Porter Square were sufficient to invoke the city; the vanishing vacant lots, with their cows and flowers, provided the rural ambiance. But once urban growth engulfed the neighborhood and filled the lots with houses, the balance was upset and the suburban illusion vanished.

Or perhaps William Dean Howells had pursued his ideal of suburbia in the wrong place. In 1858 Francis and Caroline Barrett White bought a five-acre estate in the choicest part of Brookline, where they lived for the next half century. Caroline's diary provides a unique look at the lifestyle a suburban bourgeois household experienced in the 1850s and 1860s, which turned out to be much of what in Cambridge Howells sought in vain.

Suburbia Found

Married in 1851 when Francis (Frank) White was twenty-seven and Caroline Barrett twenty-three, the Whites came from similar backgrounds. Both were youngest children of large Yankee families, and both had been born on New England farms in the 1820s. Frank's father was a prosperous farmer and storekeeper in Boylston, who had married a minister's daughter, and most of his sons became successful businessmen. Caroline was born in Ashburnham, Massachusetts (like Boylston, in Worcester County), but soon afterward her family moved to Fitchburg and later northward to another farm in Newport, New Hampshire. As a young man Frank worked in his brother's tannery in Roxbury, while Caroline taught school in rural Shirley; neither attended college. They met when one of Frank's brothers married Caroline's sister.[31]

When first married, the couple lived in Roxbury in a pair of rented furnished rooms in a boardinghouse a short walk from Frank's tannery. Following a nervous breakdown by Frank in 1854, however, and a six-month recuperative journey to Europe that mostly restored his health, they eventually leased a house in a fashionable Roxbury neighborhood. By 1857 the couple, who now had both a child and a horse and carriage, began seriously looking to buy a house of their own. "We both would like to have a house of *our own,*" Caroline wrote in her diary. "I would like to have Charley's [their year-old son] earliest recollections connected with a pleasant home."[32] With close friends in Brookline and a predilection for country driving, they gave preference to suburban properties rather than Roxbury (whose population was rapidly rising) or Boston. They seriously looked at several Brookline houses and found one they liked but felt they could not afford. Then, without warning, nearly a year later, on March 18, 1858, Caroline found herself "*amazed* when Frank came home today and said he had bought a house in Brookline, the one we had looked at and talked of so long."[33]

In Brookline they found the natural scenery they sought. Perhaps because of their now fondly recalled rural upbringings, they fully embraced the pastoral aestheticism being popularized by Downing and others.[34] Caroline's diary is filled with paeans to the beauty of nature she constantly encountered in her own backyard and elsewhere in Brookline: "Our home here has looked perfectly *beautiful* today. . . . I enjoyed sitting with my work on the balcony, listening to the sweet voices of nature." The property's attractiveness even persisted at night. "Came home by moonlight—nothing more beautiful than our lawn by moonlight, with its light & shade. I love the dancing, flickering shadows, by sunlight or moonlight." Throughout the seasons the rustic scenery provided pleasure for Caroline. "I have enjoyed sitting by my window & looking out on the many hued Autumn livery of the trees—some brilliant as crimson clouds—others like altar lighted tapers—so glowing & golden-streaming upward towards heaven—and listening to the soft music of the gently dropping leaves—& the tremulous breathing of the wind—Oh! lovely autumn time." Even when the trees were bare, nature continued to inspire her. "I never looked out upon a more splendid winter scene than has been presented today. . . . On the way to the village [I] was *amazed* at the beauty of the scenery. . . . It seemed like a fairy scene & is wholly indescribable."[35]

Cliffside, the Whites' home, proved to be as practical as it was attractive. Every modern convenience was soon available. Shortly after their arrival, Frank had a coal-fired central furnace installed to supplement the wood stoves in the parlor and library. "Mercury at 9° below this morning—tremendous cold," Caroline noted, "but our house is comfortable so it does not matter much to us insiders." In 1860 they installed a brand-new cooking range in their kitchen. When they purchased it the house was already equipped with primitive indoor plumbing, gravity fed from a roof-top cistern. In 1871 Frank added a steam-powered pump to fill the cistern, which emptied in dry spells from a stream. The house was not without its problems—unfamiliar with central heating, with Frank away Caroline sometimes let the furnace fire go out, restarting it only with great difficulty; subzero cold sometimes led pipes to freeze and leak. But on the whole, she enjoyed her estate. "The evening is splendidly moonlit and oh so lovely! Dear Cliffside looks almost paradise in the tender light—indeed I believe it is as nearly one."[36]

Although they owned but five acres and could view the Boston Common from their tower, the Whites termed their property "our little farm." They took the term seriously. Shortly after moving to Cliffside, Caroline wrote, "We shall get quite a stock of domestic animals after a while at this rate we are going on—two horses, cow & calf, five pigs, and hens—first brood of chickens hatched today." On their grounds the Whites grew peas, raspberries, strawberries, pears, apples, hay, grapes, and sweet corn, which they consumed fresh and preserved, through Caroline's labor. "Fruits & vegetables from our own garden are delicious." They actively maintained flower gardens, which in season Caroline used to transform the house into "a flower carnival—the house is filled with their delicious fragrance and bouquets of them greet the eye with their brilliant or delicate hues at every turn. I really luxuriate in them." These efforts were greatly aided by Paul

Kelly, their resident farm laborer and general hand. Kelly assisted with every farm task, from mowing and gathering hay to pruning fruit trees. He joined their household (apparently living apart from the main house) shortly after their arrival and remained with them into the 1870s. Despite his Irish birth, he elicited no complaints from Caroline.[37]

Over the next few years Caroline gave birth to three more children, while Frank pursued his leather business in Roxbury. Much of her time was occupied with hiring, supervising, and replacing her two or three live-in domestic servants. Raising children, even with help from servants, was seldom easy. Illnesses such as measles and whooping cough were all too common, and although the Whites never lost a child, their closest friends did. At one point her two-year-old daughter "when put to bed—instead of going to sleep she amused herself by pulling open a hole in her pillow—& taking out quantities of feathers & putting them on the carpet." Two weeks later she set "the water running in one of the bowls—& let . . . it overflow till it saturated the ceilings of my china closet, causing it to fall off."[38]

Caroline found the raising of her oldest child particularly vexing: "He tries us exceedingly," she complained in 1859, when he was three years old, "and I am at a loss what course to pursue." Nearly eight years later, "Charlie tries me very much—he seems to be *strenuous* to have his own way—& though we try to enforce obedience, it is very reluctantly rendered." As a committed evangelical Christian she prayed for the strength to "overcome his own will" and make him "submit lovingly to parental authority—& yield also to that Higher authority—which would secure to him that 'Peace which passeth all understanding.'"[39] Although Frank appears to have participated in their children's upbringing and supported rather than undermined his wife's efforts (at one point he wrote his sister that they were "fighting the children"), with his long hours at work the task fell mostly to Caroline.[40] "It is a great responsibility to be a parent," she wrote in her journal. At times she feared herself to be "wholly unfit to guide & direct" her children to become responsible Christian adults.[41]

Contributing to her difficulties were the high expectations that bourgeois ideology and her Christian faith placed on mothers, which Caroline had internalized. "A mother ought to learn all trades—to be able, successfully, to keep up the work of a family," she noted in her diary. "She must know all that pertains to good housekeeping—cooking, etc.—then dressmaking, millinery, tailoring, come in the repertoire of her duties—& she should also be intelligent, educated sufficiently, to instruct her children—that their minds may be clothed as well as their bodies—she must have wisdom, patience, & discretion—that the children's tempers be not spoiled &, more important than all other acquirements & accomplishments, she should have *piety*." But had she met this impossible standard? "Ah! me! Ah! me!"[42]

Perhaps because she herself had been a teacher, her children started school late: the earliest a few months shy of eight and the latest was nine and a half years old. For reasons unexplained, all attended private elementary schools in walking distance of the house. At ten or eleven they started at the town's public grammar school in Brookline Village after passing entrance examinations, and later progressed to Brookline High School. There is only scant evidence in her diaries that she home-schooled her oldest children in any systematic way; later there are indications she tutored her third son, Winthrop, after she withdrew him from the private school he was attending before gaining admission to the grammar school, and included his sister as well.[43]

Caroline was concerned with her children's success and took pride in the academic achievement of her two oldest sons. Willie, the second son, "ranked No. 1 every month since he entered" the grammar school. "Pretty good I think—for such a timid boy like him." Near the end of his first year of high school, his older brother, Charlie, "brought home his *best report* yet, since entering the High School. He attained rank *No. 2.* Pretty good for him, I think, or any one else." On the other hand, she was concerned that her third son, Winthrop, "makes slow progress in the matter of education—so far as book knowledge is concerned." Eventually, all three of her sons attended college, the second and third Harvard.[44]

Nothing in her diaries records what role Frank played in the children's education, if any. Clearly Caroline was expected to enroll their children in school at the appropriate time and attend school recitations and meetings with teachers. Given his long hours at work, the prime responsibility for rearing the children was with her, even if they were frequently under the care of servants. On the other hand, Frank obviously enjoyed spending time with his boys shooting off fireworks on Independence Day, fishing, taking his sons to the barber's or shopping for clothes, teaching them to swim in Jamaica Pond, catching a pet squirrel for their amusement, coasting with them on winter moonlit nights, and later horseback riding and visits to baseball games and circuses. (There is less evidence of his interaction with his youngest child, his only daughter, Sophia.) Still, it was their mother the children turned to first when they sought solace. When five-year-old

Willie accidentally killed his older brother's beloved pet squirrel, Caroline had to comfort two extremely distraught boys. Afterward, "Charlie carried his dead pet to his father," she wrote, "who advised him to bury it—so I helped him to select a desirable spot."[45]

To Caroline there was no better place to raise her children than Brookline. She enjoyed watching them play in their spacious yard. She was particularly happy that her youngest child "just three years old—goes out regularly to coast—with her brothers—drags the sled herself up the hill beyond the meadow and comes down alone—it is very amusing to watch her from the windows, she looks so tiny—& not knowing how to steer her sled, she sometimes goes over some hummock & impacts—I think it is very smart for the little thing." To ensure that she would keep up with her older brothers outdoors, Caroline sewed her daughter "some flannel overdrawers . . . so that she can play in the snow without getting ordinary clothes wet." As the children grew their time increasingly came under adult supervision, such as Sunday school, piano lessons (for their daughter), formal parties, and accompanying their parents on trips and to entertainment venues such as beaches, circuses, museums, concert, plays, and even to see President Ulysses S. Grant.[46]

The White household enjoyed most of the products of the nascent American consumer culture. They brought with them on their arrival from Roxbury in 1858 a two-year-old piano and wagonloads of rugs and new furniture. Over the next decade and beyond they acquired new carriages, a butter churn, crockery, a carpet sweeper, various pieces of furniture, new carpets, a silver tea service, an expensive mantle clock, a combination safe for valuables, drapery, and a stereopticon with pictures. Frank carried home from Boston an endless stream of the latest books; engravings, paintings, sculpture, and other works of art for their parlor and library; and personal items for Caroline, such as fur gloves, a work basket, and elegant fans. They also remodeled and repainted the house, and called on professional photographers for portraits of themselves, the children, and even Cliffside itself. Bourgeois consumption occasionally left Caroline with buyer's remorse: "I do not feel very well satisfied with my purchases," she lamented. "They do not seem so satisfactory now I have them all before me—as they did while making them."[47]

Whatever misgivings Caroline or her Roxbury friends might have expressed about her moving to outer suburbia were soon allayed by the hectic pace of visitation she found herself maintaining. A few weeks after their arrival at Cliffside, she complained after Frank departed on one of his frequent overnight business trips that "it is lonely always without him—perhaps more so here—so far from friends and acquaintances than it used to be in Roxbury." But less than two months later, after a hectic round of receiving guests, she could write, "People need not think I shall be lonely here—though some distance from the city."[48] With servants and housekeepers to mind the children, bourgeois women in both the city and suburbia spent a great deal of time calling and being called upon by friends and relations. During 1859, the first full year she lived in Brookline, Caroline made no less than ninety-six visits to friends, neighbors, and relations (exclusive of overnight visits); in turn, she hosted more than forty-five adult visitors (some of whom came multiple times) for times ranging from a few minutes to more than a week.[49] Additionally, she and Frank were active members of Brookline's evangelical Congregational church, attending most weekly services (both Sunday mornings and afternoons) and participating in church fairs, sewing circles, and other church-sponsored activities.

In the days before the telephone, one seldom knew if the persons one planned to visit would be home or, in turn, whom you might find at your own door. Particularly when one moved, relatives and old friends were likely to appear without notice. "This has been a regular *company* day," a tired Caroline wrote on June 9, 1858: "Davis was here this morning—& had just left when Mr. & Mrs. A. L. Howe called—& they had been gone but a few minutes when Mrs. Howard Williams Sr. came. She staid about two hours. I carried her home—& got back just in season for dinner—and this P.M. Fred & his wife grandmother Woodward, and the two children came up & made us a call." With one exception Caroline gladly welcomed company: "We like our friends very much but do not love to receive calls on the Sabbath day."[50]

In 1859 the core of their social network were three couples, all of whom they had known before their move to Brookline: Frank's business partner, Fred Guild, and his wife, Sarah, who lived in Roxbury; Mr. and Mrs. John May, also of Roxbury; and Brookline farmer Howard Williams and his wife, Sarah. That year, fifty-three of the Whites' ninety-six visits were to these three households. In turned, they received the Williamses, the Guilds, and the Mays at Cliffside a total of thirty-one times. Most of the other social calls made by the Whites that year involved other friends or Brookline neighbors near Cliffside. Both Frank and Caroline came from large families, and each had relatives in Boston, but visits to them accounted for only about a fifth of all their social calling. On the other hand, brothers, sisters, uncles and aunts, and cousins frequently appeared, often staying for days. In addition, Caroline's widowed mother lived at Cliffside for most of the year.

None of this social activity would have been possible without the excellent physical mobility the Whites and their bourgeois associates enjoyed. In 1859 Caroline ventured to Roxbury forty-six times and into Boston forty-two (sometimes on the same trip). She also traveled to Jamaica Plain, Cambridge, Dorchester, Auburndale, Brighton, Andover, Canton, Woburn, and Newton Centre. She made longer trips to the New York City area (where Frank's brothers and her own sister lived) and Boylston (Frank's home town). Her high income allowed her to take full advantage of all means of transportation: commuter trains from Brookline Village, Brighton, and Boston; the new horse-drawn street railways; and, above all, their own private carriages and wagons, which she and Frank drove themselves or had themselves chauffeured by their farm laborer, Paul Kelly. In winter they traded wagons for their sleigh. Plus, whenever she felt like it, Caroline was not averse to walking, sometimes several miles, well into her forties.

Notwithstanding all of her kin and friends, Caroline's closest relationship was with her husband, Frank. Twenty years after their marriage began, she confided to her journal, "still the anniversary is one of unmingled satisfaction—except so far as the shortcomings of our *human nature* leave something better to be desired." In most respects their marriage approached the Victorian ideal of a companionate marriage.[51] Certainly Caroline missed her husband when Frank left her on one of his frequent business trips to New York City (seven in 1859), though their duration was typically less than a week. She hated the loneliness of spending a night without him and would often write him soon after he departed.[52]

A suburban residence did not prevent the Whites from savoring the cultural events of Boston. Together they attended the opera, concerts, lectures, sermons, museums, exhibits, plays, and fairs. They saw Fanny Kemble, Wendell Phillips, performances of Verde and *Our American Cousin,* and paintings by Albert Bierstadt. They heard a sermon by Henry Ward Beecher, watched Edwin Forrest performing as Lear (typically, Caroline complained that the noted Shakespearian "rather *overacts*"), heard some of the most accomplished musicians of the day, and even encountered (at a distance) President Grant and the Prince of Wales.[53] At home, their favorite amusement after the children were asleep was reading: "Frank & I sat in the Library this evening—I sewed while he read to me—delightful way to spend an evening—I think we are *very happy.*"[54] They continued this way for many years, devouring a great variety of contemporary popular and more traditional literature, featuring both English and American authors, including Sir Walter Scott, Shakespeare, the *Atlantic Monthly*, Dinah Craik, Charles Dickens, Catherine Sedgwick, Thomas Hughes, Oliver Wendell Holmes, Lydia Maria Child, Washington Irving, and Henry Wadsworth Longfellow.

Clearly Frank White regarded his wife as his intellectual peer. Still it was Frank who appears to have made most of the decisions regarding the household unilaterally, aside from those involving the children or the servants: he bought Cliffside; ordered improvements to the house and grounds; selected, purchased, and then personally framed and hung artwork; decided when and where they would travel; purchased tickets to entertainment; and surprised her with gifts. When she shopped for furniture and wallpaper, it was typically with him. Her diary suggests that he sought her approval, which usually was tacit and after the fact. Companionship, even affection, did not imply equality.[55] Indeed Caroline herself acknowledged this, explicitly rejecting "the ultra ideas of women's rights" and women's suffrage. At the same time, her dismissal of feminism was accompanied by a keen interest in politics and current events, such as the battles of the Civil War. She was a partisan Republican, a fervent Unionist, an abolitionist who passionately hated slavery, and a champion of Reconstruction of the South, calling President Andrew Johnson (whom she would later meet in person at the White House) a traitor, poor white trash, and a fool.[56]

Although Caroline took no direct part in Frank's business affairs, his business was a constant source of concern to her. From time to time she visited him at the tannery or their Boston store, and he shared with her at least some details of his job. Early in their marriage he had experienced a nervous breakdown ("neuralgia"), presumably brought on by overwork, and as the years passed she increasingly worried that it might reoccur. "Frank is working much too hard," she wrote in 1868. "I feel he will break down under his heavy burden of *care & labor.*" Moreover, the leather business had its ups and downs, and in bad years she worried about the possibility of failure and ruin. Thus she was greatly relieved when in 1871 his partner, Fred Guild, bought out his interest, and Frank retired from active business, a rich man.[57]

In the end, was Caroline White content to be in suburbia? She certainly experienced trying times. Even with the help of servants, she found housework, especially the annual spring and fall cleaning, exhausting, growing more so as the years passed. At times she complained of the monotony of daily existence, of the rapidity of passing time, and headaches; at other points she seemed to be depressed. "I have felt '*blue,*'" she wrote on a windy fall day in 1871, "but know not the cause." She consoled herself with the Calvinistic sentiment that "every day has its duties—which if faithfully performed mark it an important day—however monotonous it may seem." Yet, taken as a whole, Caroline's writings suggest that she—and most certainly Frank—enjoyed their life in Brookline. Although they traveled widely, they always returned to Cliffside, where they spent the rest of their lives. Indeed, despite her initial fears that Brookline might be too isolated, by 1863 she was confessing, "I am glad to be back again at Cliffside—I do not think I like the city very much."[58]

The Impossible Dream?

Frank and Caroline White's experiences suggest that a distinctly suburban style of living was possible, even practical, given the ample means they enjoyed. Although her life was not always happy, there is nothing to suggest that she took any less pleasure in suburbia than he did, or that moving to Brookline was largely Frank's idea, or that her expectations of suburbia outlined in her diary were different from those held by her husband, as historian Margaret Marsh has suggested. Her diary makes it clear that transportation made it feasible for her to participate in urban social, cultural, and religious activities when she felt so inclined. Nor does she describe suburban female friends who longed for the city.[59]

Historians such as Marsh, Kenneth T. Jackson, and Mary Corbin Sies, have traced the development of what they term a suburban ideal among the bourgeoisie, which by the end of the nineteenth century, if nothing else, was well developed as a marketing concept to promote real estate and sell lawn mowers and gardening supplies. "The suburban ideal, distilled to its essence," Sies writes, "consists of the belief that the best form of shelter is the single-family detached house with a garden and ample open space located in a homogenous, locally controlled community on the periphery of a city."[60] It is clear that this was much of what William Dean Howells sought and the Whites found in their corners of suburbia, even before 1870, aside from the homogeneity.

Many nineteenth-century Brookline residents rejected some or even most of this ideal. Their preferred vision of suburbia was an orderly, urbane, and above all wealthy community of attractive neighborhoods served by every modern convenience. Largely rejecting the rustic aesthetic, they placed less importance on keeping spacious yards and gardens, and regarded the long-term preservation of farm land and other open space as impractical. Indeed, they welcomed the addition of even more affluent new residents as contributing to the town's ever-increasing prosperity (as well as helping to hold down the property tax rate). If Brookline came to resemble the best Boston neighborhoods, so be it, as long as the town retained its separate identity and moral virtue. In the end, they largely accepted the notion that they lived in an increasingly urban community.

Nevertheless, it is striking that both Howells and the Whites appear to have come to suburbia on a quest for a similar mode of living, a taste for which they apparently acquired before moving there. That Caroline and Frank White found what they were seeking and Howells did not is largely due to the former's superior resources—a larger house with more land, more servants, and more income to spend on furnishing it and supplying themselves with the latest conveniences. Perhaps even more significantly, the Whites lived in a relatively isolated neighborhood surrounded by other large estates, an area in which new houses rarely appeared. This stability contrasted vividly with the hectic pace of residential growth in Howells's streetcar suburb, which daily served as a reminder that his suburb was no longer suspended between city and country but was in fact becoming decisively urban.

On the face of it, the possibility of a distinctive suburban way of life taking hold in greater Boston seemed remote. By the 1880s the rapid growth of the region suggested that suburbia was destined to be a brief period of transition from rural countryside to urban residential district. Even if they avoided annexation to Boston, suburban towns were rapidly becoming cities in their own right. It was hard to see how anything markedly suburban could survive the urban advance. Even in Brookline, a characteristically suburban style of life had been slow to emerge, and the town had thousands of acres of land available only a few miles from Boston. Yet in the end, suburbia would prove to be surprisingly resilient.

PART 3

SUBURBIA REALIZED 1885–1900

DURING THE final fifteen years of the nineteenth century Brookline experienced yet another spurt of rapid growth. The development of Beacon Street into a grand Parisian boulevard launched the conversion of northern Brookline, hitherto a sleepy rural quarter, into a virtual extension of Boston's Back Bay neighborhood, while the nearby streets took on the appearance of high-end streetcar suburbs. Brookline Village continued to expand as well, with both commercial development and housing for the well-heeled, and working-class tenements.

Despite the fact that this development seemed to be the culmination of everything Brookline had been striving for—nearly all of the newcomers enjoyed high incomes and the buildings were undeniably stylish—this successful development touched off a debate that resulted in the emergence of a distinctly suburban aesthetic that halted further mass development elsewhere in town. Combined with the existing suburban ethic, this represented a true suburban consciousness, an ideology with great appeal for twentieth-century Americans, especially after the emergence of a full-blown automobile-based consumer culture in the 1920s with which it so nicely dovetailed.

By 1900 Brookline had become one of the nation's most prominent suburbs, and its example was studied throughout the nation, encouraged by the writings of Brookline-based authors. These accounts, often ignoring or downplaying the town's unique advantages and distinctive history, helped popularize the suburban ideal, which in turn would help launch the mass suburbanization of twentieth-century America.

CHAPTER 7

Boulevards and Trolleys

Beacon street was a lane. It appealed to [Henry M.] Whitney that the man who made that alley into a boulevard, with a street car line in the middle of it, would not only confer a tremendous blessing on posterity, but incidentally make a fortune if he happened to own the adjacent land.

—John William Denehy, *A History of Brookline, Massachusetts,* 1906

NEAR THE end of 1884 a writer in the *Brookline Chronicle* observed that Boston, particularly its "wealthy class," seemed to be poised on the brink of a major movement westward. "The year 1885," he predicted, "will witness great changes," as Boston completes the Back Bay project. "Next year the extension of Boylston Street to the Brookline line will be completed and the Jamaica Parkway will at least begin to take form. The bridges over Brookline avenue and Beacon street will then have been completed and so will the extension of Commonwealth avenue. In another year, then, Boston will be in fact, what it has been so long in theory, at our very threshold. From that time, sleepy Brookline will take on a new life and grow apace."[1] Forty years of suburbanization had changed Brookline unevenly. In and around Brookline Village the town had come to resemble a small city. The railroad tracks that cut through the heart of the district separated the crowded Irish tenements and cottages from the storefronts and streets of comfortable suburban homes. Away from the village, however, Brookline in 1885 had changed little. Broad estates mingled with scattered farmhouses, commuters' residences, and clusters of workers' houses. Meanwhile, Boston, which now surrounded Brookline on three sides, continued its explosive expansion, with thousands of new houses being built in Dorchester, Roxbury, West Roxbury, and Brighton. How much longer could it be before this growth extended into Brookline?[2]

If past patterns had continued, both the northern and southern sections of Brookline would have been gradually developed over the next few decades as new streets were laid out and horsecar and sewer lines extended. Instead, the northern section rapidly became covered with houses, apartments, and stores, while the southern remained almost entirely unaltered. This surprising course of events was brought about by a small number of men skillful in both the financial and political realms, who forced the town to decide what sort of community it had become and where it would like to go.

Beacon Street

With the one exception of Frederick Law Olmsted, no individual was more responsible for the subsequent appearance of Brookline than Henry Melville Whitney. Born in 1839 in the tiny western Massachusetts hill town of Conway (which also produced Chicago department store tycoon Marshall Field), Whitney first arrived in Brookline in 1865. His father, Gen. James S. Whitney (1811–78), an ambitious self-made politician, businessman, and militia officer, served as superintendent of the Springfield Armory, collector of the Port of Boston, and president of the Boston Water Power Company. He also owned a successful New York–to-Boston steamship line. Henry Whitney's younger brother, Yale-educated William C. Whitney (1841–1904), became a prominent and extremely wealthy New York City lawyer and investor, a mainstay of the Democratic Party who served as secretary of the navy under Grover Cleveland. William's son, sportsman Harry Payne Whitney (1872–1930), would marry a Vanderbilt and become a kingpin of New York high society.[3]

Henry Whitney entered the business world after a year in a Conway academy, working first in his father's store and later in a Boston bank. Like many a future tycoon, he was too busy making money during the Civil War years to bother serving in uniform, investing his father's money into various schemes in Boston, Iowa, and New York City. His parents had moved to Brookline in 1863, and he joined them there two years later when he was twenty-six years old. He at the time worked as the Boston agent for his father's steamship line and began to speculate in Brookline real estate, buying and selling land near his parents' house on Beacon Street.[4]

A longstanding fixture of the Massachusetts Democratic Party, James Whitney found himself drawn into Brookline politics, becoming one of the leaders of the unsuccessful annexation movement in the 1870s. Henry aided his father in this futile effort, which marked his own entry onto the local political scene. He cast himself as a reformer confronting a wasteful and inefficient town government. "I feel in duty bound to do what I can to awaken the people," Henry wrote his brother William in New York in 1875.[5] Somewhat to his surprise, the town meeting went along with his proposal to trim the public education budget. Encouraged, Whitney backed yet another attempt at annexation in 1880. "Our destiny is to be one with the city," he contended, "and the sooner it is accomplished the better for all." But a majority of town voters disagreed, and now even the most ardent supporters of consolidation lost hope of ever incorporating Brookline into Boston.[6]

But if the suburb would not join the city, why not bring the city to the suburb? Whitney now turned to other schemes to implement the union. The northern most part of the town, which lay closest to downtown Boston, seemed the logical starting place for launching further urban development, and Beacon Street was the road progress would take. Constructed in 1851 after a long controversy, Beacon Street ran from the Mill Dam at Sewall's Point (today's Kenmore Square) across northern Brookline to the Newton and Brighton lines. Beacon Street had proved a severe disappointment to its promoters, who had sought to encourage rapid growth along its way. As late as 1885 it was no more than a tree-lined, fifty-foot-wide country road fronted by a few widely spaced houses (fig. 7.1). Annexationists had argued that only Boston possessed the resources necessary to widen and improve Beacon Street. Indeed, James Whitney, who himself lived on Beacon Street, had argued back in 1873 that "another great reason for . . . annexation was that the broad and elegant avenues of the city might be extended to Brookline, under one grand plan."[7] Other annexationists specified the widening of Beacon Street as an important benefit to be gained from consolidation. Once annexation was no longer in play, Henry Whitney, along with other Beacon Street landowners, promoted an effort in 1884 to get the Norfolk County commissioners to widen the road to seventy feet and make other improvements.[8]

When the commissioners rejected this proposal, Whitney determined to bring all of his resources to bear to resolve the issue. His assets were considerable, since as a successful Boston businessman and politician he could count on the backing of some of the wealthiest and most powerful men in the city, as well as his own personal fortune. Moreover, fifteen years' involvement in Brookline politics and real estate had given him a keen appreciation of the workings of town government.[9] During the spring of 1886 Whitney quietly bought one hundred acres

FIGURE 7.1. More than thirty-five years after it had first been laid out, Beacon Street remained a country lane. The view here is looking east from the intersection of St. Paul Street in 1887. Downtown Boston is only three miles away. Soon the site would be unrecognizable. Brookline Photographic Collection, Public Library of Brookline, digitalcommonwealth.org. This work is licensed for use under a Creative Commons Attribution Non-Commercial No Derivatives License (CC BY-NC-ND).

along Beacon Street. Next he secretly assembled a syndicate of the other major landowners in the vicinity. In August, to great fanfare, he announced a stunning proposal. Landscape architect Frederick Law Olmsted, aided by the local engineering firm of Aspinwall & Lincoln, had produced for Whitney plans for "a grand boulevard of a uniform width of 200 feet, in the centre of which will be the tracks of a [street] railroad." Syndicate members pledged to donate all of the lands needed for the widening if the town would build the road. Already lined up in support were such prominent and influential residents as Amos A.

Lawrence, Henry Lee, Francis Cabot, William I. Bowditch, Robert S. Peabody, and Augustus Lowell, as well as William Aspinwall and even the town's most prominent Irishman, James Driscoll.[10]

Whitney's bold scheme overwhelmed the potential opposition. A few Beacon Street landowners objected to the impending loss of part of their property, and others denounced the project as costly and unnecessary, an unwarranted public subsidy for a private speculation. In October Whitney quieted most of these critics when he offered to donate $100,000 toward construction costs, a figure he increased in December to fully half of the total road-building cost. Only a handful of opponents bothered to show up for the hearings that followed. Both town newspapers backed the scheme (one claimed that a poll showed 90 percent approval). Olmsted's plan promised an elegant, Parisian-style boulevard lined with fashionable buildings. Such a combination of civic pride and private gain proved irresistible, and one by one the administrative hurdles were cleared. Construction began in May 1887.[11]

Integral to Whitney's plan was the street railway line to be built down the center of Beacon Street. Whitney had already established his own street railway, the West End Street Railway Company, to provide this service. When the Metropolitan Railway Company, the operator of all but one of Brookline's existing horsecar lines, put forth its own proposal to build a line on Beacon Street, Whitney quickly bought up the Metropolitan. Almost as an afterthought he then purchased control over Boston's three other horse railways, and in the spring of 1887 he merged them all into his West End company. Not only was Whitney now the streetcar czar of Boston, but he had made the city the first in the United States with a consolidated transit system. For a while the West End was the largest urban traction company in the world.[12]

When the plans for Beacon Street were unveiled in 1886, the means of propulsion for the streetcar line were unspecified, but it was assumed that they would be horses. Inventors had long been tinkering with schemes to replace the horses, the most successful being cable traction. Although adopted by a number of cities, most notably San Francisco and Chicago, cable-car systems were expensive to construct and difficult to operate. Instead of either cable or horses, Whitney decided on a new and largely unproved technology, the electric trolley. Frank Sprague, an Annapolis-trained engineer from Connecticut, had just installed what would be the first successful electric streetcar system in Richmond, Virginia, and Whitney decided to employ the Sprague system on Beacon Street. Streetcars began running down the median strip in the middle of Beacon Street in June 1888, still pulled by horses, but the electric cars took over in January. By August 1894 all Brookline streetcar lines had been converted to electric operation.[13]

Together, the widening of Beacon Street and the introduction of electric traction touched off a building boom in Brookline that boosted the town's population from 9,196 in 1885 to 12,103 in 1890. Brookline continued to grow through the terrible business depression that gripped the nation after 1893, reaching 16,164 inhabitants in 1895 and 19,935 in 1900.[14] Throughout northern Brookline new streets, subdivisions, and rows of houses arose in what had recently been pastures and orchards. Although considerable vacant land could be found near Beacon Street as late as 1900, clearly it was a only a matter of time until all of the land in that vicinity would be developed (fig. 7.2).[15]

Along Beacon Street itself much of the land belonged to Whitney's syndicate, the West End Land Company. Whitney personally held half the shares in the company, which owned eighty-seven acres of land and had options to buy twenty-eight more. As was typical of land companies, the West End dealt almost exclusively in lots, leaving construction to others. Terms of sale were cash or 25 percent down, with the balance due in three years at 5 percent interest. Covenants written into the deeds of sale restricted commercial use in some vicinities, forbade stables within one hundred feet of the street, and required twenty-foot setbacks for all construction. Land commanded a premium price, with sales reported in the late 1880s at between one and two dollars a square foot, nearly the cost in the Back Bay.[16]

As promised, Beacon Street developed into a grand urban boulevard lined by fashionable townhouses, apartment buildings, and stores. The epitome of luxury were the Beaconsfield Terraces, a series of blocks built off Beacon Street and Dean Road by Eugene Knapp. By 1892 some thirty-two townhouses, boasting fourteen or more large rooms apiece, had been built in "a combination of the English and German medieval castles' architecture, modified to insure all the modern conveniences," as a contemporary gushed. The development featured steam heating from a central boiler house, a casino, a 250-horse stable, and a sixteen-acre private park. "The residents enjoy the *summum bonum* of material comforts, with almost complete relief from the worries and cares of the average household." The going price for admission to this Valhalla was $20,000 to $35,000 per unit, expensive though less than the cost of a comparable Back Bay mansion.[17]

Most of the new development along and adjacent to Beacon Street in the

FIGURE 7.2. The new suburban frontier, circa 1900. Aspinwall Hill as seen from Corey Hill. The nearby houses are on Westbourne Terrace. The influence of Beacon Street (barely visible) is obvious; nearly all of these buildings were built after 1887. Courtesy of the Iowa State University Library Special Collections.

1890s consisted of similar if less luxurious row housing, attached townhouses that represented an extension of the dominant architectural form of the nearby Back Bay section of Boston.[18] Townhouses per se had been built in Brookline Village and Longwood as early as the mid-1850s.[19] Apartment buildings marked a more radical break with Brookline's rural past. Boston claimed one of the nation's earliest apartment houses, the Hotel Pelham, built in 1857, but this European innovation was slow to take hold. Not until the 1870s and 1880s did "French flats," as they were termed, become popular both in the city and increasingly in Brookline. Most apartment buildings squarely faced the street and had minimal setback from the sidewalk. Richmond Court, a forty-unit complex built in 1898 on lower Beacon Street, was an exception that demonstrated the possibilities of apartments. Designed in the Tudor style by the popular architect Ralph Adams Cram (best known for his churches), Richmond Court featured five separate buildings set around a twelve-thousand-square-foot courtyard. Each apartment contained nine rooms, two bathrooms, and all the latest conveniences.[20]

Commercial development also occurred along Beacon Street as two new retail districts developed. Even before the widening, the intersection of Beacon and Harvard Streets had been the location of the Coolidge general store, infamous as a hangout for southern sympathizers during the Civil War. By 1890 two groceries were in operation along Beacon Street, and a dime store was about to open. A decade later Coolidge Corner was the site of a landmark S. S. Pierce grocery (one of the Boston area's earliest examples of a downtown store opening a suburban branch—the main store was in Copley Square in the Back Bay), a savings bank, and several other stores (fig. 7.3). Another neighborhood business district was taking shape at the intersection of Beacon and Washington Streets, featuring a druggist, a fruit dealer, and offices.[21]

Critics at the outset of the Beacon Street widening had denounced the burden the project would place on Brookline taxpayers, but the outcome silenced them. Although the road construction ultimately cost the town $465,000—no mean sum at the time—lands abutting Beacon Street increased in assessed value by more than $4 million in the following decade, producing an additional $51,000 in annual tax revenue (see cover photographs).[22] Even so, in 1900, after a decade of intensive growth, sections of Beacon Street remained undeveloped, and the street would not take on much of its present appearance until well into the 1920s. By then, the large number of automobiles and the subsequent loss of elm trees to disease had seriously altered Olmsted's conception of a grand residential boulevard. Individually owned townhouses and mansions were giving way to apartments and commercial blocks, as the wealthy moved elsewhere.[23]

Streetcar Suburbs

The development of Beacon Street helped lure developers from the streetcar suburbs of Dorchester and Roxbury, who had hitherto largely avoided building in Brookline. The mostly level lands along Harvard Street northwest of Beacon proved well-suited to the system of grid streets and rectangular frontage lots these builders had long used in Boston. David H. McKay was one of the most active of these developer-builders. Born in St. John, New Brunswick, in 1846, McKay had moved to Boston as a young man, apparently working first as a lumber broker. Becoming a builder, he erected brick rowhouses in Dorchester and later detached

FIGURE 7.3. With its landmark S. S. Pierce grocery building, opened in 1899, Coolidge Corner remains Brookline's second commercial center. The original grocery closed after more than seventy years in operation. The buildings here on both sides of Beacon Street feature ground-floor stores with offices and apartments above. Courtesy of the Brookline Historical Society.

wooden houses. His stock-in-trade became a two-story frame single- or two-family house set squarely on a rectangular lot of about 4,500 square feet, facing a grid street and selling for about $6,000. Unlike most of his contemporaries McKay not only built houses but also engaged in land development, financing, and managing commercial property.

In 1888 McKay for the first time built in Brookline, erecting eleven ten-room houses off Harvard Street near Brookline Village. The success of this venture, coming at the same time as the Beacon Street improvement and the expansion of the trolley network into Brookline, led him to close his Dorchester operations and transfer his activities to Brookline. Early in 1889 he bought a 7½–acre parcel between Harvard and Winchester Streets, a third of a mile northwest of Coolidge Corner and directly off the newly opened Harvard Street trolley. He laid out two grid streets, Coolidge and Thorndike, and installed water and gas lines (fig. 7.4).

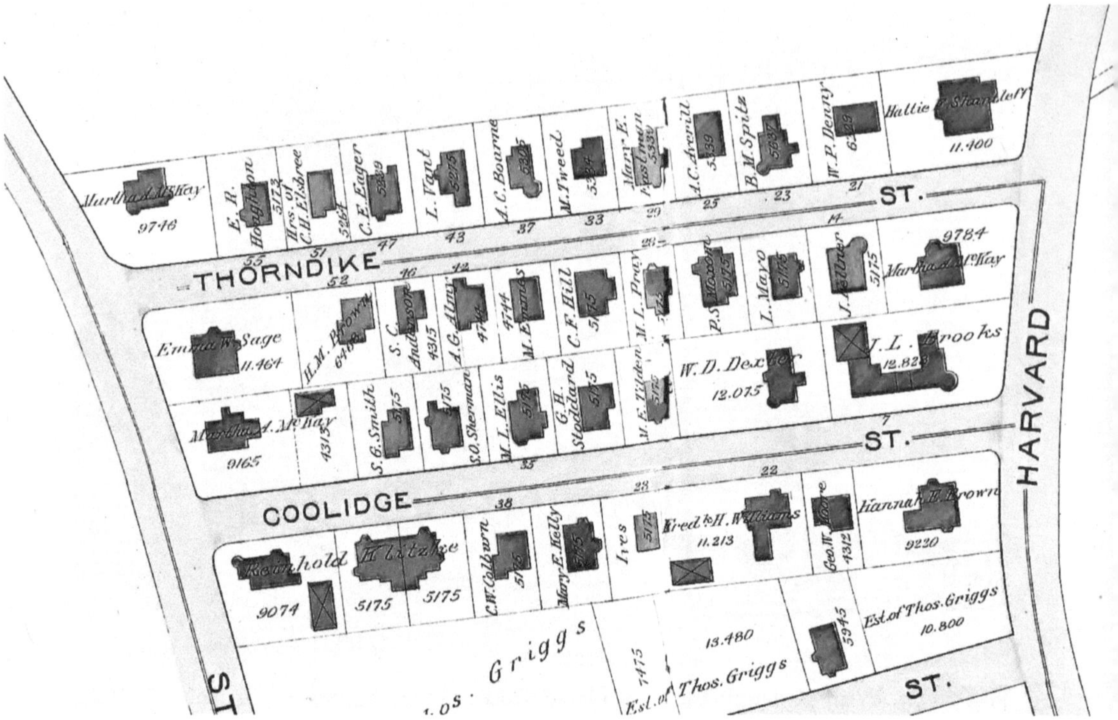

FIGURE 7.4. Developer David McKay laid out Thorndike and Coolidge Streets north of Coolidge Corner in 1890 and subsequently built many of the houses. Note that most of the houses are of similar size and are set back a uniform distance from the straight street. Lot sizes ranged from about 4,500 to 6,000 square feet. *Atlas of the Town of Brookline* (Philadelphia: Bromley, 1893), plate 7. Courtesy of the State Library of Massachusetts.

Forty-five lots, varying in size from 5,200 to 9,500 square feet (mostly near the smaller end of the range), were surveyed, and on these McKay built ten- and twelve-room wooden two-story houses selling for $7,500 to $13,000. By the end of 1891 he had sold twenty-nine of the thirty-eight houses he constructed (fig. 7.5).[24]

McKay's success in Brookline attracted other suburban developers, most notably Malden-based Peter Graffam. A Maine native who had previously built in the same part of Dorchester where McKay had been active, Graffam in April 1893 bought a twelve-acre tract off Babcock Street near McKay's subdivision. He laid out Osbourne, Naples, Abbotsford, and Manchester Roads; surveyed frontage lots; and erected houses closely resembling McKay's in style, size, and cost. Graffam eventually modified his procedures, concentrating on somewhat larger and more expensive homes, fourteen-room houses on six-thousand-foot lots selling for $14,000 to $15,000. Meanwhile, McKay had purchased another thirty acres even closer to Graffam's, where he continued to build and sell houses until his death in 1898.[25]

By 1900 some 160 new houses had been erected off Harvard Street northwest of Coolidge Corner, most of them built by McKay or Graffam. They continued the existing trend toward urban-style development already underway in Brookline Village. In these new subdivisions narrow rectangular lots, though a bit larger than the norm in Dorchester or Roxbury, were lined up along long, straight streets of uniformly sized houses, each squarely facing the road. The houses were built together in groups, without intervening vacant lots that would

FIGURE 7.5. 33 and 39 Thorndike Street, built by developer David McKay in 1890. These twelve-room single-family houses proved popular with bourgeois buyers. They sold for $7,500 to $13,000 but sat on small lots on straight streets, much as in the streetcar suburbs of Dorchester or Somerville. Photograph 2016.

provide, however temporarily, the illusion of a rustic setting. These were the traits of Boston's streetcar suburbs and were as much an innovation in Brookline as was Beacon Street itself. The ultimate inspiration of these houses was more the uniform facade of the Back Bay and the detached urban townhouse that preceded them than it was the country estate or the romantic cottage. Prosperity, convenience, fashion, and order the houses proclaimed, but not the rustic aesthetic.[26]

Despite their novelty, few in Brookline appear to have been offended by these new streetcar suburb tract developments. Both McKay and Graffam worked closely with the selectmen in laying out their streets, and no protests were heard when they were accepted as town roads.[27] Their acceptability doubtlessly had much to do with the social standing of the families who bought these houses. A sample of households in the enumeration district of the 1900 census that took in these subdivisions shows that 70 percent included live-in servants; 38 percent of the household heads were professionals or executives, with another 24 percent proprietors or other white-collar workers; 58 percent of the heads came from old Yankee stock; and only 11 percent were first- or second-generation Irish.[28] In most households some of those twelve or fourteen rooms provided sleeping space for domestics.

The household with $10,000 to spend on one of McKay's houses or $14,000 for one of Graffam's had a wide range of housing options before it, including an urban townhouse or the opportunity to live in a more genuinely rural setting than northern Brookline. That many affluent families chose to live here indicates that many in the upper middle class were willing to forgo the alleged pleasures of living in more rural, low-density borderlands, "where houses are so far apart that even in winter they cast shadows only on their own lots."[29]

The Suburban Achievement

In 1865, when Brookline had a little over five thousand inhabitants, most of the population lived within walking distance of the railroad depot in Brookline Village. The depot and its surrounding streets, with their shops and storefronts, formed the town center from which development radiated out along Walnut, Boylston, Washington, and Harvard Streets. Some parts of the village were growing crowded, particularly in the neighborhoods south of the railroad tracks, where most of the town's Irish Catholics resided. North of the tracks, the houses on newer subdivision streets grew further apart as one left the station, residential development soon yielding to fields and pastures, some of them forming commercial farmland and others the grounds of elegant estates.

Thirty-five years later in 1900, with a population of twenty thousand, many of the fields were disappearing as a new type of suburb emerged (fig. 7.6). Rapidly growing North Brookline, with its blocks of expensive apartments along the Beacon Street boulevard and adjacent streets of attractive detached houses, was becoming the bastion of the solid middle class. Here and there open fields still survived, but their days clearly were numbered as the building boom resumed after the business depression of the mid-1890s. The neighborhood had been developed to attract bourgeois families, and by every indication was a success. Streetcars on Beacon Street and across the Boston line on Commonwealth Avenue provided convenient access to downtown Boston, making this neighborhood the epitome of the streetcar suburb.[30]

The Coolidge Corner/North Brookline district formed a logical extension of Brookline Village, the boundary between the two by 1900 being no longer distinct. Even on solidly bourgeois streets, over the years lots in the village had been getting smaller, buyers willing to sacrifice land for convenient walking access to transportation and stores. Large, expensive houses on small lots were increasingly common. The village (fig. 7.7) remained separate from Coolidge Corner in that the latter was almost exclusively occupied by the Yankee upper middle class, having little of the village's social, economic, or religious diversity. On the other hand, many working-class Irish Catholics still lived in crowded tenements on largely segregated village streets and still worshiped at St. Mary's Church north of the depot. The Irish-born could take comfort that their children were likely to be materially better off than themselves. In 1900 a sample drawn from the 1900 census suggests that although 37 percent of Irish-born males still worked as laborers, this was true of only 6 percent of Massachusetts-born males with Irish-born parents. Barely one in twenty Irish-born men worked at white-collar jobs, compared to a third of the second generation.

The Irish had left their mark on the village, although with the growth of Coolidge Corner, the proportion of Brookline households headed by Irish-born persons was reduced town-wide from 40 percent in 1870 to only 22 percent in 1900. In the latter year nearly half of all village households were headed by a man or woman of Irish descent, compared to only 14 percent in the rest of the town. All in all, the village was different from the rest of Brookline, poorer and more crowded. Nearly 60 percent of village household heads were foreign-born,

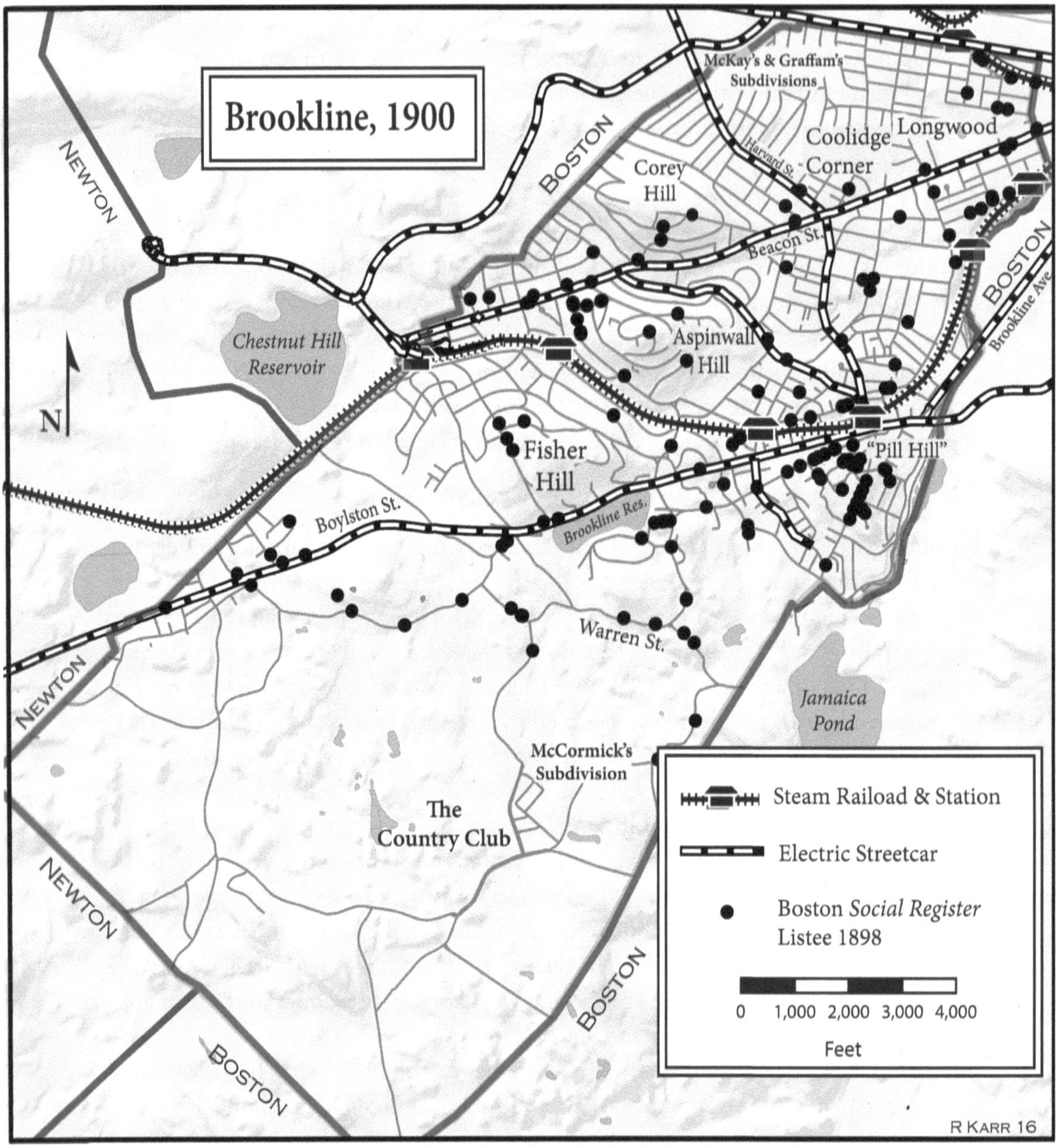

FIGURE 7.6. Map of Brookline in 1900, showing transportation routes and location of families listed in the Boston *Social Register*.

compared to only a quarter of those elsewhere. More than three-quarters of village households rented their quarters, compared to less than half of households elsewhere in town. Only 16 percent of village households included resident servants (many of them doubtless boarders); 65 percent of non-village households reported them. A majority of village heads worked at blue-collar jobs, compared to 15 percent of their counterparts outside the village.[31]

The Stamp of Fashion

In 1900 the vast majority of Brookline's inhabitants lived in the village or in the newly settled regions to the north along Beacon Street. Beyond these areas to the north closest to Boston lay the Longwood and Cottage Farm districts, the realm of the Sears and Lawrence families, who had guided the development of

FIGURE 7.7. Brookline Village looking north along Washington Street from Parker Hill, Roxbury Crossing, circa 1900. The intersection of Pond Avenue and Washington Street is in the foreground at right. Courtesy of the Brookline Historical Society.

these into high-status, low-density residential districts.[32] In the other direction lay two drumlins, Aspinwall and Fisher Hills, which were still in the process of being developed, the latter having been laid out by Frederick Law Olmsted in the 1880s. With its curvilinear hilltop lanes and half-acre lots, Fisher Hill was one of the town's most sought-after addresses, as well as the prototype for the twentieth-century upper-middle-class automobile suburb.[33]

Yet it was the remainder of the town, especially that section immediately to the south of Boylston Street and to the west of the village, that still attracted the most attention of outsiders. "Brookline is the richest suburb of Boston," a popular turn-of-the-century guidebook informed its curious readers, "and in many respects the most attractive, with numerous beautiful estates and tasteful 'villas' and charming drives." Tourists were directed to exit the Boylston Street trolley at the Brookline Reservoir and take a "stroll over [street]carless streets in Brookline's choicest parts," down Warren Street to Walnut to the old town center and burial ground, then back on Warren "between splendid estates with stately houses set in velvety lawns fringed with trees," past Frederic Law Olmsted's house to Cottage to Heath and back to Boylston.[34] Much of the town's fashionable reputation derived from these scenic historic neighborhoods, with their tree-lined, winding lanes and well-manicured, rolling lawns, shrubs, and gardens. By the 1890s it was becoming ever more apparent that this part of town had shown the greatest resilience to change.

Throughout most of the nineteenth century these estates and their Brahmin owners helped put the stamp of fashion on the entire town, even if the rest of Brookline only faintly resembled their own celebrated estates. Most middle-class commuters could not afford to emulate the lifestyles of the rich and famous, there being no way a lawyer, physician, minister, or the typical successful business owner could afford to live in a large house set on spacious grounds, maintained by a small army of servants, without inherited wealth. Early middle-class commuters therefore lived by their own standards, content to have a large, comfortable house on a modest-sized lot, with a couple of servants, near a railroad station, even if none of their neighbors or friends were Boston Brahmins and the great estates were not in view. As long as the Cabots, Lowells, Lawrences, Lees, and other great families resided somewhere in Brookline, the stamp of fashion extended to middle-class streets as well.

By 1900, however, the gap between the Brahmins and the upper-middle-class commuters was being bridged by the appearance of a new upper class, encompassing both the old proper Bostonian families and families previously considered middle class. Now the old upper-class families increasingly mingled with a select strata of the formerly lesser bourgeoisie at gentlemen's (and ladies') clubs, worshipped with them at a handful of fashionable Episcopalian or Unitarian churches, spent their summers together at swank resorts, and joined their own sons and daughters at exclusive boarding schools and coming-out parties. Many of the new members of this expanded upper class had attended Harvard—which had always had its share of middle-class and parvenu students, along with those from the best families—or had been business or professional associates of the old upper class.[35]

In 1890 the first edition of the Boston *Social Register* appeared. This directory of the new upper class listed 455 individuals and families, with 27 (6 percent) showing Brookline addresses. By 1894 the *Register* had swollen to 1,922 families, 141 (7 percent) from Brookline. Who were these listees? Examination of all 209 adult males who appeared in the 1890, 1894, and 1898 *Registers* as living in Brookline shows that they were indeed an elite lot. One-third practiced professions—mostly law, medicine, and architecture—while another 43 percent were merchants, manufacturers, brokers, and other executive occupations. Another 6 percent were gentlemen of leisure without even a pretense of gainful employment. At a time when few Americans had ever attended college, some 44 percent were Harvard graduates (another 4 percent had attended) and 9 percent had graduated from other colleges. Of the four-fifths whose birthplaces could be determined, 31 percent had been born in Boston, 12 percent in Brookline, and 11 percent in other Boston suburbs. Nearly all the rest had been born elsewhere in New England, with only ten individuals foreign-born.[36]

Less than a fifth of the *Register*-listed Brookline residents of the 1890s could claim upper-class status extending back four generations in the male line. The new expanded upper class was dominated numerically, if not socially, by individuals and families who had relatively recently climbed out of the upper middle class. Most *Social Register* listees came from urban or suburban upper-class or upper-middle-class families. No less than 63 percent of their fathers had worked as merchants, business executives, or professionals, as had 43 percent of their paternal grandfathers. At a time when the overwhelming majority of Americans were farmers, only 1 percent of these elites' fathers and 13 percent of their paternal grandfathers had worked the land. In education the listees greatly exceeded their forbearers: only 23 percent of the fathers and 11 percent of the grandfathers had been Harvard men.[37]

The new upper class in Brookline enjoyed wealth and influence disproportionate to its small numbers. In 1895 the 171 men listed in the *Social Register,* 3 percent of all taxpaying units, accounted for 14 percent of the town's total assessed real estate.[38] Five out of the sixteen men who served as selectmen between 1885 and 1900 appeared in the *Register.* The two men most active at town meetings and hearings during the 1880s and early 1890s, William Aspinwall and Harvard-educated Alfred D. Chandler, were both listed; Rufus Candage, town moderator and Republican chairman, however, was not, nor were Francis and Caroline White, despite ownership of a fine estate in an extremely desirable locale.

Whatever else they may have been, a family listed in the *Social Register* was undeniably fashionable, even if it were not fabulously wealthy. Their style of life was one that thousands of middle-class families could aspire to, and their housing choices helped establish what would become sought-after by their social inferiors. In their choice of neighborhoods the new upper class—most of whom lived in large homes on lots, not mansions on multi-acre estates—demonstrated that not all Brookline neighborhoods were equally desirable (see fig. 7.6). Most of the social elite at the end of the century clustered in a few favored neighborhoods, where they increasingly demanded larger lots, manicured lawns, professional landscaping, gardens, trees, and winding streets, not just simply large houses.

Of course, for socialites who could afford the best, an impressive mansion with extensive grounds was the ideal. In fact, even these ten-acre domains were being eclipsed by the end of the century by what amounted to mega-estates, featuring truly palatial mansions and extensive gardens. Most notable were the grounds and houses of two granddaughters of Boston shipping magnate William Fletcher Weld, Mary Pratt Sprague (the wife of Congressman Charles Sprague) and Isabel Perkins Anderson (wife of diplomat Larz Anderson). Both cousins' properties were created out of lands their Weld ancestors had owned since the eighteenth century in Brookline, Roxbury, and Newton. Their estates, which each began building at the end of the century, attracted national attention.[39]

Even among the upper class, however, great estates were exceptional. Most *Social Register* listees favored Brookline neighborhoods like Pill Hill (named for the many physicians who eventually came to live there), a bastion of the new upper class. The largest group of *Register* listees was located on the western edge of Brookline Village along Walnut and High Streets near the old town center. In 1898 nearly a third of all listees lived in this vicinity (see fig. 4.7). Three other upper-class districts—the new townhouses of upper Beacon Street, the Sears and Lawrence developments in Longwood, and South Brookline—accounted for nearly all of the rest.[40]

Whole parts of town were devoid of *Social Register* families. Naturally, Irish slums like the Marsh and Whiskey Point and the commercial center of Brookline Village were avoided. What seems especially noteworthy is the absence of upper-class families in the streetcar suburb neighborhoods in North Brookline near Coolidge Corner. McKay's and Graffam's fine new neighborhoods, with their small lots and grid streets and nearby apartments and stores, were simply not fashionable. For by and large Boston's new upper class was not leaving the city. At the turn of the century nearly half of all Boston *Social Register* listees could be found living in just one Boston neighborhood, the Back Bay, and less than a third could be found anywhere beyond the city limits.[41] A clear majority still preferred the urban style of life, and they had the resources to live wherever they wanted. For the minority who chose suburban living, most had no desire to locate in the newly built, high-density suburban neighborhoods near Beacon Street in Brookline. These must have seemed a compromise that they were not prepared to make: urban density without the convenient location, sophistication, or elegance of the Back Bay or Beacon Hill.

Many upper-class Yankees increasingly had reservations about the changes transforming the town and questioned whether development had gone too far too fast, that not enough of the old rural Brookline was being preserved. Others shrugged off such criticisms, noting that Brookline's continued wealth and fashionableness among the rich and powerful confirmed the town's basic soundness and desirability despite its population growth. The final decade of the nineteenth century would see this question constantly raised, as the inhabitants worked out the meaning of suburbia.

CHAPTER 8

Defining Suburbia

✦

Strictly suburban, that is to say, resident in detached dwellings with sylvan surroundings yet supplied with a considerable share of urban convenience.

—Frederick Law Olmsted, *Report of a Preliminary Scheme of Improvements, Staten Island Improvement Commission,* 1871

THE RAPID conversion of the fields and estates near Beacon Street into housing and commercial blocks in the 1890s raised questions among the town's bourgeoisie concerning its future. Would anything of the town's celebrated rural charm survive the onslaught of development? Was Brookline slated to follow the high-density growth of a Roxbury or Somerville, albeit with more expensive housing? Or was it possible to develop land into housing without destroying all of the features of the existing landscape? In short, could the town grow without becoming urban, retaining its distinctive suburban appearance, even if the fields and cows were gone? While they pondered these questions, Brookline's bourgeoisie faced a host of other concerns that helped shape their views regarding the town's future.

Anxious Times

As Brookline grew in the final decades of the nineteenth century, the mood of the new upper class and the broader middle class grew increasingly more conservative, insecure, anxious, even cranky, reflecting worries widely felt throughout the country that despite undoubted material progress the nation was moving in the wrong direction.[1] The exuberant confidence previously expressed by the town's newspapers in the 1870s, which, unlike much of the national press could even show sympathy for labor, women, and immigrants, now expressed an often mean-spirited conservatism. Following a series of strikes and labor demonstrations in 1886 that climaxed in the Haymarket Bombing in Chicago, the *Brookline Chronicle* saw the nation besieged by foreigners, labor agitators, and anarchist assassins, the latter, "all foreigners and recent importations. They are not to be found among native Americans, Irishmen, or Germans, who have lived among us long enough to learn the nature of our institutions. . . . They are generally Poles, Bohemians, Hungarians, Moravians, Pomeranians, Mecklenbergers, all of the Slavic or Serf races, whose ancestors have been serfs for a thousand years, and who were themselves either serfs or criminals in their native country." These new immigrants "are making necessary an American standing army in order to protect the rights of the people. . . . We must have law and order and peace here, even if our government assumes the characteristics of a despotism."[2]

Anti-immigrant sentiment continued into the 1890s. Newcomers to America should be sorted, "taking only the best and sending the others back." The literacy test should be employed to exclude "Hungarians, Polacks and Italians," a bunch of "beggars, paupers, thieves," truly "an undesirable class of people in every respect, since they intend to return home as soon as they accumulate a little money, and hence have no ambitions to become American citizens." Even though these new immigrants from southern and eastern Europe had yet to appear in Brookline in any numbers (as late as 1900 they made up less than 1 percent of the town's population), their threat was deemed so great as to demand action to save the republic. "We do not want these people; they are a nuisance and a danger wherever they gather. For the sake of us who are of American blood and for those others from the more highly civilized nations of Europe, who come here to stay," the time has now come "to withdraw the proclamation that America is the home of the poor and the asylum of the oppressed."[3]

Brookline's working class, once treated with some respect, could find scant sympathy in the *Chronicle* after 1885. Efforts by workers to secure higher pay or better conditions through collective action were now denounced as foreign-inspired innovations. Unions were condemned for calling foolish strikes that flaunted the iron law of supply and demand which governed wages and prices. The movement to secure an eight-hour day for workers was condemned as obvious folly, since a reduction in hours necessitated a corresponding reduction in pay. Piecework, the *Chronicle* suggested, was the only honest system of worker compensation, since each individual was rewarded on the basis of performance.[4]

Before the mid-1880s Brookline had alternated between a policy of tolerating the sale of liquor and half-heartedly forbidding it, a secondary concern to most voters. Beginning in 1887, however, antisaloon sentiment swept the town. In every year that followed, the question of allowing the sale of liquor in Brookline appeared before the town meeting, and in every year the prohibitionists triumphed. By 1900 the saloon, both legal and illegal, once so much a part of Brookline life, was largely a thing of the past.[5]

The movement to secure political rights for women, which had long enjoyed support in Brookline, at first sidestepped the reactionary mood. In 1877 two women, both upper-class wives, had been elected overseers of the poor, and in 1879 the town voted to allow some women to participate in the election for school committee. As early as 1871 the *Brookline Transcript* had advocated equal pay for male and female public school teachers and urged the training of women for nontraditional occupations. Its successor, the *Chronicle,* in 1877 called the lower pay received by women teachers "a blot on our civilization," and two years later advocated the election of a woman to the school committee. Although a measure endorsing municipal suffrage for all Massachusetts women failed to pass town meeting in 1881, an active women's suffrage movement was at work in the town. The number of women voting in school elections showed a sudden surge in 1889, and that same year women were admitted for the first time to the annual citizen's caucus, which nominated candidates for town offices.[6]

In 1895 the reactionary mood finally overtook the women's movement. That year antisuffrage activists had persuaded the legislature to place a nonbinding question on women's suffrage on the Massachusetts ballot that fall, with a provision to allow women to register and vote on the question as well. In response, a group of prominent local matrons circulated a petition regarding "certain obligations which we have no wish to assume." Among the signers of this antisuffrage manifesto were Mrs. Theodore Lyman, Mrs. Henry Lee, Mrs. Leverett Saltonstall, Mrs. Frederick Law Olmsted, Mrs. Henry M. Whitney, Mrs. Francis W. Lawrence, and Mrs. Alfred D. Chandler (characteristically, they signed using their husbands' names). The suffrage movement went down to a humiliating defeat, both in Brookline and throughout the state (it would take the federal Nineteenth Amendment to extend the vote to Massachusetts women). Brookline males voted 1,232 to 498 against women participating in town elections, while only 316 of the 4,000 eligible women even bothered to register to vote. "It is obvious," the *Chronicle* concluded, "that Brookline women do not believe in the expediency of municipal suffrage."[7]

The conservative reaction was starting to undermine the exuberant confidence with which nineteenth-century Americans had previously greeted the introduction of promising new technologies, mass consumer goods, and the building of new neighborhoods, towns, and even whole cities. To be sure, some had previously found the disappearance of the old ways a bit unsettling, but on the whole, despite bouts of nostalgia, few Americans had sought to derail the engine of progress. Although they may have regretted some of their losses, the benefits of change seemed to greatly outweigh its drawbacks.[8] By the 1890s, however, many Protestant Americans, especially in New England, wondered if something of value had truly been lost in the rush to modernize.

Popular writers such as Alice Morse Earle, Samuel Adams Drake, and Sarah Orne Jewett sang the praises of old-time rural New England to a receptive audience eager to rediscover the world they had lost to progress. This in turn helped spur on the Colonial Revival movement, as old-stock Americans increasingly sought houses, interior decoration, and furniture inspired by the rural, preindustrial past. Artifacts previously spurned as junk were starting to become treasured antiques. The lives of their own sturdy, hard-working, sober, and upright Puritan ancestors formed a discouraging contrast to the lazy, alcoholic, and superstitious immigrants who seemed to be displacing them. It was becoming fashionable to bemoan the passing of the traditional, rural New England landscape in growing suburbs like Brookline.[9]

An Urban Future?

With the ongoing development of North Brookline the town was fast losing its rural character. As late as 1895 26 farms still remained in operation, with a total of 672 acres (exclusive of woodlots), but ten years later there would be but 4, with only 88 acres still under cultivation.[10] The disappearance of open land to development gave a new urgency to those who shared William Dean Howells's conviction that to remain authentic, suburbia needed to preserve something of its rural heritage lest it become part of the city, regardless of its political status. In 1893 the *Chronicle* had listed the "natural beauty of surroundings and pure air" as the first reason "why Brookline attracts residents." That same year "a comparatively new resident" explained that he "was led to select this town for a residence on account of its natural beauties, its beautiful, breezy hills, wooded slopes, and rolling valleys."[11]

By the 1890s many if not most of Brookline's bourgeoisie, especially the families joining the new upper class, had adopted an aesthetic appreciation for the town's familiar landscape. If nothing else the unsettling transformation of Beacon Street would have driven home the fragility of scenery. Even the many who welcomed the widening had some reservations about the loss of open fields and trees. Although they shared an appreciation for Brookline's scenic landscape, Brookline's leaders saw no practical way to stem the loss of rustic charm. The town seemed slated to become urbanized. "Brookline's rural fate is, alas, much of it sealed," observed Alfred D. Chandler in 1893. "But laments are out of place. The new conditions of suburban life must be met."[12] As late as 1899 one of the town's leading citizens, a retired sea captain and maritime insurance inspector named Rufus G. F. Candage (1826–1912), strongly rejected the entire ruralist premise. Candage, who had been born and raised on a Maine farm, had moved to Brookline on retiring from the sea in 1867 and had held virtually every town office, including selectman, moderator, state representative, library trustee, and chairman of the Brookline Republican Party. From his house on Kent Street in Brookline Village, just north of the depot, he had witnessed the town changing over the past thirty years and overall he approved. "The change from a rural to a metropolitan community has not been without regret," he wrote in the new *Brookline Suburban.* But those "who deprecate change of any kind, and who believe that the former condition was the better condition" were wrong:

> The change has been easy and natural, and has been effected with general approval and satisfaction. Lying, as Brookline does, upon the borders of Boston on three sides (with the city of Newton on the fourth), it is in position to catch that city's overflow. Some would have felt better pleased if the town could have preserved more of its rural aspect, and that independent homes had been maintained instead of blocks and apartment houses. But with land at a dollar or two or three dollars per foot, large areas of land cannot be expected about every home.

Any loss of rural charm was more than offset by gains in wealth and the quality of its population. Brookline's inhabitants were "made up of business and professional men, principally—able, intelligent, refined, and progressive—[which] make it desirable, and its natural beauties are [still] admired by all who behold them."[13]

Indeed, many argued, it was the quality of the inhabitants that made Brookline the ideal suburb. In 1892 the *Chronicle* forgot to mention the town's natural beauty at all when it listed "the many reasons given by our newcomers, for seeking residence in Brookline":

1. Brookline is a healthy town, populated by as desirable a people as are to be found in the country.
2. It is governed by the whole people for the good of all the people.
3. It possesses the comforts of a city municipality, gained without the discomforts of political trading among the governing officers; and what the majority asks for, they get without vexatious delays.
4. It can rightfully boast of the best kept highways, well lighted; the purest of drinking water; the finest system of sewers, etc.
5. As to churches and public schools, there are none better in the land.
6. The citizens of Brookline are people of broad ideas, and liberal in the expenditure of money for public measures.
7. Taxation is kept at a reasonable rate, by the wise economy of obtaining the very best.

In Brookline none of these points seemed in dispute. The *Chronicle* had carefully sidestepped more controversial issues, such as whether continued uncontrolled growth was desirable.[14]

Some Brookline residents' vision of an ideal suburb could be reduced to a wealthy municipality with good government. At a time when large cities were becoming renowned for their corruption and inefficiency, this was no mean feat. To those fed up with big-city politics Brookline's success showed a better way. The continued political independence of the town was by now a given; annexationists had long given up the fight. "Brookline's success is not phenomenal," the *Chronicle* had proclaimed in 1890, but rather "the natural, the well-deserved result of the attention and self-sacrifice of its citizens to the town's affairs, and of a simple, sound government, free from political entanglements." Under its system of nonpartisan direct democracy, the evils of big-city corruption and boss rule were avoided, "the uneasy, restless disposition of some is held in wholesome restraint by the popular spirit which is alike conservative and yet progressive."[15]

A cynical observer would note that Brookline's success was more than wise voters choosing capable officials and rejecting partisanship. The town's attractive environment and ready location had long drawn high-income commuters, who had the time and inclination to participate in local government and use political power to shape the community to their liking. The swollen real-estate values that resulted produced a substantial tax base capable of generating huge revenue streams from a low tax rate. High-quality municipal services combined with low taxes served to attract even more high-status residents, making Brookline in turn wealthier and more desirable. For example, in 1879 Brookline's per-capita valuation was approximately $2,800, as opposed to $1,700 in Boston. Although the town's tax *rate* was lower than the city's, Brookline raised considerably more tax revenue per inhabitant. By 1898 Brookline's per-capita assessed wealth had reached $4,000, while Boston had risen to only $2,100, despite the city's vast commercial and industrial districts. In 1903 Brookline's property tax rate was only $10.00 per thousand, compared to $14.90 in the city.[16]

Brookline's leaders were all too aware of the need to keep attracting wealthy residents. Urban experience suggested that neighborhoods could change socially, not always for the better. Once-fashionable quarters, such as Boston's Beacon Hill, had been losing their attractiveness to the affluent, and the South End had declined precipitously from a would-be elite district into a near slum.[17] Overall, the numbers of upper-income households in the Boston area were limited, and Boston's city and suburban neighborhoods engaged in competition for them. "Every property owner who can be induced to settle in Brookline," Chandler himself had observed in 1881, "brings so much more taxable property to the town, and helps proportionately to reduce the rate of taxation for all." In addition to its obvious benefits, honest and effective town government also served to attract affluent urbanities disgusted at Boston's corruption.[18]

A Suburban Alternative

Back in the 1860s William Dean Howells had lamented the transience of rural features in suburbia. Unfortunately, there seemed to be no ready way to reconcile nostalgic ruralism with the reality of surburbanization. Suburbanites did not actually yearn to return to the drudgery of farming or the insipidness of small-town life. They accepted that replicating country life was impractical in the metropolis, and the high cost of land ruled out acres of open fields. Reluctantly, they acknowledged that they had no choice but to accept the inevitability of high-density, urban-style residential and commercial development. What ruralists longed for was a practical form of growth that could somehow provide at least a symbolic evocation of the now-vanished acres of open land, crops waving in the breeze, cows grazing on the meadows, and densely wooded hills, so that suburbs could still combine the best of urban and rural life.[19]

Ironically, it was the very architect of the Beacon Street widening who had already found an alternative that might achieve the goal of bringing the city and country together into a new style of suburban community. Born in Hartford in 1822, the son of a wealthy merchant, Frederick Law Olmsted graduated from Yale and dabbled in several pursuits before settling on a career in landscape architecture. One of the founders of his profession, he acquired an international reputation designing urban parks, most notably Central Park in New York City. Both repelled and attracted by cities, Olmsted designed his parks as antidotes to the baneful aspects of city life: trees, fresh air, and space would revitalize the damaged human spirit of urbanites, counter crass commercialism, uplift the masses, and provide aesthetic pleasure for those of cultivated tastes. A conservative reformer, Olmsted supported the concept of democracy but insisted on elite leadership to counter popular excesses.[20]

Olmsted viewed the suburb as another answer to the city. His involvement in suburban planning began in 1868 when the owners of a 1,600-acre tract on the Des Plaines River in Illinois, ten miles west of Chicago, commissioned him to lay out a suburban community. At Riverside, as the development was named, Olmsted produced a handsome design that featured ample park lands, irregularly shaped half-acre lots, thirty-foot setbacks, and curvilinear streets that hugged the natural contours of the land. Riverside was the antithesis of the conventional grid-street and frontage-lot development.[21]

Convinced that properly designed suburbs could help redeem the metropolis from the ills of overcrowding and overcommercialization, Olmsted decided to try suburban living for himself. A longtime resident of New York City, he first saw Brookline in 1878 on a visit to architect Henry Hobson Richardson's place on Cottage Street. Three years later he summered in the town, and in 1883 he bought a house near Richardson's at 99 Warren Street (adjacent to the Gardner's Green Hill estate and the Fairmount subdivision), which would serve as his residence and studio for the rest of his life. His first Brookline project dated from 1880, and over the next fifteen years until his retirement he helped lay out several subdivisions, widened streets (including, of course, Beacon Street), and landscaped numerous private estates. Above all, he helped turn the Muddy River from a public nuisance into a model park, one that would become renowned as part of Boston's "Emerald Necklace," an elegant solution to the drainage problems that had long plagued Brookline Village. The expansion of this Boston park network in the 1880s and early 1890s into Brookline gave the town much of the advantages of annexation with none of the drawbacks.[22]

As he had first done at Riverside, Olmsted's Brookline subdivisions were in contrast to more conventional designs, such as those employed by McKay or Graffam. His streets were curved, not straight, and the lots—twice the size of McKay's—irregularly shaped. Houses were kept far back from the streets, screened by shrubs and trees and often half-concealed by the lay of the land. The careful placement of houses on their lots was calculated to maximize the rural illusion and symbolic associations of nature. Brookline's rolling topography was well-suited for his approach.[23]

Like many successful innovators, Olmsted did not invent the tools he perfected. Curvilinear streets, as we have seen, harkened back a half century earlier to the first garden cemeteries and had been used in Brookline subdivisions as early as the 1840s. Andrew Jackson Downing had promoted the uses of landscape architecture in residential development at the very dawn of suburbanization.[24] But Olmsted had changed the rules of development by offering a clear and practical—for those with the means—alternative to conventional development. His innovative designs were popular successes. The largest subdivision that was built according to his plans, Fisher Hill (fig. 8.1), eventually became one of Brookline's most sought-after addresses for upper- and upper-middle-class families (and remains so to this day).[25] By the century's end Olmsted's formula of curvilinear streets and larger-than-average lots was becoming the suburban ideal. When fashionable Chestnut Hill began to spill over into Brookline from across the Newton line in the 1890s, its new streets were curvilinear; nearly all Brookline streets in the twentieth century have followed suit (fig. 8.2). Olmsted showed it was possible to create a commercially viable embodiment of what William Dean Howells could only dream: a distinctly suburban landscape that incorporated the best of the rural and urban without being either.

Although worked out amid the tree-shaded open rolling topography of South Brookline's great estates, Olmsted's techniques proved adaptable to other environments as well, such as the old fields adjacent to Brookline Village along High Street that would become Pill Hill. This somewhat confusing array of roads off of High and Walnut Streets southwest of Brookline Village was built up after the Civil War, partly on the holdings of the Brookline Land Company (fig. 8.3). It offers an instructive contrast to McKay's and Graffam's speculative Coolidge Corner subdivisions, built around the same time.

In the latter's subdivisions, the streets are straight, each house is (or probably was when built) the same size as its neighbor and set back a uniform distance from the street; the houses were all originally wooden-clad, and each house

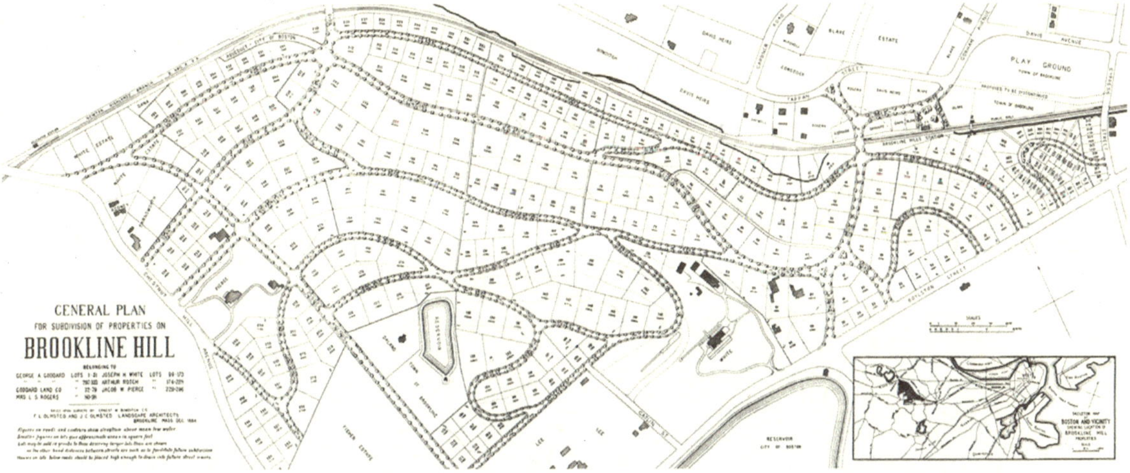

FIGURE 8.1. Frederick Law Olmsted prepared this subdivision plan for a group of Fisher Hill landowners in 1886, featuring curvilinear streets and half-acre lots. It was not fully built up until the twentieth century. Courtesy of the Public Library of Brookline.

occupied much of its lot. On Pill Hill the houses themselves—with a few notable exceptions—were roughly the same size as those near Coolidge Corner, but the lots were bigger, the houses set further back from the street—sometimes at varying distances from the curb—and some of the houses were made of brick. Unlike the Coolidge Corner streets, where the houses were often built at the same time by the same developers, the houses on Pill Hill were built over a period of several years, in differing architectural styles (see fig. 4.7). A number of prominent Boston architects lived on Pill Hill and designed their own houses. Furthermore, some of the streets, such the Olmsted-designed Maple and Upland Roads, are pleasingly curved. Howells had been right after all—city and country could be blended together to form a practical, livable, and sustainable environment. All it took was the will and power to do so, along with ample sums of money.[26]

Pill Hill clearly comes closer to the pattern of twentieth-century upper-middle-class suburban growth than does Coolidge Corner. Automobile storage and driveways soon took over significant portions of the yards of the McKay and Graffam properties, as they did in other streetcar suburbs, changing the appearance of these streets for the worse. By 1900 the concentration of upper-class residents on Pill Hill and their complete avoidance of Coolidge Corner leaves little doubt about which neighborhood was the more fashionable. Of course this does not necessarily mean that buyers were forced to settle for McKay's and Graffam's

FIGURE 8.2. A prototype of thousands of twentieth-century suburban subdivision streets, Gardner Road near Beacon Street. The houses were built in the 1890s. This demonstrates the attractiveness of curvilinear streets and larger lots, especially on hilly terrain, allowing room for landscaping, backyards, and gardens, even with large houses. Olmsted was involved in the early conceptual planning for this street but was not responsible for the final design. Brookline Photographic Collection, Public Library of Brookline, digitalcommonwealth.org.

homes when what they really wanted was to live with the social elite on Pill Hill. Social climbers may have been (temporarily in many cases) frustrated, perhaps, but for many upper-middle-class families the higher costs of a larger lot and prestigious neighbors were not a worthwhile exchange for the convenience of a comfortable house near Coolidge Corner. Even if the neighborhood were growing less fashionable, many middle-class residents had no objections to living in what was increasingly an urban district.

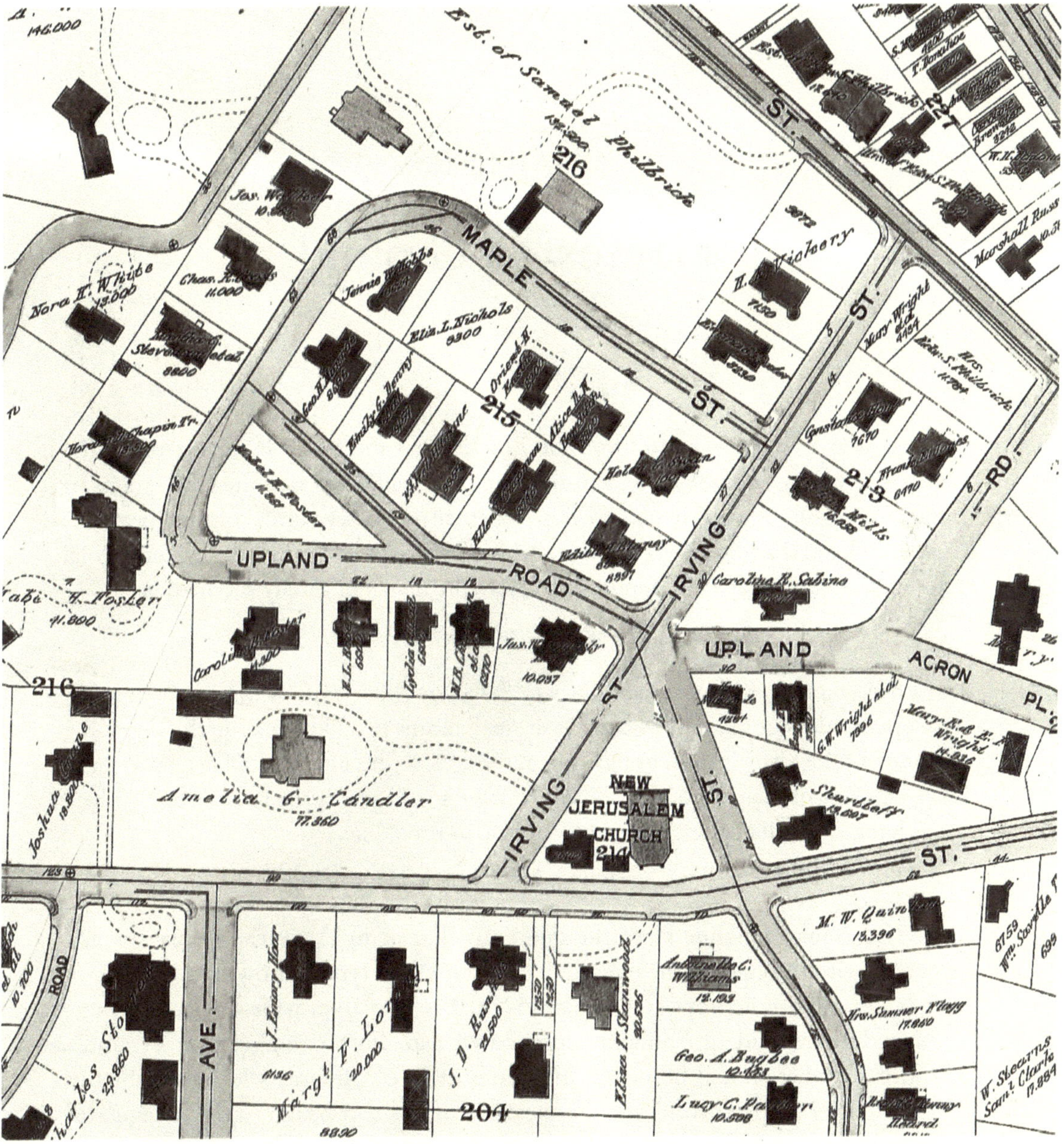

FIGURE 8.3. Laid out by Alfred D. Chandler's Brookline Land Company and the estate of Edward Philbrick, in conjunction with Frederick Law Olmsted, the High Street (Pill Hill) neighborhood offered the less-opulent members of the new upper class an attractive neighborhood convenient to Brookline Village. Most of these houses went up in the 1880s and 1890s. Here lots averaged a quarter of an acre or more, twice the size of David McKay's Coolidge Corner subdivision, and the topography is hilly. *Atlas of the Town of Brookline* (Philadelphia: Bromley, 1900), plates 16–17. Courtesy of the State Library of Massachusetts.

CHAPTER 9

Contested Ground

✦

Those who have known and loved the Brookline of the past, cannot but regret the necessity which, in some cases, and the want of a cultivated taste in others, dictates the building of crowded houses so close together that every vestige of rural beauty is sacrificed, and that the chief attractions, which have for years made our town proverbial for its charms, are rapidly disappearing before the march of greedy speculation.

—Harriet F. Woods, *Historical Sketches of Brookline,* 1874

If I have, on the whole, done an injury to the town or its property owners, by creating an opportunity for many of its citizens of small means to build homes in this charming section of the town, instead of remaining in the close and uncomfortable quarters into which many of them have been forced, I am willing to accept the responsibility. There are some, not millionaires, who choose to live in Brookline.

—John J. McCormack, 1893

In the 1890s Brookline faced the questions that many American suburbs would wrestle with throughout the twentieth century: What type of growth is desirable or to be regarded as appropriate? What was the best way to provide services for present and future residents? Should a suburb make an effort to retain its rural features, and if so, what should be done? In what sort of community did its inhabitants want to live? And above all, should questions of this sort be left to the unregulated workings of free markets or should the community intervene to determine a particular outcome? These issues provoked a series of controversies that reveal much about the varied ways in which bourgeois, middle-class, and even working-class Americans would come to interpret and define suburbia. In many cases, exactly how these questions were answered would determine a community's future.

As early as the 1870s, when modern land regulations such as zoning were far in the future, Bostonians had begun to confront the problems of controlling urban growth, forging over the next few decades a series of political tactics, innovative legal devices, and new organizations to preserve architectural landmarks, historic buildings, and precious open space from developers. Thanks to these controls, it now was becoming possible to imagine restricting and limiting development without stopping progress or undermining economic growth.[1] In Brookline the single most contentious issue arising in the 1890s was over the proper use of the town's land in general and density in particular. In 1893 Brookline lawyer Alfred D. Chandler, himself in the thick of most land use controversies, observed that "the need of co-operation between the public and the landowner is imperative. If the public allow the incoming tide of humanity to drift, it tumbles in upon a town without proper direction. If, however, suitable provision for transportation and municipal wants is anticipated, then the tide of population settles down under conditions which secure permanency and progress of a satisfactory kind; there is less waste, less annoyance, and an appreciation of advantages alike invigorating to civic pride and strengthening to civil government."[2] Clearly anticipating twentieth-century planning and subdivision control, Brookline's government, both through its town meeting and selectmen, had already started to regulate land use, selectively accepting or rejecting proposals to accept streets as town ways or lay sewer lines. The town adopted its first building code and appointed an inspector to enforce it in 1889.[3]

The problem facing local governments at the end of the century, even in Brookline, was that the wealth that funded the lavish services the town enjoyed was generated by an economic system which largely rejected regulation. Few nations had embraced economic liberalism more enthusiastically than the United States did in the nineteenth century. Americans let the marketplace allocate resources and make decisions that most other cultures had regarded as political questions. Nowhere was the hand of market-driven industrial capitalism more apparent than in the American city. Real-estate speculators, building contractors, factory owners, transit magnates, and bankers, all seeking to maximize profits, built the American metropolis with minimal interference. When the government did intervene to construct improvements, such as roads or sewers, or to provide services, such as police or fire protection, it usually acted in response to the demands of businessmen rather than offering its own agenda.[4]

Until the 1890s, despite Brookline's rapid growth, a specific building project was unlikely to generate controversy unless it catered to the lower classes or involved commercial or industrial activity, and even then only if it were located too close to a bourgeois residential neighborhood or institution. The town was usually content to let the private market—which often demanded deed restrictions forbidding commercial uses, requiring properties be set back from the street, and imposing a minimum building cost—regulate new construction aimed at the upper middle and upper classes. As yet, there was no agreement as to what was the minimum lot size for a respectable family home. Average lot sizes had been naturally shrinking as the town filled up, especially in Brookline Village, yet house sizes were not. No objections were heard when two-family houses and even row housing were built in Brookline, and the town's first apartments appeared as early as 1875.[5] Townhouses in Boston's Back Bay, with virtually no yards at all, were among the most sought-after residential properties in the city, and well into the twentieth century the small lots of McKay, Graffam, and other North Brookline builders did not discourage their purchase by affluent buyers.

By the 1890s, however, observers were increasingly associating density with lower-class tenements and other pathologies. "Massing people destroys individuality," Reverend O. P. Gifford of the Brookline Baptist Church noted in 1891. "Loss of individuality means loss of responsibility."[6] Densely packed tenement districts and streets teeming with humanity were seen as among the most repulsive features of urban life. And as the mood of the bourgeoisie turned ever more conservative and fearful, concern grew that denser development heralded Brookline's impending decline.

John J. McCormack and South Brookline

The rapid growth of northern Brookline after 1886 left the southern sector of the town as the final bastion of a traditional rural landscape. At least four competing visions emerged concerning the region's future. Some sought to convert at least some of it into a lower-middle-class streetcar suburb, along the lines of Dorchester or West Roxbury. Others hoped that southern Brookline would mirror the development of the northern part of town and feature a high-density, upper-middle-class neighborhood. A third group regarded development as inevitable but believed that much of the area's charm could be preserved if subdivided along Olmstedian lines. Finally, a small but influential band of landowners hoped to convince their neighbors to resist the developers and preserve intact the great estates.

It soon became apparent that the town would not tolerate the first proposal. John J. McCormack, the Brookline-born son of a successful Irish immigrant, one-time Boston Custom House clerk, and experienced local builder and real-estate dealer, had acquired land on Clyde Street in southern Brookline. In May 1893 he announced "a great sale of 100 building lots," not far from the failed Goddard Heights subdivision of twenty years before (fig. 9.1). He had platted seven conventional grid streets, featuring rectangular lots of 4,500 to 7,000 square feet. These closely resembled the lots being laid out at the same time by McKay and Graffam, though McCormack was only selling land, not houses. Several lots were said to have been sold before the formal announcement. Some thirty-five lots were disposed at auction, and by June sixty-eight had been purchased. The project seemed off to an excellent start.[7]

Much to McCormack's apparent surprise, his development suddenly encountered an angry swarm of opponents denouncing the project on both practical and aesthetic grounds. Some argued that McCormack's land was poorly drained, with mud six to eight feet deep laying beneath the lots. Others claimed such subdivisions were inappropriate for the town. "Brookline's successful future does not lie in the same path as that of Everett or Malden," wrote one critic. "It would be only too easy, were land owners thoughtless enough to encourage it, to hustle a large part of Brookline into another Roxbury or South Cove district." Another, an admitted newcomer to town, explained that he was drawn to Brookline by its beauty, particularly the "large and beautiful country seats which, with their open spaces, insure health-giving breezes as long as they remain intact in the hands of their fortunate owners." Now "the spell of beauty, quiet, and good order" was imperiled:

> We view with feelings of alarm and disgust any approach of popular land booming schemes in the midst of scenes we love so well. Think of the rude thumb plots and plans of streets and house-lots that will appear wherever the land may be obtained cheaply. . . . Imagine this town covered, and even crowded in places, with houses—its beautiful hills and vales obscured, its pure air contaminated, the great lungs congested—this lovely gem of nature changed from a *home* to live in to a place to merely exist in. The mere talk about a price at which some of our

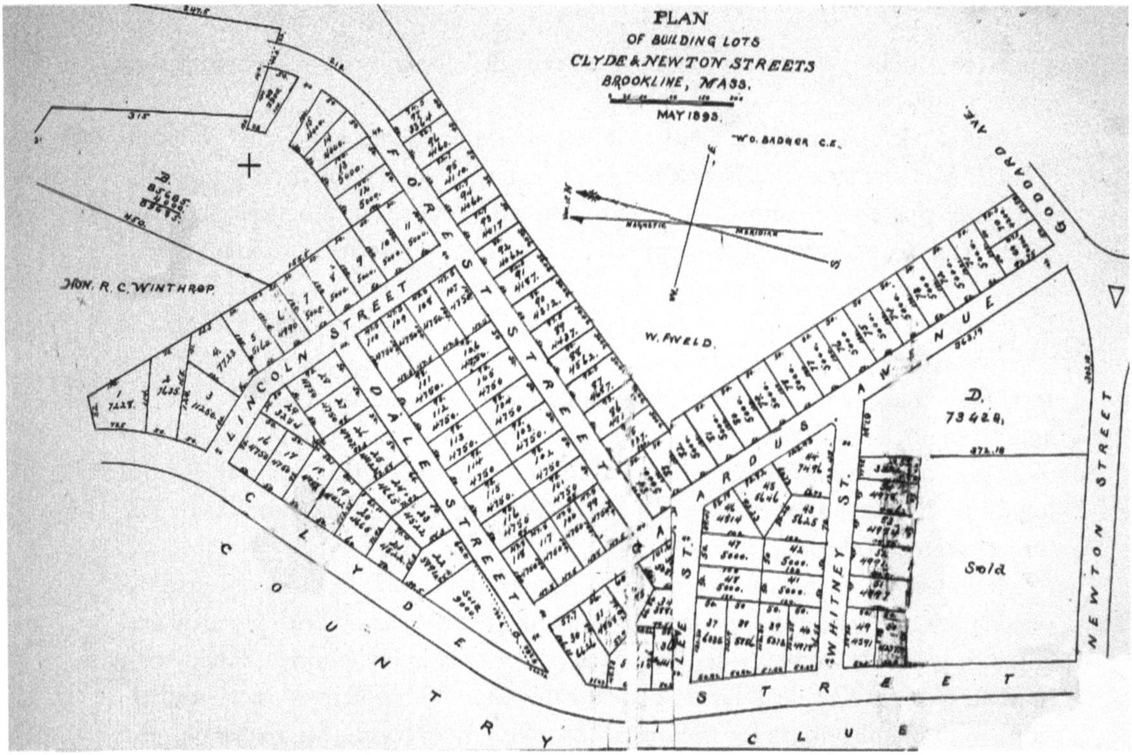

FIGURE 9.1. John J. McCormack surveyed this subdivision at the intersection of Clyde and Newton Streets in South Brookline in 1893. His abutters included The Country Club across Clyde Street; Robert C. Winthrop, former speaker of the U.S. House of Representatives; and the heirs of the late William Fletcher Weld, one of the richest men in the country. Norfolk Deeds, plan D0694–900.

> large estates might be sold to cut up into building lots sounds as sacrilegious as a bid for corner lots in paradise![8]

Why did this modest subdivision generate such a strong reaction when so many others were built without notice? As always with real estate, location made the difference. McCormack's subdivision was nearly surrounded by the estates of some of Brookline's wealthiest and most powerful families and lay adjacent to the grounds of The Country Club. Founded by a group of prominent Bostonians assembled by James Murray Forbes in 1882, The Country Club had leased the grounds of a racetrack and hotel on Clyde Street. Unlike the male-only gentlemen's city clubs, which had been gaining in popularity among the upper class, this new institution included entire families in its membership. At the onset horseracing and polo were the primary draw, but by the 1890s golf had become the main attraction, though tennis and other sports were also available for members. An ample waiting list screened by a vigilant membership committee kept out those not fortunate enough to be socially prominent Protestants. By the end of the century the club's grounds would cover more than 125 acres (by 1923 golf-course expansion had pushed the grounds to 231 acres).[9]

Locating a grid-street and frontage-lot development here was truly testing the tolerance of the town's elite for high-density development. Even worse, it was becoming apparent that the inhabitants would be predominately lower-income Irish Catholics. Archbishop John Joseph Williams of Boston bought several lots, presumably as the site for a church. While McCormack had disposed of more than eighty lots in all, they had sold for an average of ten cents a square foot as compared with fifty cents to several dollars, the typical range of prices in other parts of Brookline. Such prices, low even by contemporary Dorchester, Roxbury, and West Roxbury standards, suggested that cheap housing would be erected.[10]

Stung by the criticism, McCormack countered that Brookline did not belong solely to the elite:

> If I have, on the whole, done an injury to the town or its property owners, by creating an opportunity for many of its citizens of small means to build homes in this charming section of the town, instead of remaining in the close and uncomfortable quarters into which many of them have been forced, I am willing to accept the responsibility. There are some, not millionaires, who choose to live in Brookline, the birthplace of many of them, and there are others whose occupations make it impossible for them to live elsewhere. Have they been so often able of late to find land upon which to build their future homes at a price within their reach or without restrictions which bar out all but the wealthy?

He pointed out what everyone knew, that the town had been subsidizing the wealthy landowners by keeping taxes low on the great estates of southern Brookline, the burden of which fell on the small taxpayers in the northern part of town. Land, he contended, should be taxed at its true market value to encourage its most productive and socially desirable uses. The inhabitants of his subdivision, he assured his critics, "will be as happy and prosperous on their lots of 5,000 feet as their neighbors on their idle acres."[11]

Such arguments did little to sway his detractors. Certainly, wrote one opponent, the housing needs of the poor deserve consideration: "When there are not enough suitable, cheap and healthy places for them to own or to rent, I will agree to demolish the ideal country seats and open spaces. But there is land enough and good, pure air enough now, without encroaching upon and destroying more natural beauty for generations yet unborn." All classes had an equal stake in preserving the unspoiled suburban development, even if the poor and working classes would have to appreciate at a distance, since their very presence would erode the quality of the environment. The author continued, "Let us rejoice and be glad that we yet live in a time when the taste and cultivation of even the poorer classes is such that they love the beauties of the everlasting hills of Brookline and would vote down any attempt to mar what they feel an interest and proprietorship in."[12]

In November McCormack requested that the selectmen lay out a new town road connecting his subdivision to Boylston Street, accept his streets as town roads, and install town sewers. At the hearings that followed, McCormack found himself facing high-powered lawyers representing the large landowners of southern Brookline, including the redoubtable Alfred D. Chandler, who denounced the project as unwise, unnecessary, and the genesis of a future slum. One estate owner went so far as to hire Aspinwall & Lincoln, Brookline's premier engineering firm, to review McCormack's proposal. The engineers claimed that half of the land was suitable only as "farm land for the growth of crops not necessarily injured by flooding," and the remainder "from its nearness to the swamp, would by most persons scarcely be considered healthful building land." Only through an elaborate and prohibitively expensive combination of drainage and fill could the land be rendered usable. In vain McCormack denied that conditions on his land were as bad as his critics contended and protested that his customers were satisfied with their purchases.[13]

After mulling over McCormack's petition for nearly three months, the selectmen refused to accept the streets, install sewers, or build an access road. McCormack had no better luck when he sought to have the Norfolk County commissioners construct a county road from his subdivision to Boylston Street. When hearings before the commissioners took place a year later, he once more faced a parade of lawyers denouncing the road as expensive and unnecessary. The commissioners turned down the request.[14]

Confronted with intense, well-funded opposition, McCormack's subdivision floundered. Without sewers, finished streets, churches, stores, or access roads, and a mile from public transit, few owners built on their lots. The severe business depression that began in 1893 further discouraged construction. By 1897 many of the lots had been abandoned by their owners and seized by the town for failure to pay taxes. One bitter owner in 1900 complained that although the selectmen refused to build roads or install sewers at the development, they always seemed eager to collect taxes on it. "I think it is about time they [the selectmen] should come to understand that this Clyde Street land is in the town of Brookline, and give us some chance for our money," he wrote. "As it is now, we cannot build or do a thing, but let it lie for seven years more and pay taxes on it." Some of the unbuilt lots came into the possession of nearby estate owners, and most of the land remained vacant until after the Second World War. Today the lots are occupied by modest (at least by Brookline standards) single-family homes mostly built after World War II.[15]

John McCormack might well have pondered the very different fate a nearby project experienced. Two developers, Michael J. O'Hearn and Thomas J. Kelly, had purchased a six-acre tract in 1891 near the junction of High, Cypress, and Chestnut Streets, only a mile or so from McCormack's ill-fated subdivision. Here they surveyed streets and platted forty-eight lots, averaging a scant three thousand square feet each. In 1895 they offered the lots for sale at auction. Without controversy the streets were accepted by the town, utilities installed, and housing erected. By the end of the century a score of buildings had been constructed, mostly multifamily units. Why did this development not encounter opposition? Location, of course: O'Hearn and Kelly had wisely chosen a site adjacent to Whiskey Point, not The Country Club, close to a new streetcar barn (which stood on land they themselves had sold to the street railway!). Few objected to high-density cheap housing on such sites obviously unsuitable for higher-status residential uses.[16]

Boylston Street

Even before McCormack launched his project, others had been scheming to develop South Brookline for higher-income housing. After the rapid growth of North Brookline an air of inevitability hung in the air. "To many must come a sensation of regret at parting with the rural associations of old Brookline," the *Chronicle* noted in 1892, "but the gates are wide open, the new guests are fast heeding the invitation, they cannot be shut out, and the only sensible alternative is to meet them cheerily." Boylston Street, the old Worcester Turnpike that cut across the northern part of the region, seemed the obvious key to development. In 1891 a group of land holders commissioned Frederick Law Olmsted to prepare plans for the widening of Boylston Street and Chestnut Hill Avenue along the lines of Beacon Street. A new streetcar line would serve the entire route and join the Beacon Street line at Reservoir Station (now Cleveland Circle), presumably touching off a building boom on the adjacent lands. Supporters argued that these improvements were necessary for Brookline's continued prosperity.[17]

Olmsted was already familiar with the locale, having previously drawn up plans for the adjacent subdivision of Fisher Hill in the 1880s (see fig. 8.1). With its curvilinear streets following the natural contours of the hill and larger individual lots, the latter plan suggested that less-dense development was anticipated in areas off Boylston and Chestnut Hill Avenue. But these plans, of course, were drafted prior to the proposed widening, and there was much land in the vicinity that could have been developed at a density similar to Graffam's and McKay's North Brookline subdivisions. Olmsted was also by now well acquainted with the chief spokesman for the widening, Alfred D. Chandler.[18]

As a prominent attorney, Chandler had long represented Brahmin landowners and was sensitive to their wishes. A persuasive participant in town meetings, land improvement schemes were in his blood; his father, Theophilus, had helped found the Brookline Land Company. Moreover, Chandler had cemented his ties to presuburban Brookline through his marriage to a granddaughter of Reverend John Pierce (who also happened to be a daughter of railroad publisher Henry Varnum Poor).[19] Much like John McCormack, Chandler initially had little reason to doubt that his scheme would come to fruition, especially after the selectmen gave their blessing.

And yet, when the selectmen put the question of widening Chestnut Hill Avenue before town meeting in April 1893, the proposal was turned down "by a large majority." Shocked, the *Chronicle* warned, "If a sudden reversal of Brookline's go-ahead policy is to be persisted in, the result will be very injurious to the town, and will seriously impair the interests of all classes."[20] What had gone wrong?

Chandler and the other promoters had not reckoned with the stubborn opposition of one powerful, determined old man, Col. Henry Lee. He had been born in 1817 into one of Boston's most distinguished families: in addition to ties to other Brahmin clans like the Cabots and Jacksons, he boasted descent from Governors Thomas Dudley and Simon Bradstreet, Anne Hutchinson, and "no less than nine clergymen prominent in Colonial times," including Reverend John Cotton. In 1845 Lee had married Brookline resident Elizabeth Perkins Cabot, granddaughter of the illustrious Thomas Handasyd Perkins. Lee followed his father into the mercantile business and later became a prominent Boston banker. He acquired his military title through service in the Civil War, was active in state and national politics, and helped raise funds for his alma mater, Harvard.[21]

In 1850 Lee and his father together bought the old Zabdiel Boylston estate, with its grand mansion and sweeping lawns on Boylston Street in Brookline, close to the home of Lee's father-in-law, Samuel Cabot. The senior Lee occupied the mansion itself while the younger built a brick house for himself and his wife nearby on the site of an old barnyard, which they occupied whenever they were not at their summer home on the shore at Beverly Farms. A few years later Henry Lee and his wife moved a half mile away to his late mother-in-law's house, only to return to the Zabdiel Boylston mansion after his father's death in 1867.[22]

Among Henry Lee's many interests was the burgeoning cause of historic preservation. He was treasurer of the campaign to save the Old South Meeting House in the 1870s, the first successful preservation effort in Boston. Later he battled, though in vain, against the attempt by Henry Whitney's West End Street Railway to build a subway beneath the Boston Common, denouncing that "greedy corporation which, backed by clamorous, unscrupulous suburbans, who desire to combine the advantage of cheap land in the country with cheap conveyance through the city." Although his efforts did not always yield results, he accumulated considerable experience in appealing to public sentiment.[23]

Now in 1893 urban expansion threatened his most prized possession, the home and neighborhood he had known for more than forty years. The transformation of sleepy Boylston Street, which ran past his front door, into a grand thoroughfare would not only destroy his personal serenity but "that seclusion which is one charm of country life." Lee particularly despised the electric trolleys that would soon ply Boylston Street (and had threatened the integrity of the Boston Common). He rallied his well-heeled neighbors, including such notables as Augustus Lowell, Edward T. Cabot, Edward Atkinson, and Moorfield Storey, into joining the opposition. But Lee had learned long ago that appeals to sentiment, nostalgia, and emotion had wide resonance in Brookline beyond his own privileged set. "Mr. Chandler says my opposition is sentimental," he said at one point during the debate.

> It is partly so. My affection for my place and its value to the town are enhanced by the antiquity and history of the old Boylston House, as I have endeavored to show. It is sentiment that has moved me to plead for the preservation of the Old State House, though its removal would replenish my purse. It is sentiment which has kept me for sixteen years treasurer of the fund for the preservation of the Old South . . . and it is sentiment which makes me cherish the old trees and historic house which has passed into my possession.[24]

Lee's triumph at the 1893 annual town meeting revealed that ruralist opposition to some forms of growth was no longer confined to a handful of nostalgic cranks. The urbanization of Beacon Street and the high-intensity development of surrounding neighborhoods into upper-income streetcar suburbs, no matter how fashionable, had come at a cost that some Brookline residents were increasingly reluctant to pay, namely, losing what Henry Lee called "the rural beauty of the town."[25] Lee could never have blocked the expansion of Boylston Street and Chestnut Hill Avenue unless a large part of the community saw something worth preserving in South Brookline, a symbolic manifestation of the old Brookline now vanishing elsewhere in town. The town, which had largely applauded the widening of Beacon Street only a few years earlier, was turning against urban-style, high-density development.

After this unexpected setback, Chandler and his associates were forced to retreat, concentrating their efforts over the next few years on securing improvements for the major traffic arteries through Brookline Village. Major South Brookline landowners along Boylston Street, organized by Chandler, hired Frederick Law Olmsted's firm to lay out streets suitable for a rural suburb that would preclude streetcar suburbs when the streetcar line finally was approved.[26] In 1896 the West End Street Railway and a rival firm headed by a syndicate of Brookline residents led by Chandler each sought street railway franchises on Boylston Street and Chestnut Hill Avenue. The town refused to grant either petition, and another attempt in 1898 also failed. Not until the death of Henry Lee in November 1898 at the age of eighty-one did the project seem feasible. The following year the *Chronicle* promised that finally widening Boylston Street "will bring to us population of the most desirable classes and much wealth. There will be none of the 'undesirable classes' added to our population by it, for [real-estate] values would be too high for them. There is room for 50,000 people in Brookline, well to do, and housed in comfortable and handsome homes. Boylston Street is the thoroughfare along which a great and increasing number will come if the wheels of progress are not blocked."[27] But the town wanted more than just expensive houses in this part of town. New construction would have to be both expensive and evocative of "the rural beauty of the town" to pass public muster.

The new plan of 1899 was more in tune with popular sentiment than its predecessor. Efforts to widen Chestnut Hill Avenue were abandoned altogether, and the proposed width of Boylston Street was reduced. "In order to prevent the building up of possibly objectionable systems of street transportation hither and thither throughout the town, as the interests of real estate speculators may suggest," wrote one proponent, Osbourne Howes, "it is much better to concentrate this class of service in one relatively straight thoroughfare, running as nearly as may be through the center of the town, and in this way reserving land on either side for development along what may be termed rural lines."[28] This time, without Henry Lee to rally the opposition, the scaled-down plan sailed through town meeting by a vote of 473 to 279. Actual construction began in the spring of 1900, and the streetcar line opened in the fall.[29]

Much as Howes had predicted, the widening and new trolley line did not touch off a building boom on adjacent lands. The large landowners in the vicinity, most of them upper class, proved reluctant to sell, and when they did, took pains in laying out streets and lots along the lines Olmsted and company had designed for Fisher Hill. A century later, the section of Brookline south of Boylston Street and west of Fisher Avenue remained the wealthiest part of town but housed less than a fifth of the town's population and featured the lowest population density. Some of the great multi-acre estates survived into the 1980s or 1990s before succumbing to subdivision; by then, building lots carved out of nineteenth-century estates could fetch in excess of a million dollars apiece. Aside from the great estates, house lots here typically range in size from a quarter to a half acre, large compared to the modest-sized plots common in most parts of town, providing sufficient room for significant numbers of mature trees and wide lawns to set off a Colonial Revival or Tudor-style house.[30]

The Apartment House Menace

In 1895 George C. Lorimer, the prominent pastor of Boston's Baptist Tremont Temple, bought an expensive brick dwelling on the corner of Harvard and Vernon Streets for more than $15,000. Two years later Lorimer was horrified to learn that a brick apartment building would be replacing the house adjacent to his own, spoiling his view and presumably lowering the value of his property. This prompted an agitated letter in the *Chronicle* from one "Taxpayer" (most likely the minister himself) in January 1898: "Is it not time that Brookline opened its eyes as to the way in which private speculators are beginning to spoil the appearance of its finest streets and ruthlessly to damage their neighbors' property? Harvard Street is a case in point. The selfishness of a private enterprise is thrusting itself most offensively before the public eye in the shape of an apartment house which is definitely challenging the public rights." He went on to assert that the fact that the land was not subject to deed restrictions "does not give the private ownership absolute rights. . . . The principle that the common property of the whole community has equitable rights of control over the private property of each individual is underneath all those laws by which taxation is forcibly levied and appropriated."[31]

The spread of apartments in Brookline Village and North Brookline led to calls for closer government supervision of the building process. In 1898 the *Chronicle* suggested "prohibiting the erecting of skyscraping and ungainly apartment houses and business blocks side by side with private estates and dwelling houses." So far, however, "nothing has been done to prevent" such "offenses against good taste and the rights of others." The danger was that "men will not come to Brookline to purchase residences on quiet streets unless they are assured that their privacy is not to be encroached upon by the descent of an apartment hotel constructed after the patterns of an immense dry-goods box, or business block with its noise and confusion."[32]

The moves to restrict apartments do not seem to have been driven primarily by fears of lower-class infestation or ethnic prejudice. Residing in the new building that had given Dr. Lorimer such grief in 1900 were a physician, lawyer, stockbroker, wholesale jeweler, school teacher, clerks, managers, bookkeepers, and a piano dealer. Of the thirteen apartments reported to the census that year, ten were headed by couples in their twenties or thirties, most with a few young children, and the rest by elderly widows with their adult children. Seven of the households had one or two live-in servants. All but one of the adults had been born in New England of New England–born parents. Opponents disliked apartments because they were urban and represented nontraditional living arrangements and a rejection of ruralism, not because those opposed necessarily disdained their new neighbors. The building itself, if not an architectural gem, remains inoffensive today.

The anti-apartment movement proceeded slowly, with Alfred D. Chandler taking up the cause in 1899 amid approval from the town's two newspapers. "Is it not time," the *Brookline Suburban* asked, "that something should be done to prevent the erection of unsightly apartment houses in residential sections?" One proposed solution, which had previously been rejected by the town in 1894, would be to adopt a state law imposing a uniform twenty-five-foot setback from the street. This would have eliminated buildings rising up from the sidewalk and brought them more in line with existing houses. Others were especially upset with wooden multifamily buildings and sought to ban them outright.[33] "Restrictions heretofore existing on some large areas of land in Brookline are about to expire and . . . we may be subject to a very great increase in the number of wooden apartments in dangerous proximity to each other," wrote economist Edward Atkinson.[34] In 1900 the town meeting created a committee, including Atkinson, to study "what restrictions, if any shall be placed on the land . . . in the matter of constructing wooden apartment houses or other buildings in close and dangerous proximity to each other."[35]

Despite all of these efforts, nothing was done to curb the growth of the apartments until well into the twentieth century. The proposal to restrict wooden apartments failed at town meeting in 1900, and three-deckers were not banned until 1915.[36] Affluent suburbs in other parts of the country, such as Evanston, Illinois, accepted apartments, despite some opposition.[37] Although few openly defended apartments, even those who had reservations about them were reluctant to impose restrictions on individual property owners. Rufus Candage acknowledged that while "the apartment house to many, seems out of place in Brookline, especially on residential streets, where broad lawns predominate," restricting them would be worse. "Without restraining building laws, which in some cases work hardships to some property-holders, blocks and apartment houses must be endured."[38] As yet, zoning laws were not available to fine-tune the regulations to fit particular streets. An item from the *Boston Transcript* reprinted in the *Chronicle* thought the tempest over apartments somewhat overblown, since "for speculative building, Brookline offers little encouragement, as [deed] restrictions are too severe, land too high, and owners too exclusively inclined." Thus "Brookline has not generally suffered at the hands of the apartment-house builder." Indeed, the

Transcript noted with approval, "among apartment houses recently erected" had been a number "of a superior class, and not detrimental to the town." It concluded that "for the most part Brookline property is rightly [deed] restricted against apartments."[39]

The apartment issue divided Brookline's propertied classes. Some drew no real distinction between wooden triple-deckers and expensive brick apartment blocks, wanting both kept away from their residential streets. Others were prepared to tolerate high-class apartment buildings as long as they attracted respectable, servant-keeping neighbors, although they wanted to block the lower-middle-class and working-class three-deckers that had recently had become so popular in Boston neighborhoods. But whatever their feelings, the majority of Brookline voters were not yet ready to impose formal, far-reaching land-use controls on private property owners. The informal controls that had blocked McCormack's subdivision and encouraged the Irish to stay confined to their neighborhoods, and that had prevented Boylston Street from becoming a second Beacon Street over the objections of its residents, were still endorsed, even as their limits were being tested with each new apartment building and storefront built in North Brookline (fig. 9.2).

Toward a Suburban Consensus

By 1900 the harsh economic times and uncertainties of the mid-1890s were fading, along with some of the animosity that had previously animated political debates. The apprehensive conservatism of the middle and upper classes moderated as the Progressive movement began to gather steam. A Protestant minister in 1898 noted "the interesting change in the feeling of workmen during the past few years, whereby the spirit of a dangerous violence had been allowed to cool." The eight-hour workday, which the *Chronicle* had termed "preposterous" in 1886 and "absurd" in 1891, was by 1900 regarded as inevitable: "There is no doubt that all the trades are fast approaching the 8-hour day and there is every reason to congratulate both the men and their employers on the coming change." Diatribes against unwashed immigrants, ungrateful paupers, bomb-throwing radicals, strike-happy labor unions, and other real and imagined class enemies now rarely appeared in print.[40]

Brookline's bourgeoisie, including its new expanded upper class, was moving toward a consensus concerning the town's future. First, the town's continued

FIGURE 9.2. Wellman Street, near Coolidge Corner, 1915. Some residents of neighborhoods like these worried that apartment buildings disrupted quiet, single-family residential streets, but the town took no formal action to curb the growth of apartment buildings in North Brookline until the 1920s. Apartments remained popular with the affluent, especially the young and old. Courtesy of the National Park Service, Frederick Law Olmsted National Historic Site.

growth was convincing more residents that the process needed closer regulation from the town, even if property owners would have to surrender the right to do whatever they wanted with their property. Brookline's process of informal land regulation through deed restrictions, the approval of streets by the selectmen, and the allocation of town improvements, such as sewers, paving, and lighting, had achieved impressive results in the past. But the growth of apartments, including wooden triple-deckers, and commercial blocks, now called the process into question. If the right tools could be found, then the town should adopt them.

As defined in Brookline, the suburban ideal increasingly incorporated the belief of William Dean Howells that suburbia should combine the best features of urban and rural without becoming either. Therefore, apartments, even expensive ones, as symbols of urbanity should be kept out of most residential neighborhoods, and stores confined to busy streets. Whenever possible, houses should be surrounded by grassy yards and trees, set back an ample distance from the street. As farmland vanished, open space should be preserved in well-regulated parks and playgrounds, or by private groups such as The Country Club. No expense should be spared to provide the best in public services, such as schools, utilities, streets, and libraries.[41]

As late as 1900, however, even within the ranks of the bourgeoisie, many dissented from these views. To them, Brookline's obvious prosperity was proof that the town must be doing something right and that drastic reforms were unnecessary. Three-deckers and tenements might be unsightly, but they were largely confined to the unfashionable parts of Brookline Village. Middle-class apartments might be more of a threat to neighborhood stability, but many landowners were willing to tolerate their existence if owners retained the right to erect them on *their* property. The clearest proof of this is the fact that reforming Brookline's town meeting government and introducing effective land use controls took as long as it did, even as Progressive-Era reform politics swept the country.

Two men spearheaded the reform movement. Alfred D. Chandler had long championed Brookline's town government and had worked to enforce electoral laws to prevent illegal voting by nonqualified voters.[42] But as the town meeting continued to reject his attempts to regulate growth through restrictions on apartments and mandatory building setbacks, while at the same time turning down his schemes to improve Boylston Street, he began to fear that Brookline's open town meeting form of government, in which any legal voter (male, of course) could participate, was no longer appropriate for a municipality of more than twenty thousand. Incorporating as a city was an option, of course—other Boston suburbs had gone this route—but this would mean giving up the proud claim that Brookline remained a New England town. In 1900 Chandler advocated replacing the town meeting with an elected town council, pointing out that there was only room for 700 of the town's 3,200 voters to attend meetings at town hall.[43] After this idea went down to overwhelming defeat, Chandler advocated a third way—a system whereby the town meeting would be retained but voting would be confined to elected meeting members only. Nothing like this had ever been tried before in Massachusetts, and it was not until 1915 that Chandler was finally able to persuade the town to adopt this new form of government, which is still used today by Brookline and other larger Massachusetts towns.[44]

The second champion of tighter regulation was another *Social Register* listee, landscape architect Frederick Law Olmsted, Jr., who carried on his noted father's work. Olmsted's vision of a suburban aesthetic was much like his father's: the town should do everything to encourage high-quality buildings and discourage cheap wooden structures, embrace well-designed curving streets with lots adequate to encompass landscaped yards and trees, and promote the preservation of the scenic vistas that had made the town so attractive. Attempts to get the town to adopt uniform minimum building setbacks continued to fail. In 1914 Olmsted became chairman of the town's first Planning Board, and the following year for the first time secured a ban on wooden three-deckers. The Planning Board under Olmsted promoted street and aesthetic improvements but without much success until they persuaded the town to adopt its first zoning law in 1922 (the state had authorized zoning two years before). Zoning, with its ability to fine-tune regulations to fit individual streets, was the tool that regulators like Chandler (who died the following year) and Olmsted long had dreamed of having at their disposal.[45]

The common vision of suburbia championed by Chandler and Olmsted had prevailed. In order to combine the best features of city and country, a true suburb needed to retain its own distinctive identity. Political independence from the central city was therefore necessary, even if elite suburbs like Chestnut Hill, Philadelphia, occasionally might flourish within the bounds of a great city.[46] As much as possible, residents—ideally families with children—should live in single-family, detached homes, each house surrounded by a generous landscaped lot facing winding, tree-lined streets. Good schools, parks and private open spaces, and playgrounds should be nearby. Stores and offices should be kept out of residential neighborhoods and confined to busy streets. Public transportation in the form of commuter trains and electric trolleys should be frequent and available to all except those choosing to live in the remoter sections of town. Finally, although apartments might be appropriate for some stages of life, such as newly married couples or widows, they were generally not regarded as appropriate places to raise middle-class, suburban families. Therefore, apartment construction should be restricted to commercial streets and kept out of single-family neighborhoods.

Reality, however, defied a full realization of this vision, for in 1915 and beyond, Brookline still encompassed considerable social diversity. The Irish Catholic working class remained a presence, even though generations of upper-class Yankee Protestant leaders had done what they could to segregate blue-collar families and discourage the construction of low-income housing. Most residential streets housed few non-Yankee inhabitants except for Irish live-in maids. The development of cars and trucks would soon make it possible to dispense with resident service workers altogether, and new twentieth-century suburbs would be characterized by class homogeneity.[47]

Yet many in town, especially those not of the upper class, appreciated the higher density of North Brookline, especially the non-Yankee newcomers who increasingly were attracted to this part of town after 1900. The town had thus spawned a higher-density alternative version of the suburban ideal: a fiercely independent, affluent community with every urban amenity and convenient to the city, but with rural associations confined to street trees and parks rather than farms or landscaped yards, and with housing choices available in multiunit dwellings as well as single-family detached homes.

Even though this variation of the suburban ideal came closest to the experience of most town residents, it was the Olmstedian version that was slated to have the greatest influence on the rest of the nation. More distant Boston suburbs took notice, and many of them succeeded in preventing or sharply limiting higher-density development. For America was going suburban, and its eyes were on Brookline.[48]

CHAPTER 10

Suburbia on a Hill

✦

Wee shall be as a Citty vpon a Hill, the eies of all people are vppon vs.

—John Winthrop, "A Modell of Christian Charity," 1630

With its rare advantages and superior situation, Brookline can exhibit to the world an example of the supreme importance to a metropolis of developing a special residential district, which shall not be a mere expansion of urban conditions of life, as the metropolis grows, the usual motive in the extension of a large city, but shall be a district designed to preserve in a measure certain rural aspects, to utilize the landscape features of a diversified surface, to retain distinctive suburban characteristics, to provide ample pleasure grounds, and to give its inhabitants something more than a mere aggregation of brick and stone structures with connecting roads. A suburban residential district of such a kind is invaluable as an agent to promote civilization.

—Alfred D. Chandler, "Brookline: A Study in Town Government," 1893

By the end of the nineteenth century Brookline was gaining a national reputation as a model suburb, which other communities sought to emulate. Newspapers in Syracuse, New York City, Baltimore, and New Orleans printed breathless descriptions of what was acknowledged to be "the richest town in the world" and the lifestyles of its fortunate inhabitants: "Every resident is, you might say, well-to-do, and the majority of the inhabitants are Boston merchants."[1] Much of this reputation stemmed from the great estates of South Brookline and Longwood/Cottage Farm, so impressively close to central Boston, but statistical data suggests that Brookline actually was the most prosperous of Boston's suburbs.[2] Its system of governance, the wealth and high social standing of its inhabitants, and the aesthetic appeal of its designed and natural landscape contributed to the emergence of a widespread American conception of what "true" suburbs should be. Even while agreement within Brookline—especially over the desirability of the conversion of North Brookline into a high-class streetcar suburb—had not been reached, the town seemed to offer an alternative to the pattern of development of much of metropolitan America.

The Suburban Solution

At the onset of the twentieth century many bourgeois Americans were more than ready to consider plans for reforming and restructuring cities. Unlike some aristocratic Europeans who professed to disdain modern cities, few prosperous Americans denied that their nation could now boast some of the world's largest and richest urban conglomerations, offering cultural institutions that rivaled those of ancient European capitals. Skyscrapers, elevated railroads, urban mansions, expensive stores, and grand boulevards testified to enormous wealth and energy. Newly built museums were being filled with the artistic plunder of the Old World, while orchestras performed the latest European music in fine performance halls and opera houses. Yet cities now threatened to be overwhelmed by their own success, as millions of immigrants from overseas and migrants from rural America crowded into them. Densely packed tenement districts and streets teeming with humanity were seen as among the most repulsive features of urban life. Widespread corruption appeared to be the inevitable accompaniment to congestion, as uncouth political bosses, propped up by hordes of ignorant immigrant voters, cut deals with unscrupulous businessmen.[3] Even before the revelations of muckraking journalists confirmed the worst, Lord Bryce had made his oft-quoted observation that "the government of cities is the one conspicuous failure of the United States."[4]

To the twin plagues of congestion and corruption afflicting American cities, suburbia promised welcome relief. By the 1890s the suburbanization of the urban fringe had been underway around most North American (and English) cities for more than half a century.[5] In 1892 the Massachusetts Rapid Transit Commission envisioned "the metropolis of the future" as "a city closely built, and during the daytime densely populated, this surrounded by a semi-rural district, in which are the homes of those who work in the city, but who pass their nights, and whose families pass their lives, under the purer and healthier influences of the country." Future improvements in rapid transit—trolleys, railroads, elevated lines, and subways—would enable even the working man to "abandon the unhealthy and demoralizing life of the tenement-house, and obtain for himself and family the benefits of a suburban home." This distinctly suburban vision was echoed seven years later by Adna Ferrin Weber in his pioneering study, *The Growth of Cities.* "The most encouraging feature" of American urban expansion, he wrote, was "the tendency . . . toward the development of suburban towns. . . . Such a new distribution of population combines at once the open air and spaciousness of the country with the sanitary improvements, comforts, and associated life of the city."[6]

Champions of decentralization were convinced that moving people out of the overcrowded central cities to the suburbs would benefit both. Since many suburban residents continued to work downtown, there seemed little reason to fear that they would lose interest in the cities. "The influence of [the] suburban element upon Boston is to be encouraged," wrote the *Brookline Chronicle* in 1894. "It is often fresher, cleaner, and more advanced, than strictly urban conditions seem to allow; and if the suburbs of Boston become the more powerful of the two, the outlook is one of cheer rather than gloom, for the men may yet be found in the suburbs who will have as keen a perception of Boston's best interests as those within the city's limits."[7]

Busy Brookline attorney Alfred D. Chandler was more than happy to put forth Brookline as a model for urban reform. In an 1893 article in the popular *New England Magazine* entitled "Brookline: A Study in Town Government," he credited the town's "remarkable growth" and "unexampled" wealth—"the revenues and expenditures of Brookline last year were more than double the revenues and expenditures of the State of New Hampshire"—to "the best form of local government known." He continued, "Brookline is still a *town,* where the New England town meeting holds full sway. It has no mayor nor aldermen. . . . [It is] a town *within* a city!—a town, which, by maintaining its individuality, and by pursuing a broad and liberal policy, has reached the highest standard of municipal excellence in the very folds of a great metropolis vexed with the hard vicissitudes of American government." How did Brookline do it? "The secret is this. (1) Municipal development on broad lines as the most remunerative course for a town, where there is a strong and growing constituency to sustain it. (2) Co-operation between public and private interests, protecting the former and encouraging the latter. (3) A watchful supervision of the municipality by men and women of character and ability."[8]

Writing five years later in the *Arena,* the influential reformist magazine that he published, crusading Boston journalist Benjamin Orange Flower praised the town's fine schools and services, noting that "few if any towns or cities of America can show so credible a record as Brookline in regard to the honesty, wisdom, and economy in the management of public affairs, together with a broad and liberal policy touching all public provisions which affect the well-being and happiness of the community."[9]

As the Progressive urban reform movement spread after 1900, Brookline's example of a well-governed, efficient municipality inspired suburban residents throughout the country. According to historian Jon C. Teaford, "During the second decade of the twentieth century Chicago suburbanites cited suburban Brookline, Massachusetts, not their own central city, as the best governed city in America." After 1900, articles praising the town's governance appeared in a number of nationally circulated magazines.[10] Brookline's example showed that a suburb could remain politically independent of its central city without any negative consequences, enjoy services as good as or better than those of the city, and happily avoid the corruption of big-city political machines with their ward-heeling professional politicians (not to mention paying city taxes). This lesson would not be forgotten. Most large twentieth-century cities in the northeastern and Midwestern United States would find themselves ringed by stubbornly independent suburbs that they could not annex and whose inhabitants wanted to pay no part of the costs of supporting the city itself, while they gladly benefited from the proximity of downtown.[11]

Suburban Nation

By the beginning of the twentieth century an increasing proportion of the Anglo-American middle classes were seeking to live in suburbia. Whether or not they came pursuing a common suburban ideal, as some have suggested, is unclear.[12] Certainly more than one suburban vision was present in Brookline at the end of the century. Not everyone concurred that the single-family detached house was the only legitimate housing option for those who could afford it, nor was there agreement over what constituted sufficient open space, either for each family or for the community as a whole.

There is much to suggest that the media of the times in newspaper accounts, novels, and short stories was providing a common vision of suburbia, strongly implying that this view was widely held. Suburbs were largely inhabited by upper-middle-class families headed by commuters, presumably white and Protestant, who lived in large, centrally heated houses surrounded by trees, lawns, and gardens, enjoying easy access to the city while woods and fields lay close at hand. Those favored by wealth or high incomes could enjoy this lifestyle close to cities in towns like Brookline, while those of lesser means would have to settle for towns further away and accept longer commutes.[13]

Apartments, townhouses, and streetcar suburbs were rarely included among descriptions of suburbia. Popular writers insisted that not every development beyond the built-up portions of incorporated cities should be considered strictly suburban. One called a formerly rural district subdivided into small lots "a demoralized suburb," while another denounced "those abominable and abhorrent deserts of paved streets laid out at right angles, and all supplied with sewers and electric light wires and water-mains before the first lonely house escapes from the house-pattern books to tempt the city dweller out to that dreary, soulless waste which has the all the modern improvements and not one tree." A growing number of Brookline residents shared this aesthetic, even if they knew that most of the town's newcomer's paid dearly for their new quarters, including those in apartments or houses with small yards.[14] Such writings further promoted an aesthetic that rejected additional high-density development and encouraged the preservation of open spaces. In turn, the example of suburbs like Brookline served to inspire writers for the national media to embrace and encourage this same aesthetic of large-lot, low-density, high-social-status suburbia as the norm to which communities should strive.

What helped set aside communities like Brookline is that they were dominated by men who had finally come to share a common vision of suburbia—which they in turn helped develop—and who had the means to harness the forces of nineteenth-century American capitalism to achieve it. In most American cities, at least before the City Beautiful Movement of the Progressive Era, economic forces shaped the political agenda, and real estate was developed to maximize private gain.[15] In Brookline, making money was certainly important, but key decision-makers, such as landowners, developers, and politicians beholden to public opinion, were determined to create and sustain a community of the sort in which they and their own families wanted to live. An ideal that had emerged in Brookline and other nineteenth-century American suburbs had made practical the yearnings of William Dean Howells. Much more of the rural aspect of Brookline had survived in 1900 than anyone would have predicted thirty years earlier, even if working farms were largely gone. Cows grazing in meadows were a thing of the past, but open land survived on private estates, at The Country Club, and increasingly in parks and neighborhood playgrounds. New subdivision streets (though with the curbs, sidewalks, and utilities that Howells had once disdained) would soon bloom into tree-lined rustic lanes lined with tastefully designed houses, instead of the uniform urban grids covering much of metropolitan Boston.

Early on suburbs like Brookline and Dorchester had much in common, but by 1900 independent suburbs with large bourgeois populations and streetcar suburbs were very different places. Streetcar suburbs had become urban neighborhoods that accepted an urban political and social order, expected crowded neighborhoods that included commercial activity and blocks of three-decker apartments, and judged the quality of their streets by the size and value of their houses, access to public transportation, availability of city services, and the presence or absence of neighbors deemed undesirable. There was little demand for or expectation of the tree-lined, curvilinear streets; large landscaped lots; manicured lawns; and independent government of suburbia.

During the Progressive Era this suburban vision of the good life was embraced by the more prosperous members of the American middle class. Fine houses set in a beautiful rural setting, the latest urban amenities, a great nearby city, respectable and even distinguished inhabitants, and an efficient, cost-effective government made elite suburbs among the world's most attractive places to live.[16] This middle-class dream became a real-estate marketing tool in the 1920s, when most American metropolitan growth was taking place in the suburbs. Developers who targeted the middle and lower ranges of the market for new housing regarded the suburbs as an extension of the traditional city, and they built updated versions of the nineteenth-century streetcar suburbs. Here new streets formed extensions of existing grid patterns, lots were small and bare, and housing was uniform, drab, and modest. Yet in their marketing schemes developers of these modest tracts now used the imagery and language of suburbia to fire the imagination of their lower-middle-class clientele.[17]

In the more upscale neighborhoods—particularly in hilly regions where the lots were larger and more expensive—the street grid was broken by curvilinear roads following the natural contours of the land, evocative of earlier elite suburbs like Brookline. Although some of these new suburbs, especially in the South and West, lay within municipal limits, most in the East and Midwest fiercely maintained their political independence. Residents of these wealthy new communities, such as Beverly Hills (named after an elite Boston suburb, Beverly Farms) and Scarsdale, were anxious to retain the high standard of governmental services and residential architecture that Brookline's inhabitants enjoyed.[18]

By the 1920s the distinctly suburban attitude that had developed in Brookline and elsewhere solidified into a national consensus. For example, suburbanites by and large agreed that apartments did not belong on suburban residential streets. Brookline residents were long familiar with the sentiments expressed in 1926 by U.S. Supreme Court justice George Sutherland in the landmark case of *Euclid v. Ambler*, which upheld the constitutionality of local zoning laws, such as that recently adopted by Brookline:

> With particular reference to apartment houses, it is pointed out that the development of detached house sections is greatly retarded by the coming of apartment houses, which has sometimes resulted in destroying the entire section for private house purposes; that, in such sections, very often the apartment house is a mere parasite, constructed in order to take advantage of the open spaces and attractive surroundings created by the residential character of the district. Moreover, the coming of one apartment house is followed by others, interfering by their height and bulk with the free circulation of air and monopolizing the rays of the sun which otherwise would fall upon the smaller homes, and bringing, as their necessary accompaniments, the disturbing noises incident to increased traffic and business, and the occupation, by means of moving and parked automobiles, of larger portions of the streets, thus detracting from their safety and depriving children of the privilege of quiet and open spaces for play, enjoyed by those in more favored localities—until, finally, the residential character of the neighborhood and its desirability as a place of detached residences are utterly destroyed.[19]

Even as the Great Depression gripped the nation in the 1930s, American suburbs were beckoning families to whom they previously had no attraction. Segregated African Americans and white blue-collar workers began to construct their own scaled-down versions of suburbia, featuring modest, often self-built, detached single-family homes on the edges of cities, with minimal public and private services.[20] Some of these proved to be the precursors to a massive building wave that transformed metropolitan America following the Second World War. New federally financed highways opened millions of acres to development, and developers built countless small houses on lots large enough for a front lawn, backyard, driveway, and garage, typically facing curvilinear streets. Many of these newer suburbs remained outside of the boundaries of central cities.[21]

Post–World War II suburbia was marked by segregation by social class, race, and income. Brookline's leaders had done their best to isolate their poor and working classes, as well as control those groups' behavior by imposing discipline in the public schools, banning saloons, and hiring a paid police force, but the reality was that nineteenth-century suburbia depended on its live-in servants, laborers, and service providers, and there was no way for the affluent to avoid frequent contact with the lower classes. By 1945 the near universality of automobile ownership among the working classes (if not the poor), combined with zoning laws, meant that communities could be almost entirely segregated by class and income. Live-in servants had largely vanished after World War I from all but the households of the very rich, and service workers and municipal employees could now live elsewhere and drive in and out of town every day.[22] "A suburban town can consist of nothing but mansions and get away with it," two social scientists noted in 1975. "All the town has to do is zone its entire residential land into two-acre lots, ban industry and commerce, and establish sufficiently tough building ordinances to assure that nothing but expensive homes are built."[23]

A sociological study of a contemporary elite outer suburb of New York City reported residents strongly supporting restrictive land use controls, not merely to exclude the poor but to maintain a particular aesthetic—protecting "the rural beauty of the town." That much of this landscape is an artificial, symbolic evocation of rural life does not seem to matter. Residents take this viewpoint to its logical absurdity by opposing all development, no matter how expensive, and even demanding that some public roads remain unpaved. The authors trace this aesthetic ideology back to the arrival of wealthy New York commuters in the late nineteenth century, and note that it tends to be adopted by newcomers of various backgrounds.[24] As has been shown, similar attitudes were widespread in Brookline by the end of the nineteenth century.

Pale reflections of Brookline could even be detected in some of the new middle-class tract suburbs that came to surround every American city after 1945. Most of these modest subdivisions were aimed at the same economic classes for whom the streetcar suburbs had once been built, and the houses there typically were even smaller than their nineteenth-century predecessors. Many in fact copied the straight grid streets of the streetcar suburbs. But some of the postwar versions of suburbia, especially today after years of tree growth, seem more reminiscent of Brookline than Dorchester or West Roxbury.

Levittown, Pennsylvania, where I was raised, features tree-lined, curvilinear streets; house lots of between seven and twelve thousand square feet or more; front lawns; and a stubborn determination to resist annexation or even consolidation (the community is spread over parts of three townships and a borough, each with its own elected government).[25] Levittown's nearly all-white, middle- and even working-class residents in the 1950s expected as full a range of services as they had left behind in the cities from which many of them came, including good schools, churches and synagogues, public utilities, parks and playgrounds, public libraries, and convenient shopping, much as did Brookline's nineteenth-century commuters.[26] Yet they had no desire for Levittown to become a city, which they associated with crime, congestion, blight, and African Americans.[27] Brookline's example had promised them it was possible to enjoy a uniquely suburban lifestyle that maintained the advantages of urban living without the drawbacks.

Indeed, there is evidence that aesthetic values once largely confined to elites in high-income suburbs have spread to the broader middle class. Critics have long complained that zoning and other suburban land-use regulations have enjoyed wide support in the United States primarily because they serve to exclude the poor and persons of color from white, middle-class neighborhoods.[28] This does not explain, however, the opposition often encountered by the building of so-called McMansions in older neighborhoods of modest tract homes, even though they typically bring with them newcomers with higher, not lower, incomes than the existing residents. Middle-class opponents, championing the preservation of neighborhood ambiance, character, and history, often display aesthetic preferences recalling those of Col. Henry Lee a century earlier.[29]

Alfred D. Chandler or Frederick Law Olmsted, Sr.—not to mention Colonel Lee—would certainly have bristled at the suggestion that they were in some sense responsible for the Levittowns and other mass suburban housing developments of the later twentieth century. Indeed, attorney Chandler would have been the first to point out that curvilinear streets were not invented in Brookline or even by Olmsted. Of course, they had no way of foreseeing that the automobile and the expansion of the highway network would make vast amounts of cheap land available for low-density suburbanization, changing what had been a privilege confined to a small elite into a mass commodity. In a sense the nation became a victim of Brookline's success. For better or worse, Brookline had realized Howells's seemingly impossible, impractical dream of combining the best of urban and rural life, and once known, the awareness that this could actually be accomplished could not be unlearned. America was destined to become suburban.

Epilogue

✦

In 1914, just as Brookline was creating a Planning Board and otherwise reorganizing its government, Joseph Kennedy, a twenty-five-year-old Boston banker, purchased a home at 83 Beals Street for his fiancée. Beals Street had been named for its one-time owner, a certain James H. Beals, the wealthy publisher of the *Boston Post,* a Brookline commuter who had bought a vacant, thirteen-acre parcel off Harvard Street in 1868 as a speculation. Even after David McKay and Peter Graffam began developing the vicinity in the 1890s, Beals held onto his land, and at the time of his death in 1896 it lay undeveloped.[1]

Beals's investment proved a sound one. When his widow sold the property in November 1897 she realized $150,000 from the sale—more than ten times what her husband had paid for it thirty years before. The buyer, a real-estate developer named Benjamin B. Newhall, a newcomer to Brookline, immediately subdivided the parcel, laying out Beals Street and seventy lots, with the street forming a through route from Peter Graffam's Manchester Road eastward to Harvard Street. Most of the lots were roughly sixty feet wide and a hundred deep, in line with what Graffam had been offering. By the end of 1899 Newhall was selling these lots, sometimes only a single lot at a time. Lot 47 passed to a Cambridge resident in 1899, was seized by the town for nonpayment of taxes in 1902, and eventually came to Newton builder Robert M. Goode in 1907. Goode reduced the size of the lot to a scant 3,820 square feet and then built a nine-room house on it, which he sold in 1909 to a Boston lawyer and his wife, Daniel J. and Rosalie Kiley. In 1913 the Kileys conveyed it to another Boston commuter, Howard S. Kline, a wholesale buyer, and a year later Kline, now a resident of New York, resold it to Kennedy for a modest $6,500. Three years later a future president of the United States was born there.[2]

Because of that birth this nondescript tract house has become one of the town's best-known structures and is owned by the National Park Service. In many ways it represents the complex fabric of Brookline early in the twentieth century. Architecturally, the exterior of the house is relentlessly twentieth-century suburban Colonial Revival, with little to tie it to the older Victorian styles save for the vertical configuration forced by the narrow lot. By the time the Kennedys moved out in 1920, to a larger Peter Graffam–built house around the corner at the intersection of Naples and Abbotsford Roads, they had a full household of three—soon to be four—children, a governess, and a maid.[3]

The Brookline where John F. Kennedy spent the first ten years of his life in the late 1910s and 1920s was very much a continuation of the community of 1900. To be sure, there were unanticipated changes. The names of the successive owners of 83 Beals Street—Kiley, Kline, and Kennedy—suggest that the colonial style of their house may have been unintentionally ironic, given the owners' ancestral roots likely resided elsewhere than colonial America and England. After 1900 Brookline had begun to acquire a significant Jewish community, attracted not by opportunities for manual labor and domestic service like their Irish Catholic forerunners but for the chance to obtain more pleasant surroundings in which to live.

Jewish Brookline grew rapidly in the years between the First and Second World Wars, with most Jews settling to the north and east of Coolidge Corner in the new housing that had been built in the aftermath of the widening of Beacon Street. (In fact, Kehillath Israel, one of Brookline's two most important synagogues, was at the end of Beals Street.) Their ancestors had fled Poland or other Eastern European nations around the turn of the century, settling first in Boston proper and later in Roxbury or the Mattapan section of Dorchester. Brookline was especially attractive to upwardly mobile Jews since it boasted superior public schools, several synagogues, and numerous Jewish-operated shops and delicatessens along Harvard Street. By the beginning of World War II some especially successful Jewish professionals and businessmen lived in swank Fisher Hill as well as Coolidge Corner, although, like the Irish, they had limited social interaction with Yankee Brookline.[4]

The establishment of St. Aidan's Catholic Church on Freeman Street in 1911 was a further recognition that persons of Irish descent in Brookline were no longer confined to the Marsh and Whiskey Point. Named for an Irish saint, the fashionably Tudor structure was distant both spatially and stylistically from the massive, red-brick St. Mary of the Assumption Church in Brookline Village, which the Boston archdiocese had built in 1886 adjacent to the site of the town's first Catholic church. Joseph and Rose Kennedy were parishioners at St. Aidan's, their children were baptized there, and their sons later served as altar boys. Like the Kennedys, many of the upper-middle-class Irish Catholic elite settling around St. Aidan's likely lacked Brookline roots.[5]

By the time the Kennedy clan left Brookline for New York City in September 1927, the town had become distinctly more urban than it had been at the start of the century. Not everyone supported this change. The president of the Brookline Historical Society, Charles H. Stearns, gave annual addresses chronicling the changes seen in the town. In 1911 he reported that "the streets in and around Coolidge Corner have been paved with granite blocks, with cement grout, another evidence that the town, or the northern part of it, is fast losing its suburban character, and is becoming but an adjunct of a great city." The town's growing population, which had jumped from 19,935 in 1900 to 27,792 in 1910, had not improved the town's quality, since "a majority of the increase are residents of apartment houses, who do not always add to its real wealth or strength. We must not make a sweeping denunciation of such residents, for many, no doubt, are most desirable citizens, but a majority come to these apartments simply to sleep and have but little to do with the affairs of the town." In 1914, after describing the continued expansion of apartment houses, sometimes on the site of older houses, Stearns noted that "an immense automobile establishment has been built on Pleasant Street near the corner of Commonwealth Avenue, thus adding to the already large group of similar buildings in this vicinity." In 1917 a thirty-three-unit brick apartment building on Harvard Street featured garages in the rear, and a large block of stores was being built at the corner of Beacon and Washington Streets.[6] Still, growth continued apace, and the population reached nearly 38,000 in 1920. In 1922 alone building permits were issued for 72 stores and 168 houses and apartment buildings. With more than 250 apartments, the high-rise Longwood Towers, built in 1924, became one of the town's most prestigious addresses, and by 1930 the population stood at 47,500.[7]

Despite fears of "changes [that] threaten the character, and even the identity, of Brookline," and the departure of the Kennedys notwithstanding, the town appeared to have lost little of its appeal throughout the rest of the century.[8] It managed to gain residents even during the Great Depression, and construction resumed soon after the Second World War with new single-family homes going up in parts of South Brookline (including McCormack's unsuccessful development). Much of this more recent housing was built in the extreme southern part of the town, a hitherto isolated and unpopulated district. Population peaked in 1950 at nearly 58,000, and it has remained near this number ever since.

After World War II the town fathers took advantage of powers given to them by urban redevelopment statutes and zoning that their nineteenth-century predecessors would have drooled over. They cleared Brookline Village of most of its working-class housing. The Marsh was leveled and replaced with brick apartment blocks, parking garages, and commercial buildings, and Boylston Street lost most of its distinctive three-deckers.[9] The construction of Boston University's Riverside Campus on Commonwealth Avenue after the Second World War (and that institution's subsequent purchase of several homes in Cottage Farm) made the part of Brookline between there and Coolidge Corner attractive to generations of BU faculty, students, and staff. Brookline activists, joined by their counterparts in Cambridge and Boston, prevented the Inner Belt expressway from slashing across North Brookline in the 1970s.[10]

I was among Brookline's students, having moved to a rented room in a Coolidge Corner apartment overlooking Beacon Street in September 1970. The week I arrived the landmark S. S. Pierce store in Coolidge Corner closed its doors after more than seventy years in business. I later moved to an apartment on Westbourne Terrace, near Washington Square. Having been raised in the suburbs of Philadelphia, mostly in the notorious Levittown, I found my new neighborhood to be pleasantly urban, a welcome contrast to both my parents' postwar suburbia and the small, quaint Pennsylvania town where I had recently attended college. Forty-five years later, the older Victorian streets I explored around Coolidge Corner and Brookline Village remain attractive. Zoning has mostly succeeded in separating commercial uses and apartments from more residential neighborhoods.

Both visual evidence and statistical data confirm that Brookline continues to be, as Charles Knowles Bolton once put it, "a favored town." In 2014 the town's median family income was $145,000, 68 percent above the state's as a whole. Brookline residents are among the best-educated in the nation; in 2014 fully 81 percent of adults over the age of twenty-five were college graduates, compared to 40 percent statewide and 29 percent for the nation. Moreover, median house values had soared to over $700,000, more than twice the statewide figure. Both income and housing prices rose faster than the rest of the state, suggesting that Brookline was aging well for an inner suburb.[11] Prominent people still reside here, most notably Brookline native, former Massachusetts governor, and 1988 presidential nominee Michael Dukakis, who since 1971 has lived in a four-bedroom unit of an oversized 1870-vintage, Second Empire–style duplex near Linden Place.[12]

This is not to say that Brookline is unchanged over the past five decades. Buildings fall to the wreckers, while others are recycled: the swank private Dexter School, which John F. Kennedy attended, was torn down and replaced with a high-rise apartment building, while nearby St. Aidan's Church, closed by the Catholic archdiocese in 1999, recently reopened as condominium housing. Frederick Law Olmsted's home and office on Warren Street in South Brookline is now a federally owned National Historic Site visited by thousands each year. Many surviving Victorian twelve- and fourteen-room houses in the village and near Coolidge Corner have been carved up into pricey condominiums. Brookline has certainly become more diverse—at least racially—since when I lived there more than forty years ago. In 1970 the town's population was 97 percent white (with Chinese accounting for most of the rest). The 2010 census showed that the white population had dropped to 77 percent, with Asians now accounting for 16 percent of the town's total and blacks 3 percent (in absolute numbers, four times as many blacks now live in Brookline as did in 1970).[13]

Perhaps the most remarkable survival, however, is the so-called estates district south of Boylston Street (Route 9). In the 1970s, when some of the great estates were still intact, approaching Warren Street and vicinity from the busy traffic of Boylston Street was to cross into another world. Rolling lawns and landscaped gardens so close to downtown Boston defied any rational economic laws and seemed to have little in common with the rest of Brookline (except, perhaps, Longwood) or almost any other suburb with which I was familiar. Today few houses can be found on lots much larger than two acres, still massive by urban standards, or even compared to the half-acre lots on swank Fisher Hill. Walking up Warren Street from the Frederick Law Olmsted National Historic Site west toward Green Hill still recalls William Dean Howells's suburban idyll: "Then indeed, Charlesbridge appeared to us a kind of Paradise. . . . We were living in the country with the conveniences and luxuries of the city about us. . . . The neighborhood was in all things a frontier between city and country" (see fig. 1.2).[14] Although additional expensive houses have been built on Warren Street over the past forty years as larger properties have been subdivided, most of them have been skillfully integrated into the landscape. In one respect, the vista of Green Hill is even more striking today—the tall wooden fence that once blocked views of the mansion from the road has been removed.

The spell soon wears off. In concluding a book on American suburbanization it is de rigueur to point out that given its dependence on the automobile and its voracious appetite for land and energy, the suburban lifestyle would seem to be unsustainable; that it has encouraged segregation, inequality, and the devastation of central cities; that it has allowed suburbanites to wash their hands of responsibility for the urban poor; and that suburbia seems to be, finally, losing its popularity.[15] More difficult to answer is the question of whether Boston as a whole would be better off today if Brookline had been developed to the same density as, say, Dorchester or Somerville.

In a real sense Brookline, taken as a whole, remains a monument to the privilege, and sometimes extravagance, of American suburbia. Yet this may well guarantee its future survival even if tastes change, much as the elephantine mansions of Newport have been preserved despite their functional obsolescence, as monuments to the excesses of the Gilded Age. And unlike Marble House or the Breakers, Brookline remains eminently livable, for those who can afford it.

Abbreviations

✦

BC *Brookline Chronicle*

BI *Brookline Independent*

BSC *[Annual] Report of [the Board of] the School Committee of the Town of Brookline* (Boston: Various publishers, 1846–80)

BT *Brookline Transcript*

BTR Brookline, *Town Records of Brookline, Mass., 1838–1902,* 5 vols. (Brookline: The Town, 1888–1902)

Curtis, *Brookline*
John Guild Curtis, *History of the Town of Brookline, Massachusetts* (Boston: Houghton Mifflin, 1933)

Fishman, *Utopias*
Robert Fishman, *Bourgeois Utopias: The Rise and Fall of Suburbia* (New York: Basic, 1987)

Hayden, *Suburbia*
Dolores Hayden, *Building Suburbia: Green Fields and Urban Growth, 1820–2000* (New York: Pantheon, 2003)

Jackson, *Frontier*
Kenneth T. Jackson, *Crabgrass Frontier: The Suburbanization of the United States* (New York: Oxford University Press, 1985)

Morgan, Cushing, and Reed, *CBD*
Keith N. Morgan, Elizabeth Hope Cushing, and Roger G. Reed, *Community by Design: The Olmsted Firm and the Development of Brookline, Massachusetts* (Amherst: University of Massachusetts Press, 2013)

ND Norfolk County, Mass., Deeds, Registry of Deeds, Dedham

PBHS *Proceedings of the Brookline Historical Society*

Stilgoe, *Borderland*
John R. Stilgoe, *Borderland: Origins of the American Suburb, 1820–1939* (New Haven, Conn.: Yale University Press, 1988)

Warner, *Streetcar Suburbs*
Sam Bass Warner, Jr., *Streetcar Suburbs: The Process of Growth in Boston, 1870–1900* (Cambridge, Mass.: Harvard University Press, 1962)

WD
Caroline Barrett White, Diaries, 1855–72, American Antiquarian Society, Worcester, Mass.

Woods, *Sketches*
Harriet F. Woods, *Historical Sketches of Brookline, Massachusetts* (Boston: Davis, 1874)

Notes

✦

Introduction

1. Frank Hobbs and Nicole Stoops, U.S. Census Bureau, Census 2000 Special Reports, series CENSR-4, *Demographic Trends in the 20th Century* (Washington, D.C.: Government Printing Office, 2002), 1.

2. Karen Tongson, *Relocations: Queer Suburban Imaginaries* (New York: New York University Press, 2011), 9. This debate is well summarized in Becky M. Nicolaides and Andrew Wiese, eds., *The Suburb Reader* (New York: Routledge, 2006), 7–9.

3. U.S. Census Bureau, 2000 Census of Population and Housing, *Summary: Population and Housing Characteristics,* PHC-1–1 (Washington, D.C.: Government Printing Office, 2002), A-16; Hobbs and Stoops, *Demographic Trends,* 7, 9.

4. Jackson, *Frontier,* 5.

5. Craig Pascoe, "Metropolitan Area," in *Encyclopedia of Urban America: The Cities and Suburbs,* ed. Neil Larry Shumsky (Santa Barbara, Calif.: ABC-Clio, 1998), 2:456.

6. Hayden, *Suburbia,* 3–14; Robert Bruegmann, *Sprawl: A Compact History* (Chicago: University of Chicago Press, 2005), 7–8; Ronald Dale Karr, "Social Structure of Suburbs," in Shumsky, ed., *Encyclopedia of Urban America,* 2:720–23.

7. Robert O. Self, *American Babylon: Race and the Struggle for Postwar Oakland* (Princeton, N.J.: Princeton University Press, 2003).

8. Jackson, *Frontier,* 6.

9. Staten Island Improvement Commission, *Report of a Preliminary Scheme of Improvements Presented January 12, 1871* (New York: N.p., N.d.), 9.

10. Among the most popular of these accounts were Sloan Wilson, *The Man in the Gray Flannel Suit* (New York: Simon and Schuster, 1955); William H. Whyte, *The Organization Man* (New York: Simon and Schuster, 1956); John Keats, *The Crack in the Picture Window* (Boston: Houghton Mifflin, 1957); Jean Kerr, *Please Don't Eat the Daisies* (New York: Doubleday, 1957); and Herbert J. Gans, *The Levittowners: Ways of Life and Politics in a*

New Suburban Community (New York: Pantheon, 1967). On this literature, see Hayden, *Building Suburbia*, 92, 146–48, and Jackson, *Frontier*, 281–82. The phrase "bourgeois utopia" is from Fishman, *Utopias*.

11. Richard Harris and Robert Lewis, "The Geography of North American Cities and Suburbs, 1900–1950: A New Synthesis," *Journal of Urban History* 27 (2001): 262–84; Kevin Michael Kruse and Thomas J. Sugrue, eds., *The New Suburban History* (Chicago: University of Chicago Press, 2006); David R. Contosta, *Suburb in the City: Chestnut Hill, Philadelphia, 1850–1990* (Columbus: Ohio State University Press, 1992).

12. Nicolaides and Wiese, *Suburb Reader*, 7–9; Jackson, *Frontier*; Fishman, *Utopias*; Stilgoe, *Borderland;* Kruse and Sugrue, *New Suburban History;* Richard Harris, *Unplanned Suburbs: Toronto's American Tragedy, 1900 to 1950* (Baltimore: Johns Hopkins University Press, 1999); Becky M. Nicolaides, *My Blue Heaven: Life and Politics in the Working-Class Suburbs of Los Angeles, 1920–1965* (Chicago: University of Chicago Press, 2002); Andrew Wiese, *Places of Their Own: African American Suburbanization in the Twentieth Century* (Chicago: University of Chicago Press, 2004).

13. Nicolaides and Wiese, *Suburb Reader*, 8.

14. For examples of urban culture, see William Foote Whyte, *Street Corner Society: The Social Structure of an Italian Slum* (Chicago: University of Chicago Press, 1981); Herbert J. Gans, *The Urban Villagers: Group and Class in the Life of Italian-Americans* (New York: Free Press, 1962); Kenneth B. Clark, *Dark Ghetto: Dilemmas of Social Power* (New York: Harper and Row, 1965); and Jacob A. Riis, *How the Other Half Lives: Studies among the Tenements of New York* (1890; repr., New York: Dover, 1971). On suburban culture, see Jackson, *Frontier*, 231–82; Rachel Heiman, *Driving after Class: Anxious Times in an American Suburb* (Berkeley: University of California Press, 2015); Self, *American Babylon*; and Nicolaides and Wiese, *Suburb Reader*, 1–10, 257–497.

15. Sharon Zukin, *Landscapes of Power: From Detroit to Disney World* (Berkeley: University of California Press, 1991); James S. Duncan and Nancy Duncan, *Landscapes of Privilege: The Politics of the Aesthetic in an American Suburb* (New York: Routledge, 2004).

16. Race relations and attitudes in post–World War II Detroit show little difference between the city and suburb, except that white suburbanites had at their disposal exclusionary tools that their urban counterparts could only envy. Compare Thomas J. Sugrue, *The Origins of the Urban Crisis: Race and Inequality in Postwar Detroit* (Princeton, N.J.: Princeton University Press, 1996), with David M. P. Freund, *Colored Property: State Policy and White Racial Politics in Suburban America* (Chicago: University of Chicago Press, 2007).

17. Marc A. Weiss, *The Rise of the Community Builders: The American Real Estate Industry and Urban Land Planning* (New York: Columbia University Press, 1987); Carolyn S. Loeb, *Entrepreneurial Vernacular: Developers' Subdivisions in the 1920s* (Baltimore: Johns Hopkins University Press, 2001).

18. Edwin M. Bacon, *Boston: A Guide Book* (Boston: Ginn, 1903), 109.

19. On Llewelyn Park and Riverside, see John Archer, *Architecture and Suburbia: From English Villa to American Dream House, 1690–2000* (Minneapolis: University of Minnesota Press, 2005), 221–28, and Stilgoe, *Borderland*, 52–55, 258–59.

20. Fishman, *Utopias*, 134–54; Ann Durkin Keating, *Chicagoland: City and Suburbs in the Railroad Age* (Chicago: University of Chicago Press, 2005); Contosta, *Suburb in the City*; Michael H. Ebner, *Creating Chicago's North Shore: A Suburban History* (Chicago: University of Chicago Press, 1988); Estelle F. Feinstein, *Stamford in the Gilded Age: The Political Life of a Connecticut Town, 1868–1893* (Stamford, Conn.: Stamford Historical Society, 1973).

21. Archer, *Architecture and Suburbia*, 41–169; Nicolaides and Wiese, *Suburb Reader*, 13–97; Fishman, *Utopias*, 18–154; Jackson, *Frontier*, 20–102; Henry C. Binford, *The First Suburbs: Residential Communities on the Boston Periphery, 1815–1860* (Chicago: University of Chicago Press, 1985); Ronald Dale Karr, "Suburban Land Development in Antebellum Boston," *Journal of Urban History* 41 (September 2015): 862–80.

22. Studies of pre-1850 suburbs are rare; two of the best examine the Boston area: Binford, *First Suburbs*, and Alexander Von Hoffman, "Weaving the Urban Fabric: Nineteenth-Century Patterns of Residential Real Estate Development in Outer Boston," *Journal of Urban History* 22 (1996): 191–230.

23. L. H. Bailey quoted in *Suburban Life*, September 1906, 122. For studies of late nineteenth-century railroad suburbs, see Jackson, *Frontier*, 87–102; Fishman, *Utopias*, 134–54; and Keating, *Chicagoland*.

24. Arthur I. Raymond, "A Study in Contrasts," *Suburban Life*, November 1906, 219.

25. Stilgoe, *Borderland*, 22–220.

26. Warner, *Streetcar Suburbs;* Binford, *First Suburbs*; Hayden, *Suburbia*, 71–96.

27. Binford, *First Suburbs;* Von Hoffman, "Weaving the Urban Fabric."

28. Stilgoe, *Borderland*, 152; Douglas Shand-Tucci, *Built in Boston: City and Suburb, 1800–2000* (Amherst: University of Massachusetts Press, 1999). For another study that demonstrates the essentially urban character of the streetcar suburbs, see Alexander Von Hoffman, *Local Attachments: The Making of an American Urban Neighborhood, 1850 to 1920* (Baltimore: Johns Hopkins University Press, 1994). By the mid-twentieth century the suburban character of Boston's Dorchester and Roxbury neighborhoods, two of Warner's original streetcar suburbs, was long gone. Gerald H. Gamm, *Urban Exodus: Why the Jews Left Boston and the Catholics Stayed* (Cambridge, Mass.: Harvard University Press, 2001).

29. Stilgoe, *Borderland*, 156; Nicolaides and Wiese, *Suburb Reader*, 99–116; Graham Taylor, *Satellite Cities: A Study of Industrial Suburbs* (New York: Appleton, 1915); Harlan Paul Douglass, *The Suburban Trend* (New York: Century, 1925). This is not to deny that the blue-collar residents of these industrial suburbs may have shared some traits associated with suburban living, such as raising livestock or keeping gardens.

30. Jackson, *Frontier*, 87–102; Fishman, *Utopias*, 134–54; Ronald Dale Karr, "Brookline and the Making of an Elite Suburb," *Chicago History* 13 (Summer 1984): 36–47.

31. See, for example, William H. Wilson, *The City Beautiful Movement* (Baltimore: Johns Hopkins University Press, 1989), 41–44, and Nancy Kleniewski, *Cities, Change, and Conflict: A Political Economy of Urban Life* (Belmont, Calif.: Wadsworth, 2002), 289–311.

32. The closest studied twentieth-century elite suburbs are those of Westchester County, New York. See Carol A. O'Connor, *A Sort of Utopia, Scarsdale, 1891–1981* (Albany: State University of New York Press, 1983); Zukin, *Landscapes of Power*, 136–74; and Duncan and Duncan, *Landscapes of Privilege*.

33. Allan Kulikoff, *Agrarian Origins of American Capitalism* (Charlottesville: University Press of Virginia, 1992); Charles G. Sellers, *The Market Revolution: Jacksonian America, 1815–1846* (New York: Oxford University Press, 1991); James A. Henretta, *The Origins of American Capitalism: Collected Essays* (Boston: Northeastern University Press, 1991).

34. Harvey Molotch, "The Political Economy of Growth Machines," *Journal of Urban Affairs* 15 (1993): 29–53; Robert J. Kolesar, "The Politics of Development: Worcester, Massachusetts in the Late Nineteenth Century," *Journal of Urban History* 16 (1989): 3–28.

1. New England Town

1. Woods, *Sketches*, 18–20, 25–27, 125–28, 130–31; Theodore F. Jones, *Land Ownership in Brookline from the First Settlement*, Publication No. 5, Brookline Historical Society (Brookline: Brookline Historical Society, 1923), map 7; "Plan of the Town of Brookline . . . Taken in August 1830," Edward W. Baker Papers, Brookline Historical Society. Henry C. Binford, *The First Suburbs: Residential Communities on the Boston Periphery, 1815–1860* (Chicago: University of Chicago Press, 1985), 1–43, points out that a transitional zone of tanneries, factories, and shops had developed throughout this urban fringe, such as in Cambridge and Charlestown.

2. W. J. Latimer et al., "Soil Survey of Norfolk, Bristol, and Barnstable Counties, Massachusetts," in U.S. Department of Agriculture, *Field Operations of the Bureau of Soils, 1920* (Washington, D.C.: Government Printing Office, 1925), 1033–1120, map 31; Clifford A. Kaye, *The Geology and Early History of the Boston Area of Massachusetts: A Bicentennial Approach* (Washington, D.C.: Government Printing Office, 1976), 1–7, 65–68; Bradford Kingman, "Brookline," in *History of Norfolk County, Massachusetts*, ed. D. Hamilton Hurd (Philadelphia: Lewis, 1884), 2:783–84, 790–91; Jones, *Land Ownership*, map 7.

3. U.S. Secretary of State, *Sixth Census or Enumeration of the Inhabitants of the United States* (Washington, D.C.: Blair and Rives, 1841), 39; John Pierce, *An Address at the Opening of the Town Hall in Brookline, on Tuesday 14 October 1845* (Boston: White and Potter, 1846), 24–25.

4. City of Boston, *Report of the Record Commissioners* (Boston: Municipal Printing Office, 1902), 2:6 (quotation); Town of Brookline, *Muddy River and Brookline Records* (Boston: Farwell, 1875), 9–26; John F. Sly, "A History of Muddy River from 1630 to 1705,"

unpublished manuscript, 1930, 5–59, Public Library of Brookline; Darret B. Rutman, *Winthrop's Boston: Portrait of a Puritan Town, 1630–1649* (Chapel Hill: University of North Carolina Press, 1965), 34–40, 68–70, 76–94.

5. Sly, "Muddy River," 67–75; Rutman, *Winthrop's Boston,* 79–96. On outlivers, see Richard L. Bushman, *From Puritan to Yankee: Character and the Social Order in Connecticut, 1690–1765* (New York: Norton, 1967), 54–72. By the eighteenth century Muddy River's pattern of dispersed settlement had become the norm in Massachusetts; see Joseph S. Wood, *The New England Village* (Baltimore: Johns Hopkins University Press, 1997), 52–70.

6. Brookline, *Muddy River Records,* 57–58, 62–63, 78–89, 91; Sly, "Muddy River," 118–22, 125–29, 133, 150–59; Kingman, "Brookline," 804–6.

7. Walter Muir Whitehill, *Boston: A Topographic History* (Cambridge, Mass.: Harvard University Press, 1968), 37–38, 47–48.

8. Based on a reconstruction of the 1770 population using genealogical and tax records. See also Ronald Dale Karr, "The Transformation of Agriculture in Brookline, 1770–1885," *Historical Journal of Massachusetts* 15 (1987): 33–34. On household production, see Allan Kulikoff, "Households and Markets: Toward a New Synthesis of American Agrarian History," *William and Mary Quarterly,* 3rd ser., 50 (1993): 348–51.

9. Daniel Vickers, "Competency and Competition: Economic Culture in Early America," *William and Mary Quarterly,* 3rd ser., 47 (1990): 3–29; James A. Henretta, *The Origins of American Capitalism: Collected Essays* (Boston: Northeastern University Press, 1991), 71–120; Virginia DeJohn Anderson, *New England's Generation: The Great Migration and the Formation of Society and Culture in the Seventeenth Century* (Cambridge: Cambridge University Press, 1991), 131–76.

10. Karr, "Transformation of Agriculture," 33–34.

11. Ronald Dale Karr, "Two Centuries of Oligarchy in Brookline," *Historical Journal of Massachusetts* 13 (1985): 117–20. On ties with the provincial hierarchy, see Edward M. Cook, Jr., *The Fathers of the Towns: Leadership and Community Structure in Eighteenth-Century New England* (Baltimore: Johns Hopkins University Press, 1976), 143–63. On a per-capita basis Brookline accounted for more members of the provincial elite than any of the seventy-five New England towns sampled by Cook.

12. Karr, "Two Centuries."

13. Gen. John Heath quoted in Charles Knowles Bolton, "The First Harvard Graduate Killed in the American Revolution," *New England Magazine,* new ser., 12 (1895): 111.

14. Brookline, *Muddy River Records,* 247–50; Bolton, "First Harvard Graduate," 110–11; Curtis, *Brookline,* 144–48.

15. Two of the Loyalists, however, Henry Hulton and Samuel Sewall, held extensive real estate. In 1781, after their flight to England, their lands were confiscated by the state and sold, Hulton's to a man from Roxbury and Sewall's to Brookline farmer John Heath and Edward K. Wolcott, Sewall's brother-in-law. Jones, *Land Ownership,* 22, 24–25;

Rufus G. F. Candage, *Jeremy Gridley* (Brookline, Mass.: Brookline Historical Society, 1903), 5–7.

16. Calculated from *Church Records of Baptisms, Marriages and Deaths for 100 Years* (Brookline, Mass.: Brookline Historical Publication Society, 1897). On these epidemics, see Lee Nathaniel Newcomer, *The Embattled Farmers: A Massachusetts Countryside in the American Revolution* (New York: Russell and Russell, 1971), 69, 94–95.

17. Newcomer, *Embattled Farmers,* 88–131; Howard S. Russell, *A Long, Deep Furrow: Three Centuries of Farming in New England* (Hanover, N.H.: University Press of New England, 1976), 216–29.

18. Calculated from 1771 valuation, Brookline, Massachusetts Archives, 132:160–62, Boston; 1784 valuation (microfilm), State House Library, Boston. On the effect of the Revolution on eastern Massachusetts agriculture, see Russell, *Long, Deep Furrow,* 224–26, and Winifred Barr Rothenberg, *From Market-Places to a Market Economy: The Transformation of Rural Massachusetts, 1750–1850* (Chicago: University of Chicago Press, 1992), 214–40.

19. 1783 census return for Brookline, Massachusetts Archives; U.S. Bureau of the Census, *Heads of Families at the First Census of the United States Taken in the Year 1790: Massachusetts* (Washington, D.C.: Government Printing Office, 1908), 196–97. Wealth distribution calculated from 1770 tax list, Massachusetts Archives, 130:421–24, and from a 1787 tax list, Brookline Historical Society Papers. On the increasing use of farm labor, see Rothenberg, *From Market-Places,* 181–212.

20. Newcomer, *Embattled Farmers,* 131–32; Jones, *Land Ownership,* 24–26; Brookline, *Muddy River Records,* 344–47.

21. Karr, "Transformation of Agriculture," 36–37.

22. Brian Donahue, *The Great Meadow: Farmers and the Land in Colonial Concord* (New Haven, Conn.: Yale University Press, 2004), 214–20; Carolyn Merchant, *Ecological Revolutions: Nature, Gender, and Science in New England* (Chapel Hill: University of North Carolina Press, 1989), 162–67.

23. Karr, "Transformation of Agriculture," 37; calculated from 1770, 1812, and 1826 Brookline tax assessments.

24. John Pierce, "Brookline in 1817," *Proceedings of the Massachusetts Historical Society,* 2nd ser., 19 (1905): 425.

25. Karr, "Transformation of Agriculture," 37–39.

26. Russell, *Long, Deep Furrow,* 295–96, 374–78, 451; Percy Wells Bidwell and John I. Falconer, *History of Agriculture in the Northern United States, 1620–1860* (Washington, D.C.: Carnegie Institution of Washington, 1925), 242.

27. George Rogers Taylor, *The Transportation Revolution, 1815–1860* (New York: Rinehart, 1951), 32–36, 74–103, 132–75; Andrew H. Baker and Holly V. Izard, "New England Farmers and the Marketplace, 1780–1865: A Case Study," *Agricultural History* 65 (1991):

29–52; Russell, *Long, Deep Furrow,* 332–38; Massachusetts Bureau of Labor Statistics, *History of Wages and Prices in Massachusetts, 1750–1883* (Boston: Wright and Potter, 1885), 181–82; Winifred B. Rothenberg, "A Price Index for Rural Massachusetts, 1750–1855," *Journal of Economic History* 39 (1979): 975–1001.

28. Brookline, *Muddy River Records,* 588.

29. Brookline, *Muddy River Records,* 588–90; Curtis, *Brookline,* 80–83, 188–89. On roads in rural New England, see Edward C. Kirkland, *Men, Cities and Transportation: A Study in New England History, 1820–1900* (Cambridge, Mass.: Harvard University Press, 1948), 1:34–37.

30. Karr, "Two Centuries," 123; Jones, *Land Ownership,* 29; Charles H. Stearns, "President's Annual Address," *PBHS,* 1911, 11; Curtis, *Brookline,* 121; Emma Downing Coolidge, *Descendants of John and Mary Coolidge of Watertown, Massachusetts* (Boston: Wright and Potter, 1930), 40, 215.

31. Jones, *Land Ownership,* 12, 14; Woods, *Sketches,* 109–12; Curtis, *Brookline,* 93–94; Samuel Eliot Morison, *Builders of the Bay Colony* (Boston: Houghton Mifflin, 1958), 135–82.

32. John Archer, *Architecture and Suburbia: From English Villa to American Dream House, 1690–2000* (Minneapolis: University of Minnesota Press, 2005), 46–168; Fishman, *Utopias,* 18–72.

33. James C. O'Connell, *The Hub's Metropolis: Greater Boston's Development from Railroad Suburbs to Smart Growth* (Cambridge, Mass.: MIT Press, 2013), 17–18.

34. Carl Bridenbaugh, *Cities in Revolt: Urban Life in America, 1743–1776* (New York: Capicorn, 1964), 24–25, 95, 144–46; Candage, *Jeremy Gridley,* 3; Jones, *Land Ownership,* 19, map 4; Curtis, *Brookline,* 111–14; Woods, *Sketches,* 297–301, 347.

35. *American National Biography,* s.v. "Gridley, Jeremiah"; Jones, *Land Ownership,* 24; Candage, *Jeremy Gridley,* 3–4; Brookline, *Muddy River Records,* 180–217.

36. Curtis, *Brookline,* 121, 128–30; Jones, *Land Ownership,* 24–25; Candage, *Jeremy Gridley,* 4–5; E. Alfred Jones, *Loyalists of Massachusetts* (London: St. Catherine Press, 1930), 167.

37. Calculated from the manuscript returns of the direct tax of 1798 for Brookline, New England Historic Genealogical Society, Boston. On upper-class Boston in the postrevolutionary period, see Samuel Eliot Morison, *The Maritime History of Massachusetts, 1783–1860* (Boston: Houghton Mifflin, 1961), 119–33.

38. Frances Rollins Morse, *Henry and Mary Lee: Letters and Journals with Other Family Letters, 1802–1860* (Boston: N.p., 1926), 300; Mrs. Thomas Doliber, "Two Old Brookline Homesteads," *PBHS,* 1905, 50–53; Curtis, *Brookline,* 186–87; Jones, *Land Ownership,* 32–34; Julia Goddard, "The Goddard House," *PBHS,* 1903, 20–26.

39. Woods, *Sketches,* 345; Jones, *Land Ownership,* 33–34, maps 5, 6; Nina Fletcher Little, *Some Old Brookline Houses Built in This Massachusetts Town before 1825 and Still Standing in 1948* (Brookline, Mass.: Brookline Historical Society, 1949), 55–57, 87, 89.

40. Carl Seaburg and Stanley Paterson, *Merchant Prince of Boston: Col. T. H. Perkins,*

1764–1854 (Cambridge, Mass.: Harvard University Press, 1971), 141, 276, 388–89; Woods, *Sketches*, 355–60; Jones, *Land Ownership*, map 6.

41. Morgan, Cushing, and Reed, *CBD*, 199–225.

42. Tamara P. Thornton, *Cultivating Gentlemen: The Meaning of Country Life among the Boston Elite, 1785–1860* (New Haven, Conn.: Yale University Press, 1989).

43. Woods, *Sketches*, 258–63; Doliber, "Two Brookline Homesteads," 46–53; Mary W. Poor, "Recollections of Brookline," *Publications of the Brookline Historical Society* (1903): 20–24.

44. Calculated from 1826 tax return, Town Assessor's Office, Brookline.

45. Jeremiah Spofford, *Gazetteer of Massachusetts* (Newburyport, Mass.: Whipple, 1828), 170.

46. Detailed statistics on Brookline occupations before 1850 are not available. The list of tradesmen circa 1812 presented here is derived from Samuel Aspinwall Goddard, *Recollections of Brookline: Being an Account of the Houses, the Families, and the Roads, in Brookline, in the Years 1800 to 1810* (Birmingham, Eng.: E. C. Osborne, 1873), written from memory sixty years later. See also Woods, *Sketches*, 25–27, 39, 50, 125, 130–31, 150, 354, 375. The data for 1820 and 1840 are from U.S. Secretary of State, *Census for 1820* (Washington, D.C.: Gales and Seaton, 1821), 7, and U.S. Secretary of State, *Sixth Census*, 39.

47. Whitehill, *Boston*, 4–9, 26, 46–52, 76–78; Kirkland, *Men, Cities and Transportation*, 1:7–8, 34–59, 62–66; Frederic J. Wood, *The Turnpikes of New England and Evolution of the Same through England, Virginia, and Maryland* (Boston: Marshall Jones, 1919), 80–198; Russell, *Long, Deep Furrow*, 236–37, 264–69, 326–32.

48. Curtis, *Brookline*, 188–97; Wood, *Turnpikes*, 160–66.

49. Binford, *First Suburbs*, 15–44; James Driscoll, "Industry in Brookline," *PBHS*, 1952, 12; Charles F. Read, "President's Annual Address," *PBHS*, 1908, 9–10; U.S. Census, 1840, Manufacturing Schedules, Brookline.

50. "Plan of the Town of Brookline"; Jones, *Land Ownership*, maps 7, 8; Wood, *New England Village*.

51. Woods, *Sketches*, 18–20; Kingman, "Brookline," 865–66.

52. Jones, *Land Ownership*, map 7; Driscoll, "Industry in Brookline," 12; Woods, *Sketches*, 25–27, 125–28, 130–31; Goddard, *Recollections of Brookline*, 13–14; "Plan of the Town of Brookline."

53. Wood, *New England Village*, 122–23.

54. Edward W. Baker, "Brookline Volunteer Fire Department," *PBHS*, 1904, 20–21; Kingman, "Brookline," 817–18; Alisa Belinkoff, "Everyone Who Was Anyone in Brookline, Mass., 1705–1875" (B.A. thesis, Brandeis University, 1975), 183–84; Pierce, *Address at Town Hall*, 5, 15, 33, 36.

55. Woods, *Sketches*, 175–78; Rufus G. F. Candage, "President's Annual Address," *PBHS*, 1905, 15–16; Jones, *Land Ownership*, 30, 39, 41, map 6; John Pierce, *A Discourse Delivered at*

Brookline, 24 November 1805, the Day Which Completed a Century from the Incorporation of the Town (Cambridge, Mass.: William Hillard, 1806), 26; Ebenezer Clapp, *History of the Town of Dorchester* (Boston: E. Clapp, Jr., 1859), 139, 197–200, 322–23.

56. Brookline, *Muddy River Records;* Woods, *Sketches*, 21, 176–79, 205, 354.

57. John Pierce, *Reminiscences of Forty Years* (Boston: Minot Pratt, 1837), 14; Woods, *Sketches*, 252–55; William H. Lyon, *The History of the First Parish in Brookline: As a Mirror of the History of the Town: A Sermon* (Brookline, Mass.: First Parish in Brookline, 1905), 17–19; Daniel Walker Howe, *The Unitarian Conscience: Harvard Moral Philosophy, 1805–1861* (Cambridge, Mass.: Harvard University Press, 1970), 216–21.

58. Pierce, *Forty Years,* 14.

59. Lyon, *First Parish,* 17–19; Seaburg and Paterson, *Merchant Prince of Boston*, 383–84, 388, 408; Brookline, *Muddy River Records*, 467, 493, 471.

60. John Pierce, "Memoirs," 3 (1818): 36, Massachusetts Historical Society, Boston; Lyon, *First Parish,* 20–21.

61. Pierce, "Memoirs," 3 (1818): 36–39.

62. Pierce, "Memoirs," 5 (1828): 101–7; Pierce, *Forty Years,* 12.

63. Kingman, "Brookline," 820; Ashley Day Leavitt, "An Account of the Founding and Development of the Harvard Church, Brookline, Mass.," *PBHS,* 1951, 13.

64. Richard D. Brown, "The Emergence of Urban Society in Rural Massachusetts, 1760–1820," *Journal of American History* 61 (1974): 29–51.

65. Baker, "Fire Department," 25–29; Woods, *Sketches,* 136–38. Between 1790 and 1845 only four Brookline houses were destroyed by fire. Pierce, *Address at Town Hall,* 24, 41–42.

66. Kingman, "Brookline," 827; Curtis, *Brookline,* 228–30. On the diffusion of culture in rural New England, see Brown, "Emergence of Urban Society," and, more generally, David Jaffee, *A New Nation of Goods: The Material Culture of Early America* (Philadelphia: University of Pennsylvania Press, 2010).

67. Kingman, "Brookline," 827 (quotation); Curtis, *Brookline,* 229; Pierce, *Address at Town Hall,* 13. On the rise of the national lecture circuit, see Donald M. Scott, "The Popular Lecture and the Creation of a Public in Mid-Nineteenth-Century America," *Journal of American History* 66 (1980): 791–809. On the role of popular culture in promoting market-oriented values, see Charles G. Sellers, *The Market Revolution: Jacksonian America, 1815–1846* (New York: Oxford University Press, 1991), 237–68, 364–95.

68. Pierce, *Address at Town Hall,* 28–29, 52; Pierce, "Memoirs," 6 (1833): 16. On the Washingtonians, see Ian R. Tyrrell, *Sobering Up: From Temperance to Prohibition in Antebellum America* (Westport, Conn.: Greenwood, 1979), 159–90.

69. Curtis, *Brookline,* 257–59; Pierce, "Memoirs," 7 (1837): 70–71; James R. McGovern, *Yankee Family* (New Orleans: Polyanthos, 1975), 35–36.

70. Brown, "Emergence of Urban Society"; Sellers, *Market Revolution.*

2. Commuters and Immigrants

1. Charles G. Sellers, *The Market Revolution: Jacksonian America, 1815–1846* (New York: Oxford University Press, 1991); Christopher Clark, *The Roots of Rural Capitalism: Western Massachusetts, 1780–1860* (Ithaca, N.Y.: Cornell University Press, 1990), 151–313; Theodore Steinberg, *Nature Incorporated: Industrialization and the Waters of New England* (Cambridge: Cambridge University Press, 1991), 77–186.

2. Oscar Handlin, *Boston's Immigrants, 1790–1880: A Study in Acculturation*, rev. and enl. ed. (Cambridge, Mass.: Harvard University Press, 1991), 1–87, 239; Peter R. Knights, *The Plain People of Boston, 1830–1860: A Study in City Growth* (New York: Oxford University Press, 1971), 33–47; Walter Muir Whitehill, *Boston: A Topographic History* (Cambridge, Mass.: Harvard University Press, 1968), 95–140.

3. Knights, *Plain People*, 33–47, 84; Warner, *Streetcar Suburbs*, 5, 8–9, 129.

4. Glenna Matthews, *"Just a Housewife": The Rise and Fall of Domesticity in America* (New York: Oxford University Press, 1987), 3–65; Laurel Thatcher Ulrich, *A Midwife's Tale: The Life of Martha Ballard, Based on Her Diary, 1785–1812* (New York: Knopf, 1990); Nancy F. Cott, *The Bonds of Womanhood: "Woman's Sphere" in New England, 1780–1835* (New Haven, Conn.: Yale University Press, 1977).

5. David Jaffee, *A New Nation of Goods: The Material Culture of Early America* (Philadelphia: University of Pennsylvania Press, 2010); Jack Larkin, *Where We Lived: Discovering the Places We Once Called Home: The American Home from 1775 to 1840* (Newtown, Conn.: Taunton Press, 2006), 8–111; Richard L. Bushman, *The Refinement of America: Persons, Houses, Cities* (New York: Knopf, 1993); Jane C. Nylander, *Our Own Snug Fireside: Images of the New England Home, 1760–1860* (New Haven, Conn.: Yale University Press, 1993).

6. Margaret Marsh, *Suburban Lives* (New Brunswick, N.J.: Rutgers University Press, 1990), 13–16.

7. Jackson, *Frontier*, 68–72.

8. Nylander, *Our Own Snug Fireside.*

9. John Archer, *Architecture and Suburbia: From English Villa to American Dream House, 1690–2000* (Minneapolis: University of Minnesota Press, 2005), 46–168; Jackson, *Frontier*, 20–44.

10. Cott, *Bonds of Womanhood*, 20–30, 43–45, 60–83; Handlin, *Boston's Immigrants*, 15–16, 93–94; Whitehill, *Boston*, 111–20.

11. Henry C. Binford, *The First Suburbs: Residential Communities on the Boston Periphery, 1815–1860* (Chicago: University of Chicago Press, 1985), 84–88; Warner, *Streetcar Suburbs*, 15–21; Edward Pessen, *Riches, Class, and Power before the Civil War* (Lexington, Mass.: Heath, 1973), 189–201.

12. Binford, *First Suburbs*, 88–90; Jackson, *Frontier*, 33–35.

13. Charles J. Kennedy, "Commuter Services in the Boston Area," *Business History Review* 36 (1962): 153–59; Binford, *First Suburbs*, 91–92.

14. Kennedy, "Commuter Services," 158–62, 158 (quotation); Knights, *Plain People*, 103–18; Binford, *First Suburbs*, 91–95, 128–31.

15. Massachusetts Bureau of Statistics of Labor, *The Census of Massachusetts, 1885* (Boston: Wright and Potter, 1887–88), vol. 1, part 1:72–73.

16. Of the 818 adult males listed on the 1850 manuscript U.S. Census population returns for Brookline, 111 had a business address listed in *Directory of the City of Boston* (Boston: George Adams, 1850). These constitute the commuters as used in this analysis.

17. Woods, *Sketches*, 21; *Boston Almanac for the Year 1839* (Boston: Sampson and Murdock, 1839), 68; *Boston Almanac for the Year 1845* (Boston: Sampson and Murdock, 1845), 125; George Adams, *An Almanac and Business Directory of the Citizens of Cambridge, Charlestown, and Roxbury, and the Towns of Chelsea, Dorchester, and Brookline* (Boston: David Clapp, 1848), 122.

18. *Report of the Directors of the Boston and Worcester Rail-Road Corporation to the Stockholders at Their Twelfth Annual Meeting* (Boston: A. J. Wright, 1843), 10–11; *Boston Almanac for 1845*, 131; Thomas J. Humphrey and Norton D. Clark, *Boston's Commuter Rail: The First 150 Years* (Cambridge, Mass.: Boston Street Railway Association, 1985), 21.

19. *Report of the Directors of the Boston and Worcester Railroad to the Stockholders at the Seventeenth Annual Meeting* (Boston: Dutton and Wentworth, 1847), 16; *Report of the Directors of the Boston and Worcester Railroad to the Stockholders at the Eighteenth Annual Meeting* (Boston: Dutton and Wentworth, 1848), 3–4; Charles Knowles Bolton, *Brookline: The History of a Favored Town* (Brookline, Mass.: Spencer, 1897), 55–56; Humphrey and Clark, *Boston's Commuter Rail*, 21.

20. *Twenty-Ninth Annual Report of the Directors of the Boston and Worcester Railroad* (Boston: David Clapp, 1859), 4–5; *Thirty-Eighth Annual Report of the Directors of the Boston and Worcester Railroad* (Boston: David Clapp, 1868), 16.

21. James M. Driscoll, "Railroads in Brookline," *PBHS*, 1963–66, 39–40; Tom Nelligan, "Mr. Kneilling, Meet Messrs. Goss and Munson," *Trains*, October 1977, 28–30; Humphrey and Clark, *Boston's Commuter Rail*, 43–44.

22. Kennedy, "Commuter Services," 162–68; Binford, *First Suburbs*, 146–48.

23. R. C. F. Candage, "Brookline Changes—Street Car Accommodations," *Brookline Suburban*, June 29, 1899; *BT*, October 15, November 19, 1870.

24. Ronald Dale Karr, "Suburban Land Development in Antebellum Boston," *Journal of Urban History* 41 (September 2015): 862–80.

25. Karr, "Suburban Land Development," 870–72.

26. As before, commuters are defined as those 111 adult males listed on the 1850 manuscript U.S. Census population returns for Brookline who had a business address listed in the *Directory of Boston*, 1850.

27. Amory, Gardiner, Gardner, Sargent, and Weld are all shown with Boston residential

addresses in the *Directory of Boston,* 1850. The census shows only Amory and Gardner with coachmen residing at their Brookline estates, but there seems little doubt the others employed drivers. (The census lists another three coachmen as heads of their own households.) Altogether twenty Brookline households had live-in coachmen; of these nine were commuters (including Amory and Gardner). Concerning the great wealth and high social standing of Amory, Gardiner, Gardner, Sargent, and Weld, see Pessen, *Riches, Class, and Power,* 56, 114–15, 215, 224, 333–34.

28. In 1851 only 11 percent of the men listed in Boston's directory were commuters, and 53 percent of these resided in Cambridge, Charlestown, or Roxbury. By 1860 commuters made up 18 percent of those listed, with only 43 percent in the three innermost suburbs. Binford, *First Suburbs,* 130–31.

29. Unlike with later censuses, the 1850 population census schedules do not specify relationships to the household head. I have considered any persons listed directly after the head and his wife as children of the head if they shared the same surname and were at least eighteen years younger. On the cult of domesticity and the feminine sphere, see Matthews, *"Just a Housewife,"* 3–65, and Cott, *Bonds of Womanhood,* 20–30, 43–45, 60–83.

30. Handlin, *Boston's Immigrants,* 88–112; Whitehill, *Boston,* 111–18; Binford, *First Suburbs,* 126; Warner, *Streetcar Suburbs,* 17–20. Pessen, *Riches, Class, and Power,* 189–201, shows that although most wealthy Bostonians remained in Boston proper in the 1840s, they were becoming more concentrated on a few elite streets, most notably on Beacon Hill. It seems likely that this would have pushed rents and land values even higher in these neighborhoods, which in turn might have provided some of the 111 Brookline commuters who had lived on Beacon Hill in 1840 with an additional incentive to leave.

31. There were fifty-four commuting household heads living within a half mile of the depot. Of these, fifty-two appear on the 1851 tax list, with a median holding of $8,000 (mean, $10,927) of assessed real and personal property. Another twenty-one lived further away (nineteen on the tax list), with a median holding of $34,000 (mean $36,900). The addresses of four commuting heads could not be determined.

32. In 1850 the mean size of households headed by a commuter was 8.01 persons, compared to a mean of 6.17 for all Brookline households (calculated from manuscript U.S. Census population schedules).

33. In 1850 households headed by commuters had a mean of 3.13 children, compared to 2.17 for all households. The 1850 census does not distinguish between relatives, boarders, and servants, and the occupations of females are not listed, but the fact that 78 percent of commuting households contained at least one person born in Ireland suggests that few lacked domestic help. Sixty-two of seventy-nine commuting households had at least one Irish-born member. Only four commuting households did not include persons in addition to the head, his wife, and their children.

34. Of the seventy-nine commuting household heads of 1850, thirty-two appear in *The*

Brookline, Jamaica Plain and West Roxbury Directory for 1871 (Boston: Dean, Dudley, 1871) and another four are represented by widows. The rate is somewhat higher for the fifty-five heads under fifty years old in 1850: twenty-five persisted and three widows remained.

35. Bradford Kingman, "Brookline," in *History of Norfolk County, Massachusetts*, ed. D. Hamilton Hurd (Philadelphia: Lewis, 1884), 811, 819–22, 835–41, 867.

36. A special census taken in 1844 showed only two household heads with Irish surnames (a copy appears in John Pierce, "Memoirs," 2nd ser., 2 (1844): 401–12, Massachusetts Historical Society, Boston). The 1850 U.S. Census showed 608 residents born in Ireland (tabulated from manuscript population returns). Although the census did not record religious affiliation, there seems little doubt that few of the Irish immigrants were Protestants. Among the evidence supporting this is the absence of a Presbyterian church or other Irish Protestant organizations and the predominance of typically Irish Catholic given names. See Theodore Dockhorn, "Record Linkage," *Historical Methods Newsletter* 9 (1976): 150–57.

37. Handlin, *Boston's Immigrants*, 25–53; Kevin Kenny, *The American Irish* (Harlow, Essex, U.K.: Longman, 2000), 45–130; Kerby A. Miller, *Emigrants and Exiles: Ireland and the Irish Exodus to North America* (New York: Oxford University Press, 1985).

38. Handlin, *Boston's Immigrants*, 54–87. There is only indirect evidence to date the initial appearance of the Irish. From the *Vital Records of Brookline, Massachusetts, to the End of the Year 1849* (Salem, Mass.: Essex Institute, 1929), the births of individuals with Irish surnames or who are listed as natives of Ireland are as follows: 1705–1843: two; 1844: zero; 1845: ten; 1846: six; 1847: thirteen; 1848: eighteen; 1849: eighteen. At the town meeting of March 10, 1845, a committee noted that a proposed poor farm would attract "inmates from the foreign population, with which our country is flooded, and this class is daily coming within our borders." *BTR*, 1:162–63. The Brookline School Committee reported a sudden surge of attendance in the North District School in the 1848–49 school year and noted that Irish pupils made up one-third of the enrollment at that school by the year's end. *BSC*, 1849, 4–5, 9. That unskilled jobs were the primary lure for Irish males is indicated by the fact that in Boston in 1850, 48 percent of Irish men were listed as laborers; in Brookline the proportion was 78 percent. Handlin, *Boston's Immigrants*, 57–60; U.S. Census, 1850, Population Schedules, Brookline.

39. U.S. Census, 1850, Population Schedules, Brookline.

40. In 1850, 633 persons lived in households headed by commuters and 388 in households headed by an Irish native. These 1,021 individuals represent 40.6 percent of Brookline's population.

41. *BTR*, 1:15, 42. On school reform in the 1830s, see Carl F. Kaestle, *Pillars of the Republic: Common Schools and American Society, 1780–1860* (New York: Hill and Wang, 1983), 62–117, and Michael B. Katz, *The Irony of Early School Reform: Educational Innovation in Mid-Nineteenth Century Massachusetts* (Boston: Beacon, 1970), 1–112.

42. *BTR*, 1:77–80; Curtis, *Brookline*, 76–80, 220–21.

43. "Petition to Town of Brookline," February 16, 1842, Brookline Historical Society. Occupations are from the 1850 manuscript U.S. Census population and agriculture returns. By then each of the six owned at least $10,000 worth of real estate.

44. *BTR,* 1:48–49.

45. For example, in 1849–50, of the two high school teachers, the male was paid a salary of $1,000; the female, $394. At the intermediate schools, the male received $588; the female, $325. *Brookline Auditor's Report, 1850* (Boston: John Wilson, 1850), 4.

46. *BTR,* 1:114.

47. *BTR,* 1:77–80, 89–90, 95, 113–16; *BSC,* 1846, 7–9; John Pierce, *A Discourse Delivered in Brookline at the Request of Its Inhabitants on 15 March 1847, the Day Which Completed Half a Century from His Ordination* (Boston: James Monroe, 1847), 28; Kaestle, *Pillars of the Republic,* 103–35; Katz, *Irony of Early School Reform,* 53–60.

48. Michael Rawson, *Eden on the Charles: The Making of Boston* (Cambridge, Mass.: Harvard University Press, 2010), 76–128.

3. The Great Divide

1. Elias Nason, *A Gazetteer of the State of Massachusetts* (Boston: Russell, 1874), 132–33.

2. Lawrence quoted in William Lawrence, *Life of Amos A. Lawrence: With Extracts from His Diary and Correspondence* (Boston: Houghton Mifflin, 1888), 23–24. The term *Boston Associates* was coined by a twentieth-century historian, Vera Shlakman, in her *Economic History of a Factory Town: A Study of Chicopee, Massachusetts* (Northampton, Mass.: Smith College, 1935).

3. Lawrence, *Amos Lawrence,* 26–104; Robert F. Dalzell, Jr., *Enterprising Elite: The Boston Associates and the World They Made* (New York: Norton, 1987), 211–24; Betty G. Farrell, *Elite Families: Class and Power in Nineteenth-Century Boston* (Albany: State University of New York Press, 1993), 39–75; Thomas H. O'Connor, *Lords of the Loom: The Cotton Whigs and the Coming of the Civil War* (New York: Scribner, 1968), 102–14, 134–44, 155–59; Louise Hall Tharp, *The Appletons of Beacon Hill* (Boston: Little, Brown, 1973), 266–68.

4. Walter Muir Whitehill, *Boston: A Topographical History* (Cambridge, Mass.: Harvard University Press, 1968), 88–94; Curtis, *Brookline,* 198; Woods, *Sketches,* 109–13, 124; Theodore Francis Jones, *Land Ownership in Brookline from the First Settlement, Illustrated by Six Maps, 1635, 1667, 1693, 1746, 1786, 1822* (Brookline, Mass.: Riverdale Press, 1923), 27–29; Bradford Kingman, "Brookline," in *History of Norfolk County, Massachusetts,* ed. D. Hamilton Hurd (Philadelphia: Lewis, 1884), 2:859; Charles H. Stearns, "The Sewall House," *PBHS,* 1903, 39–40; Frederic J. Wood, *The Turnpikes of New England and Evolution of the Same through England, Virginia, and Maryland* (Boston: Marshall Jones, 1919), 163, 188–91, 193–94.

5. Lawrence, *Amos Lawrence,* 59–61; ND, 192:fol. 232, 233; Plan Book 55:2606, 2607; Anne Wardwell, "'Longwood' and 'Cottage Farm' in Brookline," in *Victorian Boston Today:*

Ten Walking Tours, ed. Pauline Chase Harrell and Margaret Supplee Smith (Boston: Victorian Society in America, 1975), 56–79.

6. Lawrence, *Amos Lawrence*, 61–62; William Lawrence, *Memories of a Happy Life* (Boston: Houghton Mifflin, 1926), 4.

7. U.S. Census, 1870, Population Schedules, Brookline, 70–71.

8. John S. Lawrence, *Amory Appleton Lawrence* (Boston: N.p., 1914); ND, 10649:390.

9. The appearance of Pearl Place is conjecture based on early property atlases such as *Atlas of the Town of Brookline, Massachusetts* (Philadelphia: Hopkins, 1874), since I have been unable to locate contemporary photographs or detailed descriptions. The street was demolished after the Second World War as part of an urban renewal project. Although the 1870 manuscript U.S. Census returns for Brookline do not include street addresses, comparison with the addresses given in *The Brookline, Jamaica Plain and West Roxbury Directory for 1871* (Boston: Dean, Dudley, 1871) allowed me to identify likely Pearl Place residents.

10. U.S. Census, 1870, Population Schedules, Brookline, 82; marriage record, John O'Hare and Mary Lavery, Boston, March 3, 1851; birth record, Patrick O'Hare, Brookline, February 8, 1855; birth record, Mary O'Hare, Brookline, December 11, 1861; death record, Catherine Lavery, Brookline, July 26, 1871, all in *Massachusetts: Vital Records, 1841–1910* (Boston: New England Historic Genealogical Society, 2004), www.americanancestors.org.

11. Lawrence, *Memories of a Happy Life*, 5; *BC*, June 23, 1877.

12. Death record, Mary O'Hare, Brookline, August 22, 1882; death record, John O'Hare, Brookline, October 3, 1884, both in *Massachusetts: Vital Records;* U.S. Census, 1900, Population Schedules, Brookline.

13. E. J. Hobsbawm, *The Age of Capital, 1848–1875* (New York: Scribner, 1975), 2.

14. Jane G. Carter and Susie P. Holmes, *Genealogical Record of the Dedham Branch of the Avery Family in America* (Plymouth, Mass.: Avery and Doten, 1893), 62–74; Laura Wasowicz, "The Quest for Home: The Early Married Life of Caroline and Frank White, 1851–1859," 1992, 12–20, American Antiquarian Society, Worcester.

15. U.S. Census, 1850, Manufactures Schedule, Roxbury, Massachusetts, microfilm T1204, roll 8; Carter and Holmes, *Genealogical Record*, 62–74; Wasowicz, "Quest for Home," 12–20.

16. WD, January 10, 1863.

17. WD, *passim;* U.S. Census, 1860, Manufactures Schedule, Roxbury, Massachusetts, microfilm T1204, roll 15. The tannery is shown on the *Combined Atlas of the County of Suffolk, Massachusetts*, vol. 2, *Roxbury* (Philadelphia: Hopkins, 1873), plate L. On the development of the American tanning industry, see Peter C. Welsh, *Tanning in the United States to 1850: A Brief History* (Washington, D.C.: Museum of History and Technology, Smithsonian Institution, 1964), and Charles H. McDermott, *A History of the Shoe and Leather Industries of the United States* (Boston: Denehy, 1920), 1:33–49. On the tanning process, see Charles Thomas Davis, *The Manufacture of Leather* (Philadelphia: Baird, 1897).

18. U.S. Census, 1860, Manufactures Schedule, Roxbury, Massachusetts, microfilm T1204, roll 15. In 1850 the two predecessor firms produced $2,800 per each worker (and paid $468 in wages). By 1860 each Guild, White worker produced $4,286 and was paid an average of $343. Whether this apparent productivity gain resulted from the introduction of new machinery, more effective management, or simply rising leather prices is difficult to say.

19. Although the title of the *land* from Perkins to Waldo Maynard in 1851, to William Dwight, Jr., in 1856, to Nathaniel Goddard in 1857, to White in 1858 is not in dispute, it is not clear which of the owners built the house. Both Leslie Larkin and Carla Benka, "'Cliffside': 222 Warren Street, Brookline," form B-Building, May 1983, Massachusetts Historical Commission, Boston, and Morgan, Cushing, and Reed, *CBD*, 216, suggest the house was reconstructed by Nathanial Goddard when he owned it in 1857–58. But Caroline White wrote in her diary, "We had a call from Mr. Samuel Gardner Perkins & his little clan this P.M. Mr. P. built this house, & was once the owner of the whole estate formerly." Also, the Whites had seen the house the previous spring *before* Goddard purchased it, and Caroline gives no indication it had changed significantly. WD, August 24, 1858.

20. Federal Reserve Bank of St. Louis, "Median Sales Price for New Houses Sold in the United States," https://research.stlouisfed.org/fred2/series/MSPNHSUS.

21. Technically, they only put down $6,000 in cash and assumed a $12,000 mortgage on the balance due, but Francis White discharged this mortgage shortly afterward. ND, 582:fol. 273; 619:fol. 58.

22. Wasowicz, "Quest for Home," 38, suggests that some of the purchase money may have come from Frank White's brothers.

23. Andrew Jackson Downing, *A Treatise on the Theory and Practice of Landscape Gardening* (New York: Putnam, 1850), 56.

24. This is based on numerous WD entries, 1858–65.

25. WD, March 15, April 3, 1871; *Incomes of the Citizens of Boston and Other Cities and Towns in Massachusetts* (Boston: Williams, 1866), 21. On changes in the leather industry following the Civil War, see McDermott, *Shoe and Leather Industries*, 1:158–70.

26. U.S. Census, 1870, Population Schedules, Brookline; Carter and Holmes, *Avery Family*, 74; Morgan, Cushing, and Reed, *CBD*, 216–17.

27. Obituary of Theophilus Parsons Chandler, *BC*, December 25, 1886; W. Woodford Clayton, *History of Cumberland County, Maine* (Philadelphia: Everts and Peck, 1880), 326–27, 337; Mary Chandler Lowell, *Chandler-Parsons; Edmund Chaundeler, Geoffrey Parsons and Allied Families* (Boston: Marvin and Sons, 1911); David Jaffee, *A New Nation of Goods: The Material Culture of Early America* (Philadelphia: University of Pennsylvania Press, 2010), 47–146.

28. Obituary of Theophilus Parsons Chandler; Lowell, *Chandler-Parsons;* John H. Campbell, *History of the Friendly Sons of St. Patrick and of the Hibernian Society for the Relief*

of Emigrants from Ireland March 17, 1771–March 17, 1892 (Philadelphia: Hibernian Society, 1892), 516–17.

29. *Stimpson's Boston Directory, 1845* (Boston: Stimpson, 1845); *The Boston Directory, 1848–9* (Boston: George Adams, 1848).

30. ND, 179:fol. 222, 223; *PBHS,* 1905, 12. Here I have assumed that the "new modern built elegant House" mentioned in Craft's ad in the *Boston Atlas,* May 15, 1844, is this house, which is not shown on the subdivision plan drawn up the previous fall.

31. U.S. Census, 1850, Population Schedules, Brookline; ND, 217:fol. 160; Charles H. Stearns, "President's Annual Address," *PBHS,* 1905, 12; *Atlas of the Town of Brookline,* plate E; *Tax List of the Town of Brookline for the Year 1870* (Boston: Farwell, 1871) 11.

32. Lowell, *Chandler-Parsons,* 42–43.

33. *Boston Directory, 1885* (Boston: Simson, Murdock, 1885); David Hackett Fischer, *Growing Old in America* (New York: Oxford University Press, 1977), 43–46, 142–43.

34. For alternative definitions of the American bourgeoisie, contrast Fishman, *Utopias,* 12, with Sven Beckert, *The Monied Metropolis: New York City and the Consolidation of the American Bourgeoisie, 1850–1896* (Cambridge: Cambridge University Press, 2001), 6–8.

35. On the use of resident domestic servants as a marker for the upper middle class, see Michael B. Katz, *The People of Hamilton, Canada West: Family and Class in a Mid-Nineteenth Century City* (Cambridge, Mass.: Harvard University Press, 1975), 27, 77, 141, 158–59, and E. J. Hobsbawm, *The Pelican Economic History of Britain,* vol. 3, *Industry and Empire from 1750 to the Present Day* (Baltimore: Penguin, 1969), 157. "Employing a servant also represented the attainment of middle-class status in a community, not just for the woman of the house but for the man as well. . . . Middle-class lifestyle required servants." David M. Katzman, *Seven Days a Week: Women and Domestic Service in Industrializing America* (New York: Oxford University Press, 1978), 149.

36. John Archer, *Architecture and Suburbia: From English Villa to American Dream House, 1690–2000* (Minneapolis: University of Minnesota Press, 2005), 126–42, 185–209.

37. Clifford Edward Clark, *The American Family Home, 1800–1960* (Chapel Hill: University of North Carolina Press, 1986), 42–50, 167–68; William Seale, *American Interiors through the Camera's Eye, 1860–1917* (New York: Praeger, 1975); WD, September 17, 19, December 15, 1858; November 16, 1859; January 10, 1861; January 4–8, 1863; Briann Greenfield, *Out of the Attic: Inventing Antiques in Twentieth-Century New England* (Amherst: University of Massachusetts Press, 2009).

38. Massachusetts State Census, 1865, Population Schedules, Brookline, Familysearch .org. Theophilus Chandler was living in Newton in 1870.

39. When Elizabeth Mason Cabot inherited a share in her father's estate worth $600,000 in 1867, her brother advised her "she could safely spend $14,000 during 1868. She thought this an underestimate, and he relaxed the limit to $18,000. More importantly, he pointed out that later, when formalities and legal fees would have come to an end, she

would have $30,000 or even $40,000 a year." Elizabeth Rogers Mason Cabot, *More Than Common Powers of Perception: The Diary of Elizabeth Rogers Mason Cabot*, ed. P. A. M. Taylor (Boston: Beacon Press, 1991), 8.

40. Computed from Brookline, *Tax List of the Town of Brookline for the Year 1870*. Also included were the holdings of the Sears family, technically nonresidents. On the Boston upper class, see Dalzell, *Enterprising Elite*; Cleveland Amory, *The Proper Bostonians* (New York: Dutton, 1947); Farrell, *Elite Families*; and Frederick Cople Jaher, *The Urban Establishment: Upper Strata in Boston, New York, Charleston, Chicago, and Los Angeles* (Urbana: University of Illinois Press, 1982).

41. The development of a distinctive upper class is discussed below.

42. *BT*, November 26, December 17, 24, 1870; January 21, February 11, October 28, 1871; April 27, December 14, 1872; January 4, 1873; *BC*, December 25, 1875; January 29, February 19, July 15, 1876.

43. *BC*, July 21, 1900; *BT*, November 15, 23, 1872. For examples of some Brookline-owned businesses that failed during the 1870s depression, see *BC*, October 6, 1876; August 11, 1877; August 7, 1878.

44. Occupations were obtained by matching individuals listed in *Incomes of the Citizens of Boston*, 19–21, with the 1870 U.S. Census population schedules and *The Brookline, Jamaica Plain and West Roxbury Directory for 1871* (Boston: Dean Dudley, 1871).

45. In 1870, 93 percent of Brookline's household servants were women. Employing one of Brookline's sixty-one live-in male servants—mostly coachmen or gardeners—was largely restricted to the truly wealthy. Only fifty-three households (4 percent) enjoyed this perk.

46. Most of the white-collar workers who headed Brookline households kept live-in servants, as did 13 percent of those deemed skilled workers. Although their occupational titles—bank teller, carpenter, jeweler, and the like—may have suggested lower-middle-class status, the presence of servants and often substantial real-estate and personal property holdings indicated their standing as corporate managers, successful contractors, and thriving Boston businessmen. There were twenty-one Irish-headed households in 1870 with resident domestic servants, though doubtless many of these were boarders who worked elsewhere.

47. *Incomes of the Citizens of Boston*, 19–21. The first $600 of income were exempt from the tax in 1866. Brookline physicians typically charged $2.00 a visit in 1879. *BC*, January 25, 1879. In 1878 the typical Brookline lawyer was said to earn $5,000 a year. *BC*, April 13, 1878.

48. For a classic Marxist definition of social class structure, see T. B. Bottomore, *Classes in Modern Society* (New York: Vintage, 1968). Sven Beckert also draws a distinction between professionals and mercantile-manufacturers and finds them distinct from the bourgeoisie proper until the 1880s. Beckert, *Monied Metropolis*, 7–8, 253–60.

49. Dennis L. Gilbert, *The American Class Structure in an Age of Growing Inequality* (Los Angeles: Pine Forge Press, 2008); Leonard Beeghley, *The Structure of Social Stratification in the United States* (Boston: Allyn and Bacon, 2000).

50. Gilbert, *American Class Structure,* 20–30.

51. Of the 370 servant-keeping household male heads on the 1870 census, 230 could be linked to a Boston business address in the *Brookline Directory for 1871* or *Boston Directory 1871* (Boston: Sampson, Davenport, 1871).

52. Here I have omitted from the calculations one New England–born "carpenter" who reported assets of $206,000. Including him jumps mean Yankee-born holdings to $8,365.

53. *BT,* May 6, 1871; *BC,* June 26, 1875; February 12, April 15, July 15, 1876; March 13, April 24, 1880; Kevin Kenny, *The American Irish* (Harlow, Essex, U.K.: Longman, 2000), 61–64, 109–10; Stephan Thernstrom, *Poverty and Progress: Social Mobility in a Nineteenth Century City* (New York: Atheneum, 1970), 15–32.

54. Kenny, *American Irish,* 111, 145–47.

55. *BTR,* 2:125–26; *BT,* December 24, 1870; April 22, 1871; *BC,* February 12, July 29, 1876.

56. *The Story of St. Mary of the Assumption Parish and the History of Catholic America* (Hackensack, N.J.: Custombook, 1977), 4–9.

57. Kenny, *American Irish,* 71–80, 76 (quotation).

58. I compiled a database of Brookline selectmen, 1845–55, and used census, biographical, and genealogical sources to identify their occupations, origins, and the number of resident servants listed.

59. Warner, *Streetcar Suburbs,* 53.

60. The organizations were compiled from those mentioned in *BT,* 1870–71, and in *BC,* 1887, On Brookline churches, see Charles Knowles Bolton, *Brookline: The History of a Favored Town* (Brookline, Mass.: Spencer, 1897), 130–57, and Kingman, "Brookline," 2:820–25.

4. Building Blocks

1. Nathaniel S. Keith, *Politics and the Housing Crisis since 1930* (New York: Universe Books, 1973), 17–19; Roy Lubove, *Community Planning in the 1920s: The Contribution of the Regional Planning Association of America* (Pittsburgh: University of Pittsburgh Press, 1963), 17–22.

2. Ronald Dale Karr, "Suburban Land Development in Antebellum Boston," *Journal of Urban History* 41 (2015): 862–80.

3. *Boston Evening Transcript,* May 22, 1843. An announcement also appeared in the *Boston Post,* May 22, 1843. For a plan of Linden Place, see ND, 141:fol. 105.

4. *An Almanac and Business Directory of the Citizens of Cambridge, Charlestown, and Roxbury, and the Towns of Chelsea, Dorchester, and Brookline* (Boston: George Adams, 1848), 129; ND, 142:fols. 31–34, 47, 172; 143:fol. 64; 147:fol. 307; 149:fol. 92; 150:fol. 70; 163:fol. 312; Woods, *Sketches,* 63–65; Brookline, *List of Taxes Assessed in the Town of Brookline . . . for the Years 1851, 1852, 1853* (Boston: Wilson, 1854); *The Brookline, Jamaica Plain and West Roxbury Directory for 1871* (Boston: Dean Dudley, 1871).

5. Clifford Edward Clark, Jr., *The American Family Home, 1800–1960* (Chapel Hill: University of North Carolina Press, 1986), 3–71; Gwendolyn Wright, *Building the Dream: A Social History of Housing in America* (New York: Pantheon, 1981), 73–113.

6. ND, plan 13:593.

7. *Boston Atlas,* May 15, 1844; ND, 147:fols. 226–33; 148:fol. 261; 149:fols. 24–26; 150:fol. 288; 151:fol. 204; 154:fol. 109; 157:fol. 205.

8. *BC,* January 24, 1880. In 1870 nonresidents accounted for only 15 percent of the assessed value of Brookline real estate; trustees, estates, land companies, and other non-individual owners made up another 11 percent, but some of these were undoubtedly locally controlled. Computed from *Tax List of the Town of Brookline for the Year 1870* (Boston: Farwell, 1871).

9. Computed from *Tax List of the Town of Brookline for the Year 1870.* Contemporaries were fully aware of this practice and generally approved. See *BT,* January 20, 1872.

10. *BT,* March 2, 1872; May 17, 1873; *BC,* May 9, 1874 (quotation).

11. ND, 281:fol. 146; 285:fol. 5; *BC,* March 12, 1881. Land companies had already appeared in neighboring Newton in the late 1840s. James C. O'Connell, *The Hub's Metropolis: Greater Boston's Development from Railroad Suburbs to Smart Growth* (Cambridge, Mass.: MIT Press, 2013), 44–46.

12. Anne Wardwell, "'Longwood' and 'Cottage Farm' in Brookline," in *Victorian Boston Today: Ten Walking Tours,* ed. Pauline Chase Harrell and Margaret Suplee Smith (Boston: Victorian Society in America, 1975), 56–58; Cynthia Zaitzevsky, "Frederick Law Olmsted in Brookline: A Preliminary Study of His Public Projects," *PBHS,* 1975–78, 46.

13. Wardwell, "'Longwood,'" 58–79; Zaitzevsky, "Frederick Law Olmsted in Brookline," 46; Brookline Assessors, "Atlas of Brookline, 1872," Public Library of Brookline; *Atlas of the Town of Brookline* (Philadelphia: Hopkins, 1874); *Atlas of the Town of Brookline, Massachusetts* (Philadelphia: Hopkins, 1884); Herbert L. Fletcher, *A History of the Church of Our Saviour, Protestant Episcopal, in Longwood, Mass., from Its Founding of 1868 to 1936* (Brookline: Church of Our Saviour, 1936), 5–8.

14. Jackson, *Frontier,* 73–76; Keith Thomas, *Man and the Natural World: Changing Attitudes in England, 1500–1800* (New York: Oxford University Press, 1983), 221, 261–63; David Schuyler, *The New Urban Landscape: The Redefinition of City Form in Nineteenth-Century America* (Baltimore: Johns Hopkins University Press, 1986), 22–23, 37–56.

15. Morgan, Cushing, and Reed, *CBD,* 13–14; *Atlas of Brookline,* 1874, plate J. For the lot sales, see ND, 188:fol. 247ff.

16. Karr, "Suburban Land Development," 873–74.

17. Woods, *Sketches,* 198; *BT,* December 24, 1870; April 22, 1871; *BC,* February 12, 1876; May 16, 1891; Curtis, *Brookline,* 265; ND, 211:fol. 69; 213:fol. 278.

18. Zaitzevsky, "Olmsted in Brookline," 48–52; ND, 354:fols. 81, 83; 390:fol. 171; 392:fol. 162; 517:fols. 281, 311; *BC,* August 10, 1878; March 6, 20, August 7, 28, November 27, 1880;

April 23, August 6, 1881; January 14, February 4, April 8, 1882; December 1, 1883; January 5, 1884; *Atlas of Brookline*, 1874; *Atlas of Brookline*, 1884; Morgan, Cushing, and Reed, *CBD*, 150–51.

19. "Catalog of 76 Lots of Land," Brookline Historical Society Papers, Public Library of Brookline; *BI*, July 4, 1873; *Atlas of Brookline*, 1884; *Atlas of the Town of Brookline* (Philadelphia: Bromley, 1888). Most of what was to be Goddard Heights is now part of Larz Anderson Park and remains unbuilt.

20. For a good example of an 1884 five-lot commuter subdivision, see ND, plan D0549:604 (corner of Harvard and Babcock Streets); for a twenty-one-lot subdivision in Irish Whiskey Point, see ND, plan 9:395 (Sewall Place).

21. The actual patterns of streets, lots, and house placement can be seen in the various atlases of Brookline already cited.

22. Ann Durkin Keating, *Building Chicago: Suburban Developers and the Creation of a Divided Metropolis* (Columbus: Ohio State University Press, 1988); Warner, *Streetcar Suburbs*, 117–52.

23. Sarah Zimmerman and Carla Wyman Benka, "Historic Resources of the Town of Brookline, Massachusetts (Partial Inventory: Historical and Architectural Resources, 1632–1930)," National Register of Historic Places Inventory—Nomination Form, 1985, Massachusetts Historical Commission, Boston; Brookline Historical Commission, *Brookline Village Walking Tours*, 2nd ed. (Brookline: Brookline Historical Commission, 1981); Warner, *Streetcar Suburbs*, 141–52; Douglas Shand-Tucci, *Built in Boston: City and Suburb, 1800–2000* (Amherst: University of Massachusetts Press, 1999), 46–100.

24. Warner, *Streetcar Suburbs*, 92–101.

25. ND, 142:fols. 31–34. Similar language was included in the deeds to lots in the Harvard Place subdivision; see, for example, ND, 179:fol. 122.

26. Wardwell, "Longwood," 63. In looking at hundreds of Brookline deeds between 1840 and 1900, this is the only example I know of deed restrictions aimed at an ethnic or religious group.

27. ND, 372:fol. 122; 374:fol. 150; 376:fol. 150; 535:fol. 124; 541:fol. 61; 583:fol. 255; "Catalog of 76 Lots"; *BI*, July 4, 1873. In Dorchester, Roxbury, and West Roxbury, restricted covenants did not come into general use until later, at the end of the century. Warner, *Streetcar Suburbs*, 122. For the history of restrictive covenants, see Robert M. Fogelson, *Bourgeois Nightmares: Suburbia, 1870–1930* (New Haven, Conn.: Yale University Press, 2005).

28. *BC*, March 20, 1875.

29. Curtis, *Brookline*, 213, 230–37, 284–89, 292–93; Charles Knowles Bolton, *Brookline: The History of a Favored Town* (Brookline, Mass.: Spencer, 1897), 158–59; *BSC*, 1872, 7–10; *BC*, April 17, 1875; Desmond Fitzgerald, *Brookline Playgrounds* (Brookline, Mass.: Merrymount Press, 1907), 1–7.

30. Michael Rawson, *Eden on the Charles: The Making of Boston* (Cambridge, Mass.:

Harvard University Press, 2010), 75–128; Curtis, *Brookline*, 235–37; *BT*, November 26, 1870; April 12, 1872; January 17, March 22, 29, 1873; *BI*, October 25, November 22, 29, 1873; *BC*, May 9, June 6, 27, 1874; July 3, 10, September 11, 1875; October 11, November 8, 1879; July 10, 1880; August 20, 1892; December 29, 1900.

31. Curtis, *Brookline*, 238, 289–90; *BT*, July 13, 1872; *BC*, March 6, 1875; January 15, 29, July 29, October 21, December 16, 1876; January 27, March 3, July 28, 1877; August 23, 1879; November 13, 1880; September 17, 1881. On popular beliefs and the origins of the urban sanitation movement, see Peterson, *Birth of City Planning*, 30–39.

32. *BSC*, 1847, 6; 1880, 4; *BC*, April 17, 1875.

33. *BSC*, 1846, 8–9; 1847, 5–7; 1853–54, 10; 1854–55, 3–4; 1855–56, 3–4; 1872, 7–10; 1873, 6, 11–14, 37–38; 1874, 17–23; 1875, 5. On education in nineteenth-century Massachusetts, see Carl F. Kaestle and Maris A. Vinovskis, *Education and Social Change in Nineteenth-Century Massachusetts* (New York: Cambridge University Press, 1980).

34. *BSC*, 1849, 14.

5. The New Landscape of Suburban Politics

1. Brookline, *Muddy River and Brookline Records* (Boston: Farwell, 1875), 630; *BTR*, 1:323.

2. Michael Rawson, *Eden on the Charles: The Making of Boston* (Cambridge, Mass.: Harvard University Press, 2010), 136–43.

3. In 1870 Brookline's tax rate per $1,000 was $7.55, compared to $15.30 in Boston. *Tax List of the Town of Brookline for the Year 1870* (Boston: Farwell, 1871), cover; Charles Phillips Huse, *The Financial History of Boston, from May 1, 1822, to January 1, 1909* (Cambridge, Mass.: Harvard University Press, 1916), 146. In 1875 Brookline spent nearly three times the state average per pupil on education. *BC*, April 17, 1875; *BTR*, 1:22; 3:436.

4. On naturalization, see Oscar Handlin, *Boston's Immigrants, 1790–1880: A Study in Acculturation* (Cambridge, Mass.: Harvard University Press, 1991), 191–92.

5. *BT*, March 15, April 19, 26, 1873.

6. This analysis is based on accounts of Brookline politics in *BT*, 1870–73; *BI*, 1873; and *BC*, 1874–85.

7. John W. Candler, *BT*, March 15, 1873.

8. Henry M. Whitney to William C. Whitney, April 21, 1875, William C. Whitney Papers, Library of Congress, Washington, D.C.

9. Rawson, *Eden on the Charles*, 135–62.

10. *BT*, December 16, 1871; January 6, 12, 1872; March 15, 22, April 19, May 3, 1873.

11. *BT*, January 27, 1872.

12. *BT*, March 15, 1873.

13. *BI*, July 25, 1873.

14. *BI,* August 9, 1873.

15. *BI,* October 4, 18, 1873.

16. *BT,* March 22, 1873.

17. *BT,* January 13, 1872; April 26, 1873.

18. *BT,* March 22, 1873.

19. Rawson, *Eden on the Charles,* 149–62; Warner, *Streetcar Suburbs,* 164; James Everett Clark, "The Impact of Transportation Technology on Suburbanization in the Chicago Area, 1830–1920" (Ph.D. diss., Northwestern University, 1977), 118–21, 137–38.

20. Brookline Assessors, "Atlas of the Town of Brookline, 1872," Public Library of Brookline; *Atlas of the Town of Brookline, Massachusetts* (Philadelphia: Hopkins, 1874).

21. *BC,* December 6, 1879; January 17, 1880; December 3, 1883.

22. *BI,* October 11, 1873.

23. *BI,* March 6, 27, November 6, 1875; February 22, October 25, 1879; January 31, March 13, 27, 1880.

24. Rawson, *Eden on the Charles,* 176–78; Warner, *Streetcar Suburbs,* 163–64.

25. *BT,* March 16, June 22, 1872; *BC,* December 25, 1875; January 1, 1876 (quotation); September 20, 1879; Kevin Kenny, *The American Irish* (Harlow, Essex, U.K.: Longman, 2000), 112–15, 145–49, 158.

26. *BT,* October 29, 1870; July 15, 1871; October 26, 1872; *BI,* November 29, 1873; *BC,* May 13, 20, July 29, 1876; July 28, 1877.

27. *BC,* November 16, 1878.

28. *BC,* July 4, November 28, December 4, 1874; August 7, December 4, 1875; December 23, 1876; February 3, October 13, 1877; January 19, 1878; April 12, 1879; March 20, 1880. Although Margret Driscoll was the first Irish woman on that board, she was not the first Catholic; back in 1873 the Industrial Union had among its directors Mrs. Amelia R. Finotti, the wife of the Italian consul, G. M. Finotti, and the sister-in-law to the then-pastor of St. Mary's. *BT,* April 12, 1873.

29. *BSC,* 1846, 11; 1848, 15; 1853–54, 9–10; 1880, 7.

30. *BSC,* 1849, 4–5, 9; 1850, 8.

31. *BSC,* 1850, 17; 1851, 7; 1852–53, 4–5, 7–8; 1853–54, 6; 1854–55, 3–5; 1855–56, 8–9; 1863–64, 6–7; 1870–71, 11.

32. Calculated from statistics in *BSC,* 1856–57, 1860–61.

33. *BSC,* 1875, 5–6; 1859–60, 5–6; 1869–70, 9–10, 12; 1848, 14; 1849, 11–12; 1852–53, 3–4.

34. *BSC,* 1872, 38–39; 1870–71, 10–12; 1873, 36–37. The report for 1874 does not mention it.

35. *BSC,* 1877, 8; 1876, 10; 1880, 4; John H. Drum, "A History of the First Hundred Years of St. Mary's of the Assumption," *PBHS,* 1952, 29–30. Thanks in part to new state laws, the 1870s and 1880s saw statewide reduction in truancy. Marvin Lazerson, *Origins of the Urban School: Public Education in Massachusetts, 1870–1915* (Cambridge, Mass.: Harvard University Press, 1971), 16.

36. Few Irish names appear on the lists of Brookline High School graduates. *BC*, July 1, 1882; June 30, 1883. On the question of the public schools and social control in Massachusetts, see Michael B. Katz, *The Irony of Early School Reform: Educational Innovation in Mid-Nineteenth Century Massachusetts* (Boston: Beacon Press, 1970), 24–50, 129–31, and Lazerson, *Urban School*, 1–35.

37. Faye E. Dudden, *Serving Women: Household Service in Nineteenth-Century America* (Middletown, Conn.: Wesleyan University Press, 1983); David M. Katzman, *Seven Days a Week: Women and Domestic Service in Industrializing America* (New York: Oxford University Press, 1978); Daniel E. Sutherland, *Americans and Their Servants: Domestic Service in the United States from 1800 to 1920* (Baton Rouge: Louisiana State University Press, 1981).

38. *The Census of Massachusetts, 1875*, vol. 1, *Population and Social Statistics* (Boston: Wright, 1876). Boston, Cambridge, Worcester, Salem, Springfield, Newton, Lowell, New Bedford, Brookline, Lynn, Somerville, and Chelsea accounted for 25,716 of the state's 42,942 female domestics (59.9%), although they only contained 39.4% of the state's families. Throughout the United States, servants disproportionately lived in urbanized areas. Katzman, *Seven Days*, 59; Sutherland, *Americans and Their Servants*, 46.

39. Kenny, *American Irish*, 62–63, 110–11, 151–54.

40. The 1870 U.S. Census indicates if a person's parents were foreign born but does not list where. I counted a woman as Celtic if she were born in Ireland or if she was foreign-born with a Celtic (Irish or Scottish) surname. (This undoubtedly underestimates the actual number.) The census that year did not record marital status, but as late as 1900 American white female domestics were overwhelmingly single. Katzman, *Seven Days*, 87.

41. "Domestics were the largest single occupational group among the depositors in antebellum savings banks. . . . It was this ability to accumulate cash that recommended service to dutiful immigrant daughters who wanted to send remittances home." Dudden, *Serving Women*, 222.

42. WD, October 4, 1865.

43. Elizabeth Rogers Mason Cabot, *More Than Common Powers of Perception: The Diary of Elizabeth Rogers Mason Cabot*, ed. P. A. M. Taylor (Boston: Beacon Press, 1991), 268.

44. WD, November 20, 1860. For other examples of Caroline White's dismissing unsatisfactory domestics, see entries for September 23, 1857; April 10, 1858; November 19, 1860.

45. WD, October 26, 1865. See also entries for April 10, 13, May 8, 1858; June 19, 1859; March 30, April 2, June 4, July 2, 1860; August 30, October 16, 1861.

46. Carol Lasser, "The Domestic Balance of Power: Relations between Mistress and Maid in Nineteenth-Century New England," *Labor History* 87 (1987): 5–22; Dudden, *Serving Women*, 44–71, 155–83; Katzman, *Seven Days*, 146–83; Sutherland, *Americans and Their Servants*, 26–30.

47. WD, January 10, 1862; Dudden, *Serving Women*, 155–83.

48. For example, see WD, April 20, May 21, June 8, 1859; April 19–21, 1860; January 10, 1862. Faye Dudden's claim that "Mrs. White did not share the work with her servants" seems overstated. Dudden, *Serving Women,* 56.

49. WD, April 10, 1858; November 19, 1860; October 21, 1861.

50. "I had never appeared to be even so intelligent as I really was. This all colored people at the south, free and slaves, find it peculiarly necessary for their own comfort and safety to observe." Ex-slave Lunsford Lane, 1848, as quoted in Gilbert Osofsky, *Puttin' on Ole Massa: The Slave Narratives of Henry Bibb, William Wells Brown, and Solomon Northrop* (New York: Harper and Row, 1969), 9.

51. Dudden, *Serving Women,* 143, 198; Sutherland, *Americans and Their Servants,* 91–94.

52. Dudden, *Serving Women,* 58–59.

53. Clifford Edward Clark, *The American Family Home, 1800–1960* (Chapel Hill: University of North Carolina Press, 1986), 42, 167.

54. Dudden, *Serving Women,* 150.

55. Kenny, *American Irish,* 119; Curtis, *Brookline,* 258–59.

56. John Pierce, *An Address at the Opening of the Town Hall in Brookline on Tuesday 14 October 1845* (Boston: White and Potter, 1846), 28–29; John Pierce, "Memoirs," May 2, 1833, 6:16, Massachusetts Historical Society, Boston.

57. Michael H. Ebner, *Creating Chicago's North Shore: A Suburban History* (Chicago: University of Chicago Press, 1988), 94–95.

58. Curtis, *Brookline,* 246–47; *BC,* November 18, 1874; October 30, 1875; July 22, September 9, 1876; July 7, December 22, 1877; January 5, February 16, April 6, 13, May 4, 11, 1878; May 22, 1880; May 20, 1882; December 13, 1884; April 4, August 8, 1885; Martin Kingman, "Brookline Village, 1865 to 1902," *Publications of the Brookline Historical Society* 2 (1903): 33.

59. *BC,* February, 16, 23, 1878; June 19, 1880.

60. *BC,* August 8, September 19, October 10, November 7, December 12, 1885.

61. *BC,* December 12, 1885.

6. Suburbia Real and Imagined

1. William Bradford, *Of Plymouth Plantation,* ed. Samuel Eliot Morison (New York: Modern Library, 1967), 62; Keith Thomas, *Man and the Natural World: Changing Attitudes in England, 1500–1800* (New York: Oxford University Press, 1983), 192–200, 243; Michael Rawson, *Eden on the Charles: The Making of Boston* (Cambridge, Mass.: Harvard University Press, 2010), 18–19.

2. Thomas, *Man and the Natural World,* 250–52.

3. Thomas, *Man and the Natural World,* 266–301; John Archer, *Architecture and Suburbia: From English Villa to American Dream House, 1690–2000* (Minneapolis: University

of Minnesota Press, 2005), 52–169; Fishman, *Utopias,* 18–38; Michael Bunce, *The Countryside Ideal: Anglo-American Images of Landscape* (London: Rutledge, 1994), 1–44.

4. Leo Marx, *The Machine in the Garden: Technology and the Pastoral Ideal in America* (New York: Oxford University Press, 1964), 116–44; Rawson, *Eden on the Charles,* 131–33.

5. Warner, *Streetcar Suburbs,* 10–12; Rawson, *Eden on the Charles,* 17–21, 129–36; James S. Duncan and Nancy Duncan, *Landscapes of Privilege: The Politics of the Aesthetic in an American Suburb* (New York: Routledge, 2004), 33–50; Andrew Lees, *Cities Perceived: Urban Society in European and American Thought, 1820–1940* (New York: Columbia University Press, 1985), 6–10, 91–96.

6. Andrew Jackson Downing, *A Treatise on the Theory and Practice of Landscape Gardening* (New York: Putnam, 1850), 53–54, 56; Hayden, *Suburbia,* 26–35.

7. Downing, *Landscape Gardening,* 54.

8. Lees, *Cities Perceived,* 91–104.

9. Stilgoe, *Borderland,* 69–92; Jack Larkin, *Where We Lived: Discovering the Places We Once Called Home: The American Home from 1775 to 1840* (Newtown, Conn.: Taunton Press, 2006), 8–58, 75–82, 97–103.

10. Warner, *Streetcar Suburbs,* 11–14; Thomas Bender, *Toward a New Urban Vision: Ideas and Institutions in Nineteenth-Century America* (Lexington, Ky.: University Press of Kentucky, 1975), 76–78, 85–90; Lees, *Cities Perceived,* 6–10, 91–96.

11. *BT,* January 13, July 13, 1872; May 24, 31, 1873.

12. Woods, *Sketches,* 405; *BC,* August 16, 1879.

13. *BC,* August 23, 1879.

14. *BT,* March 30, 1872.

15. *BC,* May 9, 1874; September 11, 1875; January 15, 1876; *BT,* October 15, 1870; January 11, 1872; *BI,* October 18, 1873.

16. Douglas Shand-Tucci, *Built in Boston: City and Suburb, 1800–2000* (Amherst: University of Massachusetts Press, 1999), 84.

17. Shand-Tucci, *Built in Boston,* 73–199; Warner, *Streetcar Suburbs.*

18. *Atlas of the Town of Brookline* (Philadelphia: Bromley, 1888), plate 2. A well-preserved example of a block from this period is Elm Street (formerly Jones Street) in Brookline Village, built in early 1886 as rental housing.

19. *BT,* October 15, 1870.

20. *BC,* September 11, 1875. For more examples of this sentiment, see *BC,* May 9, 1874; October 9, November 20, 1880; May 14, 1881; May 5, 1883; December 12, 1885.

21. *BT,* February 25, April 29, 1871; January 2, 1875; *BC,* January 1, 1876; Desmond Fitzgerald, *Brookline Playgrounds* (Brookline, Mass.: Merrymount Press, 1907), 1–7.

22. For example, see *BT,* April 12, 1872; March 22, 1873; *BC,* July 18, 1874; December 16, 1876; August 10, 1878; March 8, 1879; October 20, 27, 1883; December 6, 1884; January 3, 1885;

November 13, December 11, 1886. At one point Chandler had Aspinwall arrested for criminal libel.

23. *BT,* March 15, 1873.

24. Ronald Dale Karr, "Evolution of an Elite Suburb: Community Structure and Control in Brookline, Massachusetts, 1770–1900" (Ph.D. diss., Boston University, 1981), 211–14. One long-serving selectman, Horace James, was himself a building contractor.

25. Ronald Dale Karr, "Suburban Land Development in Antebellum Boston," *Journal of Urban History* 41 (2015): 871–72; Becky M. Nicolaides and Andrew Wiese, eds., *The Suburb Reader* (New York: Routledge, 2006), 14–26; Stilgoe, *Borderland,* 165–220.

26. William D. Howells, *Suburban Sketches* (New York: Hurd and Houghton, 1871), 12–14.

27. Howells, *Suburban Sketches,* 14–15.

28. Howells, *Suburban Sketches,* 14, 220–21.

29. Elif S. Armbruster, *Domestic Biographies: Stowe, Howells, James, and Wharton at Home* (New York: Lang, 2011), 56–57; Jackson, *Frontier,* 45–46.

30. Charles M. Sullivan, *Landmark Designation Study Report: William Dean Howells House, 41 Sacramento Street* (Cambridge, Mass.: Cambridge Historical Commission, 2009).

31. Laura Wasowicz, "The Quest for Home: The Early Married Life of Caroline and Frank White, 1851–1859," 1992, 12–20, American Antiquarian Society, Worcester, Mass.

32. WD, May 2, 1857.

33. WD, March 18, 1858; April 24, May 2, 1857; Wasowicz, "Quest for Home," 12–20.

34. Wasowicz, "Quest for Home," 8.

35. WD, June 30, July 19, October 17, 1858; March 22, 1861.

36. WD, January 8, 1856; August 9, 10, 17, October 12, November 13, December 25, 1858; January 10, March 31, 1859; February 2, 11, August 15, 17, 1860; July 26, 1866; October 1, 1870; January 26, April 5, 1871.

37. WD, April 3, May 27, 28, June 28, July 17, August 16, September 26, 1858; January 3, May 4, 9, July 4, 1859; May 18, June 19, July 9, August 26, 1860; June 11, 20, 24, September 28, 1861; June 13, 1864; August 5, 1865; August 9, 1867.

38. WD, July 16, 29, 1865.

39. WD, August 2, 1859; May 23, 1867.

40. Francis A. White to Mary Davis, July 8, 1860, Caroline Barrett White Papers, American Antiquarian Society.

41. WD, August 2, 1859; February 12, 1860; June 1, 1861.

42. WD, April 1, 1865. In this White echoed contemporary bourgeois advice literature of such writers as Lydia Maria Child, Catherine Sedgwick, and Catharine Beecher, authors that Caroline herself had read. Margaret S. Marsh, *Suburban Lives* (New Brunswick, N.J.: Rutgers University Press, 1990), 22–29.

43. WD, February 23, 24, 1864; September 4, 8, 1866; February 15, 1867; April 20, June 30,

September 7, 1868; September 6, 7, 1869; July 1, September 5, 1870; January 31, June 7, 8, 30, September 4, 11, 1871.

44. WD, March 26, April 24, May 21, 1867; November 1, December 7, 1869; February 1, June 30, October 4, December 17, 1870; June 29, 1871.

45. WD, July 22, 1859; October 27, 1861; August 14, 1863; June 4, 5, 1864; February 9, July 6, 1865; July 4, 1866; February 10, 1868; February 19, June 21, 1869; June 14, July 7, 1870.

46. WD, June 5, 1865; January 4, March 23, May 1, July 4, May 9, 1866; September 8, 1867; May 30, June 12, 1869; February 2, April 21, June 14, 1870; April 27, 1871.

47. WD, December 24, 1855; February 21, March 14, 23, May 11, 14, June 28, September 1, December 7, 1859; March 28, August 7, 1860; November 27, 1862; June 1, 1864; December 12, 1866; November 30, 1867; November 16, 1868; March 9, 1869; February 7, 19, 1870.

48. WD, April 16, June 9, 1858.

49. Calculated from entries in WD for 1859.

50. WD, August 12, 1860; Jane C. Nylander, *Our Own Snug Fireside: Images of the New England Home, 1760–1860* (New York: Knopf, 1993), 235–37.

51. Marsh, *Suburban Lives,* 24–25, 49–56.

52. WD, April 16, May 24, 1858; February 4, June 4, August 10, 1859; September 3, 1862.

53. WD, October 11, 1861.

54. WD, September 2, 1858.

55. WD, March 18, May 1, 29, August 9, 1858; January 13, March 23, 28, May 29, September 1, 1859; October 24, 1860; Marsh, *Suburban Lives,* 25–29.

56. WD, July 5, 1858; November 2, 9, 1864; February 3, March 4, 1865; February 20, 24, March 28, 1866; January 15, February 24, 25, 1868; May 14, 1871.

57. WD, February 25, 1856; September 30, 1857; March 9, 20, August 24, 1858; January 14, March 7, 8, 1859; April 25, 1860; January 9, February 4, August 15, 1861; January 10, March 6, 9, 1863; July 28, August 1, November 26, 1866; January 1, November 7, 1867; January 4, April 23, 27, 30, July 10, 22, 1868; January 7, 1869; January 6, 10, April 6, December 12, 23, 1870; January 6, March 15, 1871.

58. WD, August 12, 1861; February 18, October 3, 1862; November 11, 1863; April 4, 23, 1864; February 15, 1865; November 17, 1866; March 9, April 15, 1867; April 22, 29, June 18, October 3, December 11, 15, 21, 1868; May 17, 1870; March 10, April 27, October 20, 1871.

59. "The suburban ideal . . . was largely male-defined, and had at its center a physical space, the residential suburb. Middle-class women embraced urban life in the second third of the nineteenth century. The city, not its periphery, offered them significant opportunities for social interaction, for participation in reform or religious organizations, and for relative freedom from domestic drudgery." Marsh, *Suburban Lives,* xiii–xiv, 14–15, 41–42.

60. Mary Corbin Sies, "Suburban Ideal," in *Encyclopedia of Urban America: The Cities and Suburbs,* ed. Neil L. Shumsky (Santa Barbara, Calif.: ABC-Clio, 1998), 2:754–56; Marsh, *Suburban Lives;* Jackson, *Frontier;* Fishman, *Utopias.*

7. Boulevards and Trolleys

1. *BC*, November 22, 1884.

2. Warner, *Streetcar Suburbs.*

3. Mark D. Hirsch, *William C. Whitney: Modern Warwick* (New York: Dodd, Mead, 1948), 5–8, 10–11, 18; John W. Denehy, *A History of Brookline, Massachusetts, from the First Settlement of Muddy River until the Present Time, 1630–1906* (Brookline, Mass.: Brookline Press, 1906), 127–30; *American National Biography*, s.v. "Whitney, William Collins," "Whitney, Harry Payne."

4. Hirsch, *William C. Whitney*, 28–32; Denehy, *History of Brookline*, 127–30; Sam Bass Warner, Jr., "Residential Development of Roxbury, West Roxbury, and Dorchester, Massachusetts, 1870–1900" (Ph.D. diss., Harvard University, 1959), 69–79; *BT*, December 31, 1871; January 6, 1872; March 15, 1873; *BI*, October 11, 1873.

5. Henry M. Whitney to William C. Whitney, April 21, 1875, William C. Whitney Papers, Library of Congress, Washington, D.C.

6. *BC*, January 31, 1880. See also *BC*, January 24, 1880.

7. *BT*, March 15, 1873.

8. *BC*, December 6, 1879; January 17, 1880; December 8, 1883; July 19, September 13, 1884.

9. Charles W. Cheape, *Moving the Masses: Urban Public Transit in New York, Boston, and Philadelphia, 1880–1912* (Cambridge, Mass.: Harvard University Press, 1980), 113–15; Geoffrey Blodgett, *The Gentle Reformers: Massachusetts Democrats in the Cleveland Era* (Cambridge, Mass.: Harvard University Press, 1966), 12, 58, 85, 89, 109–13.

10. *BC*, August 7, 1886; Morgan, Cushing, and Reed, *CBD*, 140–43.

11. *BC*, August 14, 21, September 4, October 23, 30, December 4, 11, 18, 25, 1886; January 22, 29, February 5, 19, March 19, April 2, 9, May 14, 1887; *Brookline News*, December 18, 1886; February 12, 1887.

12. Warner, *Streetcar Suburbs*, 25–29; *BC*, August 7, December 18, 25, 1886; January 1, March 19, April 30, July 9, 1887; Cheape, *Moving the Masses*, 113–17.

13. Frank Rowsome, Jr., *Trolley Car Treasury* (New York: Bonanza, 1956), 35–94; *BC*, August 7, December 4, 1886; January 1, March 19, September 24, December 10, 1887; April 28, June 2, July 21, August 18, 1888; January 5, 19, 1889; August 4, 1894; Cheape, *Moving the Masses*, 117–19.

14. Massachusetts Bureau of Statistics of Labor, *Census of the Commonwealth of Massachusetts, 1895* (Boston: Wright and Potter, 1896), 1:188; U.S. Census Office, *Twelfth Census of the United States: Population, Part 1* (Washington, D.C.: Government Printing Office, 1901), 620.

15. Compare *Atlas of the Town of Brookline* (Philadelphia: Bromley, 1888) with *Atlas of the Town of Brookline* (Philadelphia: Bromley 1900). For a contemporary survey of the boom, see *BC*, February 7, 1891.

16. Warner, "Residential Development," appendix D. ND, 585:568, contains the articles of association and the names of initial stockholders of the West End Land Company. On the size of the company's holdings, see *BC*, January 15, 1887. For examples of deed restrictions, sales prices, and terms of sales, see ND, 596:151, and *BC*, September 17, 1887; February 2, 1889; January 30, 1892.

17. John Waterman, "Beaconsfield Terraces," *New England Magazine*, new ser., 5 (1892): 625–36; *BC*, September 6, 1890; June 22, 1895. On the prices of Back Bay houses, see Bainbridge Bunting, *Houses of Boston's Back Bay* (Cambridge, Mass.: Harvard University Press, 1967), 368–70.

18. Bunting, *Houses*.

19. For an example, see Monmouth Street and Court (1876). Anne Wardwell, "'Longwood' and 'Cottage Farm' in Brookline," in *Victorian Boston Today: Ten Walking Tours*, ed. Pauline Chase Harrell and Margaret Suplee Smith (Boston: Victorian Society in America, 1975), 61, 64.

20. Douglass Shand-Tucci, *Built in Boston: City and Suburb, 1800–2000* (Amherst: University of Massachusetts Press, 1999), 101–30; Warner, "Residential Development," 72–73, 148; *BC*, September 18, 25, 1897; Gwendolyn Wright, *Building the Dream: A Social History of Housing in America* (New York: Pantheon Books, 1981), 135–51.

21. *BC*, December 27, 1890; January 7, 1899; April 14, 1900.

22. Curtis, *Brookline*, 300.

23. Morgan, Cushing, and Reed, *CBD*, 143–44.

24. Warner, "Residential Development," 54–55, appendix C; *BC*, April 2, 1888; May 25, June 1, 1889; October 10, 17, 24, 31, 1891; Warner, *Streetcar Suburbs*, 132–41.

25. Warner, "Residential Development," appendix C; *BC*, April 29, 1893; February 3, April 7, 28, July 21, September 15, 1894; May 11, 25, September 14, 28, November 2, 23, 1895; June 6, July 25, 1896; October 1, 15, 1898.

26. *Atlas of Brookline*, 1900; Shand-Tucci, *Built in Boston*, 77–108; Warner, *Streetcar Suburbs*, 145, 149–51; Clifford Edward Clark, Jr., *The American Family Home, 1800–1960* (Chapel Hill: University of North Carolina Press, 1986), 72–102; Wright, *Building the Dream*, 96–113. More than a century later, McKay's and Graffam's houses, many converted into two units, typically sold for well over a million dollars.

27. *BC*, September 15, 1894; June 8, 1895.

28. These numbers are derived from a 20-percent systematic sample of each fifth household as listed on the 1900 census manuscript population returns for Brookline.

29. Stilgoe, *Borderland*, 11.

30. Shand-Tucci, *Built in Boston*, 75, 77; Morgan, Cushing, and Reed, *CBD*, 143–44; *BC*, January 7, 1899; April 14, 1900; *Historic Resources of the Town of Brookline: Massachusetts Partial Inventory: Historical and Architectural Resources, 1632–1930*, National Register of

Historic Places, Inventory—Nomination Form, NPS Form 10–900, September 4, 1985, U.S. Department of the Interior, National Park Service, Washington, D.C.

31. These have been calculated from a 20-percent sample of the 1900 U.S. Census returns for Brookline. Brookline Village has been defined as Enumeration Districts 1021 through 1025, the area encompassed by Aspinwall Avenue, School Street, Cypress Street, and the Boston line.

32. Wardwell, "Longwood," 56–69.

33. Morgan, Cushing, and Reed, *CBD*, 151–55.

34. Edwin M. Bacon, *Boston: A Guide Book* (Boston: Ginn, 1903), 109–13.

35. On the expansion of the American urban upper class in the late nineteenth century, see E. Digby Baltzell, *Philadelphia Gentlemen: The Making of a National Upper Class* (Glencoe, Ill.: Free Press, 1958), 21–24, 301–5; C. Wright Mills, *The Power Elite* (New York: Oxford University Press, 1956), 47–70; James McLachlan, *American Boarding Schools: A Historical Study* (New York: Scribner, 1970), 189–96; and G. William Domhoff, *The Higher Circles: The Governing Class in America* (New York: Random House, 1970).

36. Various historical and genealogical sources were used to compile information on the listees, including city directories, the Harvard *Quinquennial Catalogue*, newspaper obituaries, published vital records, town histories, family genealogies, and biographical directories. On the *Social Register*, see Ronald Dale Karr, "Social Register," in *Class in America: An Encyclopedia*, ed. Robert E. Weir (Westport, Conn.: Greenwood, 2007), 3:798–99.

37. I was able to determine the occupations of 80 percent of the listees' fathers and 68 percent of their paternal grandfathers.

38. Computed from Brookline Assessors, "Tax List of the Town of Brookline for the Year 1895," in *Annual Report of the Town Officers of Brookline, Massachusetts* (Brookline, Mass.: Riverdale Press, 1896).

39. "Faulkner Farm," *The Downeast Dilettante*, January 19, 2011, http://thedowneastdilettante.blogspot.com/2011/01/faulkner-farm.html; *Wikipedia*, s.v. "Isabel Weld Perkins."

40. I was able to identify the addresses of all but nine of the Brookline residents listed in the 1898 *Boston Social Register.*

41. Walter Firey, "Sentiment and Symbolism as Ecological Variables," *American Sociological Review* 10, no. 2 (1945): 141.

8. Defining Suburbia

1. John Higham, *Strangers in the Land: Patterns of American Nativism, 1860–1925* (New York: Atheneum, 1972), 52–58; Richard Hofstadter, *The Age of Reform: From Bryan to FDR* (New York: Vintage, 1955), 131–73.

2. *BC,* May 15, 22, 1886. Contrast the earlier more favorable attitude toward immigration just four years earlier; *BC,* March 18, 1882.

3. *BC,* February 25, March 31, May 5, 1888; April 11, 1891.

4. *BC,* March 13, April 24, May 8, 15, 29, June 5, July 10, 1886; January 1, February 19, July 30, 1887; May 9, 1891; February 17, 1894.

5. *BC,* June 5, 1886; April 5, 1890; April 4, 18, May 9, 1891; March 30, May 4, 11, 25, August 17, November 9, 1895; April 4, 1896; March 25, April 1, 1899; March 31, 1900; Martin Kingman, "Brookline Village, 1865 to 1902," *Publications of the Brookline Historical Society* 2 (1903): 33.

6. *BT,* October 7, 1871; March 9, 1872; *BC,* March 17, 24, 1877; March 29, July 5, 1879; February 12, April 2, 1881; March 23, April 27, 1889.

7. *BC,* February 9, July 20, November 9, 1895; James J. Kenneally, "Woman Suffrage and the Massachusetts 'Referendum' of 1895," *Historian* 30 (1968): 617–33.

8. Andrew Lees, *Cities Perceived: Urban Society in European and American Thought, 1820–1940* (New York: Columbia University Press, 1985), 189–255; Michael Holleran, *Boston's "Changeful Times": Origins of Preservation and Planning in America* (Baltimore: Johns Hopkins University Press, 1998), 15–61.

9. Joseph A. Conforti, *Imagining New England: Explorations of Regional Identity from the Pilgrims to the Mid-Twentieth Century* (Chapel Hill: University of North Carolina Press, 2001), 203–62; Alen Axelrod, ed., *The Colonial Revival in America* (New York: Norton, 1985); William B. Rhoads, *The Colonial Revival* (New York: Garland, 1977); Briann G. Greenfield, *Out of the Attic: Inventing Antiques in Twentieth-Century New England* (Amherst: University of Massachusetts Press, 2009), 6–10, 19–25.

10. Massachusetts Bureau of Statistics of Labor, *Census of the Commonwealth of Massachusetts, 1895* (Boston: Wright and Potter, 1896–1900), 6:268, 435, 440–510 *passim*, 546–47, 556–57; *Census of the Commonwealth of Massachusetts, 1905* (Boston: Wright and Potter, 1908–10), 4:58–59, 97–250 *passim*, 266–67, 282–83, 298, 336–456 *passim.*

11. *BC,* August 26, September 16, 1893.

12. *BC,* February 25. 1893.

13. R. G. F. Candage, "Some Brookline Changes," *Brookline Suburban,* May 6, 1899; Edward Wild Baker, "Rufus George Frederick Candage," *New England Historical and Genealogical Register* 67 (1913): 3–6.

14. *BC,* November 26, 1892.

15. *BC,* September 13, 1890; February 28, 1891.

16. *BC,* October 18, 1879; March 12, 1898; B. O. Flower, "Democracy and Municipal Government; or, How the Richest Town in the World Is Governed by the Referendum," *Arena* 32 (1904): 382.

17. Holleran, *Boston's "Changeful Times,"* 42, 262–63.

18. *BC,* April 2, 1881.

19. Peter J. Schmitt, *Back to Nature; The Arcadian Myth in Urban America* (New York: Oxford University Press, 1969), 3–32, 56–65; Marvin Lazerson, *Origins of the Urban School: Public Education in Massachusetts, 1870–1915* (Cambridge, Mass.: Harvard University Press, 1971), 24–30; Geoffrey Blodgett, *The Gentle Reformers: Massachusetts Democrats in the Cleveland Era* (Cambridge, Mass.: Harvard University Press, 1966), 119–20.

20. Morgan, Cushing, and Reed, *CBD,* 19–39; Laura Wood Roper, *FLO: A Biography of Frederick Law Olmsted* (Baltimore: Johns Hopkins University Press, 1973); Thomas Bender, *Toward an Urban Vision: Ideas and Institutions in Nineteenth-Century America* (Lexington: University Press of Kentucky, 1975), 161–87; Geoffrey Blodgett, "Frederick Law Olmsted: Landscape Architecture as Conservative Reform," *Journal of American History* 62 (1976): 869–89.

21. Roper, *FLO,* 321–24; Hayden, *Suburbia,* 61–65.

22. Morgan, Cushing, and Reed, *CBD,* 32–39; Cynthia Zaitzevsky, *Frederick Law Olmsted and the Boston Park System* (Cambridge, Mass.: Harvard University Press, 1982).

23. Morgan, Cushing, and Reed, *CBD,* 35–37; Cynthia Zaitzevsky, "Frederick Law Olmsted in Brookline: A Preliminary Study of His Public Projects," *PBHS,* 1975–78, 42–65.

24. David Schuyler, *The New Urban Landscape: The Redefinition of City Form in Nineteenth-Century America* (Baltimore: Johns Hopkins University Press, 1986).

25. Morgan, Cushing, and Reed, *CBD,* 151–55; Zaitzevsky, "Olmsted in Brookline," 52–54, 56.

26. *Brookline Village Walking Tours* (Brookline, Mass.: Brookline Historical Commission, 1981), 16–28; Morgan, Cushing, and Reed, *CBD,* 68–69, 155–57, 198.

9. Contested Ground

1. Michael Holleran, *Boston's "Changeful Times": Origins of Preservation and Planning in America* (Baltimore: Johns Hopkins University Press, 1998), 84–164; Walter Firey, *Land Use in Central Boston* (Cambridge, Mass.: Harvard University Press, 1947).

2. Alfred P. Chandler, "Brookline: A Study in Town Government," *New England Magazine,* new ser., 8 (1893): 791.

3. *BC,* March 2, 1889.

4. Sam Bass Warner, Jr., *The Private City: Philadelphia in Three Periods of Its Growth* (Philadelphia: University of Pennsylvania Press, 1968), 3–157; Robert J. Kolesar, "The Politics of Development: Worcester, Massachusetts in the Late Nineteenth Century," *Journal of Urban History* 16 (1989): 3–28.

5. *Historic Resources of the Town of Brookline, Massachusetts: Partial Inventory: Historical and Architectural Resources, 1632–1930,* National Register of Historic Places, Inventory—Nomination Form, NPS Form 10–900, September 4, 1985, 38–39, U.S. Department of the Interior, National Park Service, Washington, D.C.

6. *BC*, May 9, 1891.

7. *BC*, November 7, 1874; January 16, 1875; January 1, February 5, 12, 1876; June 12, 1886; September 29, 1888; January 5, October 26, 1889; July 19, December 27, 1890; May 2, 1891; January 9, 1892; May 27, June 3, 17, 24, 1893; ND, 694:900 (plan); 700:202 (plan).

8. *BC*, July 29, August 26, 1893.

9. Elmer Osgood Cappers, *Centennial History of The Country Club* (Brookline, Mass.: The Country Club, 1981), 1–40; David Alan Mittell, *The Country Club: Physical Evolution, 1882–2001* (Brookline, Mass.: N.p., 2001), 15–26; James M. Mayo, *The American Country Club: Its Origins and Development* (Brunswick, N.J.: Rutgers University Press, 1998), 7–66. From the beginning, prospective members of The Country Club had to have "the recommendation of two members, followed by notice to all members requesting opinions as to the applicant's character, and finally . . . approval by the Membership Committee and the Board of Governors." Cappers, *Centennial History*, 129.

10. *BC*, January 30, March 5, May 14, November 19, 1892; March 3, December 1, 1894. In Dorchester, Roxbury, and West Roxbury, ordinary building lots sold for ten to thirty cents a square foot, with prices on fashionable streets reaching sixty to eighty cents. Sam Bass Warner, Jr., "Residential Development of Roxbury, West Roxbury, and Dorchester, Massachusetts, 1870–1900" (Ph.D. diss., Harvard University, 1959), appendix D.

11. *BC*, July 22, August 5, 1893.

12. *BC*, August 26, 1893.

13. *BC*, November 18, 1893. For what it is worth, current GIS maps of flood hazards, wetlands, and other environmental concerns do not indicate any problems with drainage in this section of Brookline. "MassGIS Online Mapping," Commonwealth of Massachusetts, http://www.mass.gov/anf/research-and-tech/it-serv-and-support/application-serv/office-of-geographic-information-massgis/online-mapping/.

14. *BC*, February 3, July 7, 1894; June 29, July 27, 1895.

15. *BC*, May 15, 1897; *Brookline Suburban*, February 15, 1900; *Atlas of the Town of Brookline* (Philadelphia: Bromley, 1900); Morgan, Cushing, and Reed, *CBD*, 146–47. In one 1911 transaction heiress Isabel Anderson, wife of diplomat Larz Anderson, whose palatial estate lay close at hand, purchased six of McCormack's vacant lots, which she retained until 1947. ND, 1181:177; 2680:586.

16. *BC*, July 18, 1891; May 25, 1895; *Atlas of the Town of Brookline*, 1900.

17. *BC*, January 16, March 12, April 23, 30, May 7, 14, 1892; Morgan, Cushing, and Reed, *CBD*, 147–48; Cynthia Zaitzevsky, "Frederick Law Olmsted in Brookline: A Preliminary Study of His Public Projects," *PBHS*, 1975–78, 60.

18. Zaitzevsky, "Olmsted in Brookline," 53–60; Morgan, Cushing, and Reed, *CBD*, 147, 151–55.

19. On Chandler, see Conrad Reno, *Memoirs of the Judiciary and Bar of New England for the Nineteenth Century* (Boston: Century Memorial 1901), 2:276–78, and *Harvard*

College Class of 1868 Fortieth Anniversary Secretary's Report No. 8 (Boston: Cockayne, 1909), 30–34.

20. *BC,* April 15, 22, 1893.

21. John T. Morse, Jr., *Memoir of Colonel Henry Lee, with Selections from His Writings and Speeches* (Boston: Little, Brown, 1905), 3–20, 91–150.

22. Morse, *Henry Lee,* 190–92. The deed conveyed the 5.35 acre property to the senior Lee alone, at a price of $22,026.90. ND, 193:fol. 112.

23. Morse, *Henry Lee,* 180–90; Holleran, *Boston's "Changeful Times,"* 94–109, 115–22.

24. Morse, *Henry Lee,* 196; *BC,* May 21, 28, June 4, 11, November 17, December 3, 1892; April 15, 22, 1893.

25. *BC,* May 28, 1892.

26. Morgan, Cushing, and Reed, *CBD,* 147.

27. *BC,* September 30, 1899; November 16, 1895; January 25, February 15, 22, 1896; March 5, 19, 1898.

28. *BC,* September 23, 1899.

29. *BC,* October 7, November 4, 11, 18, December 16, 1899; January 20, 27, February 3, April 28, September 29, October 26, 1900.

30. Morgan, Cushing, and Reed, *CBD,* 147–50. In 2000 Census Tract 4011, the old upper-class district off Warren, Cottage, Heath, and Boylston Streets, and Fisher Hill Avenue (often termed part of Chestnut Hill by real-estate agents) contained 3,804 residents (7 percent of the town's total), with a median family income of $158,457 (compared to a town-wide median of $92,993). U.S. Census Bureau, American Fact Finder, http://www.census.gov.

31. *BC,* October 2, 1897; January 15, 1898; ND, 739:583; *Atlas of the Town of Brookline* (Philadelphia: Bromley, 1893), plate 14; *Atlas of the Town of Brookline, Norfolk County, Massachusetts* (Philadelphia: Bromley, 1907), plate 14; Morgan, Cushing, and Reed, *CBD,* 168–72. On Lorimer, see Wikipedia, s.v. "George C. Lorimer." His son became the long-serving editor of the *Saturday Evening Post.*

32. *BC,* January 22, 1898.

33. *Brookline Suburban,* April 19, June 7, 1900.

34. *Brookline Suburban,* June 15, 1900.

35. *Annual Report of the Town Officers of Brookline, Massachusetts* (Brookline, Mass.: Riverdale Press, 1901), 68–69; *BC,* November 10, 1900.

36. *Annual Report of the Town of Brookline,* 1901, 90; Morgan, Cushing, and Reed, *CBD,* 168–69.

37. Michael H. Ebner, *Creating Chicago's North Shore: A Suburban History* (Chicago: University of Chicago Press, 1988), 96.

38. *Brookline Suburban,* May 6, 1899.

39. *BC,* July 14, 1900.

40. *BC,* February 12, 1898; May 8, 1886; May 9, 1891; March 3, 1900.

41. On playgrounds, see Desmond Fitzgerald, *Brookline Playgrounds* (Brookline, Mass.: Merrymount Press, 1907).

42. Chandler, "Brookline," 787–88.

43. *BC*, January 13, 1900.

44. Curtis, *Brookline*, 325–26; Ken Liss, "November 1915: Brookline Votes for Representative Town Meeting," *Muddy River Musings*, November 2, 2009, http://brooklinehistory.blogspot.com/2009/11/november-1915-brookline-votes-for.html.

45. Morgan, Cushing, and Reed, *CBD*, 165–75. On American zoning, see Michael Allan Wolf, *The Zoning of America: Euclid v. Ambler* (Lawrence: University Press of Kansas, 2008), and Seymour Toll, *The Zoned American* (New York: Grossman, 1969).

46. David R. Contosta, *Suburb in the City: Chestnut Hill, Philadelphia, 1850–1990* (Columbus: Ohio State University Press, 1992).

47. Jackson, *Frontier*, 172–89.

48. James C. O'Connell, *The Hub's Metropolis: Greater Boston's Development from Railroad Suburbs to Smart Growth* (Cambridge, Mass.: MIT Press, 2013), 84–86.

10. Suburbia on a Hill

1. *Baltimore Sun*, October 5, 1897 (reprinted in *BC*, October 16, 1897); *New York Tribune*, August 8, 1898 (quotation, reprinted from *Syracuse Post*, reprinted in *BC*, August 13, 1898); *New Orleans Daily Picayune*, September 12, 1897. "Richest Town in the World" referred to the town's total property valuation of some $62 million (1892), said to be the largest of any municipality under a town form of government. Alfred P. Chandler, "Brookline: A Study in Town Government," *New England Magazine*, new ser., 8 (1893): 778–89; B. O. Flower, "Democracy and Municipal Government; or, How the Richest Town in the World Is Governed by the Referendum," *Arena* 32 (1904): 382.

2. Although modern statistical measures, such as median family or household income, do not exist for nineteenth-century Boston, some surviving data can be used to illustrate Brookline's wealth and high income. For example, if Boston suburbs in 1895 are ranked by the mean number of female servants per 100 households, Brookline comes off first with 68.9 (Milton is a distant second, with 44.8; Newton, 41.6). Similarly, Brookline ranked highest for male servants per 100 households. Ronald Dale Karr, "The Evolution of an Elite Suburb: Community Structure and Control in Brookline, Massachusetts, 1770–1900" (Ph.D. diss., Boston University, 1981), 361–62.

3. Andrew Lees, *Cities Perceived: Urban Society in European and American Thought, 1820–1940* (New York: Columbia University Press, 1985), 105–255.

4. James Bryce, *The American Commonwealth* (London: Macmillan, 1889), 1:608.

5. Jackson, *Frontier*, 20–115; John Archer, *Architecture and Suburbia: From English Villa to American Dream House, 1690–2000* (Minneapolis: University of Minnesota Press, 2005).

6. Massachusetts Rapid Transit Commission, *Report of the Rapid Transit Commission to the Massachusetts Legislature, April 5, 1892* (N.p.: N.p., 1892), 15–17; Adna Ferrin Weber, *The Growth of Cities in the Nineteenth Century: A Study in Statistics* (1899; Ithaca, N.Y.: Cornell University Press, 1967), 458–59, 469–75; William H. Wilson, *The City Beautiful Movement* (Baltimore: Johns Hopkins University Press, 1994), 20–22. On the spread of railroad suburbs in Chicago, see Ann Durkin Keating, *Chicagoland: City and Suburbs in the Railroad Age* (Chicago: University of Chicago Press, 2005).

7. *BC*, August 4, 1894.

8. Chandler, "Brookline," 777–96.

9. B. O. Flower, "Brookline: A Model Town under the Referendum," *Arena* 19 (1898): 505–19. On Flower, see Arthur Mann, *Yankee Reformers in the Urban Age: Social Reform in Boston, 1880–1900* (Cambridge, Mass.: Harvard University Press, 1954), 163–69.

10. Jon C. Teaford, *City and Suburb: The Political Fragmentation of Metropolitan America* (Baltimore: Johns Hopkins University Press, 1979), 83; Flower, "Democracy," 377–91; "An American Municipality for Two Hundred Years under Direct-Legislation," *Arena* 35 (1906): 70–71; "Practical Democracy as Illustrated in the Government of the Richest Town in the World," *Arena* 35 (1906): 531–32; Thomas F. Anderson, "A Model Suburban Town," *Suburban Life* 3 (1906): 115–17, 142; Thomas F. Anderson, "The Wealthiest Town in the World and the Best Governed," *New England Magazine*, new ser., 39 (1908): 265–77.

11. Jackson, *Frontier*, 138–56.

12. Mary Corbin Sies, "Suburban Ideal," in *Encyclopedia of Urban America: The Cities and Suburbs*, ed. Neil Larry Shumsky (Santa Barbara, Calif.: ABC-CLIO, 1998), 754–56.

13. Stilgoe, *Borderland*, 165–220, extensively surveys this literature, which first appeared as early as 1855. My own reading of selected books and articles describing American suburbs from the 1860s through 1910 confirms his findings.

14. Stilgoe, *Borderland*, 180.

15. Wilson, *City Beautiful Movement*, 75–95.

16. On the attractions of elite suburban life at this period, see Michael H. Ebner, *Creating Chicago's North Shore: A Suburban History* (Chicago: University of Chicago Press, 1988).

17. Carolyn S. Loeb, *Entrepreneurial Vernacular: Developers' Subdivisions in the 1920s* (Baltimore: Johns Hopkins University Press, 2001).

18. Jackson, *Frontier*, 138–89, 278; Fishman, *Utopias*, 134–81; Carol A. O'Connor, *A Sort of Utopia: Scarsdale, 1891–1981* (Albany: State University of New York Press, 1983); David R. Contosta, *Suburb in the City: Chestnut Hill, Philadelphia, 1850–1990* (Columbus: Ohio State University Press, 1992); Roger Panetta, ed., *Westchester: The American Suburb* (New York: Fordham University Press, 2006). For early twentieth-century bourgeois-dominated suburbs, see Anne Marie T. Cammarota, *Pavements in the Garden: The Suburbanization of Southern New Jersey Adjacent to the City of Philadelphia, 1769 to the Present* (Madison, N.J.: Fairleigh Dickinson University Press, 2001); Richardson Dilworth, *The Urban Origins*

of Suburban Autonomy (Cambridge, Mass.: Harvard University Press, 2005); Michael J. Birkner, *A Country Place No More: The Transformation of Bergenfield, New Jersey, 1894–1994* (Rutherford, N.J.: Fairleigh Dickinson University Press, 1994); and James Borchert and Susan Borchert, *Lakewood: The First Hundred Years* (Norfolk, Va.: Downing, 1989).

19. 262 U.S. 365, at 394.

20. Andrew Wiese, *Places of Their Own: African American Suburbanization in the Twentieth Century* (Chicago: University of Chicago Press, 2004); Becky M. Nicolaides, *My Blue Heaven: Life and Politics in the Working-Class Suburbs of Los Angeles, 1920–1965* (Chicago: University of Chicago Press, 2002); Hayden, *Suburbia*, 97–127.

21. Jackson, *Frontier*, 231–45; Hayden, *Suburbia*, 128–53.

22. Daniel E. Sutherland, *Americans and Their Servants: Domestic Service in the United States from 1800 to 1920* (Baton Rouge: Louisiana State University Press, 1981), 182–99.

23. K. H. Schaeffer and Elliot Sclar, *Access for All: Transportation and Urban Growth* (Baltimore: Penguin, 1975), 50–51. "Since all classes are willing to commute, purely residential towns of modest homes are possible too, and many exist" (51).

24. James S. Duncan and Nancy Duncan, *Landscapes of Privilege: The Politics of the Aesthetic in an American Suburb* (New York: Routledge, 2004).

25. Richard Longstreth, "The Levitts, Mass-Produced Houses, and Community Planning in the Mid-Twentieth Century," in *Second Suburb: Levittown, Pennsylvania,* ed. Dianne Harris (Pittsburgh: University of Pittsburgh Press, 2010), 123–74.

26. Longstreth, "The Levitts," 149–59.

27. Thomas J. Sugrue, "Jim Crow's Last Stand: The Struggle to Integrate Levittown," in Harris, ed., *Second Suburb,* 175–99; David M. P. Freund, *Colored Property: State Policy and White Racial Politics in Suburban America* (Chicago: University of Chicago Press, 2007); Jackson, *Frontier*, 231–45.

28. Jackson, *Frontier*, 241–43.

29. Willow Lung-Amam, "That 'Monster House' Is My Home: The Social and Cultural Politics of Design Reviews and Regulations," *Journal of Urban Design* 18 (2013): 220–41. Because most of the McMansions in the community she describes are being built by Asian immigrants, at times Lung-Amam implies that the opposition from less-affluent whites is racially motivated. Nonetheless, she shows that opponents cited a coherent ideology grounded in aesthetic concerns and suggests that opposition appears to have been motivated more by cultural than by racial differences.

Epilogue

1. ND, 337:fol. 44; 369:fol. 1; 413:fol. 429; plan D0369–2 (online); U.S. Census, 1870, Population Schedules, Brookline; Massachusetts Vital Records; *The Brookline, Jamaica Plain, and West Roxbury Directory for 1871* (Boston: Dean Dudley, 1871).

2. ND, 803:201; 859:225; 923:622; 989:639; 1068:571; 1121:266; 1239:251; 1289:478; plans D0800–640, D0800–900; 1080–461; 21–90; Alexander von Hoffman, *John F. Kennedy Birthplace: A Presidential Home in History and Memory: A Historic Resource Study* (N.p.: N.p., 2004), 27–29.

3. For plans and interior photographs and other useful information, see the Historic American Buildings Survey/Historic American Engineering Record/Historic American Landscapes Survey, "John Fitzgerald Kennedy Birthplace, 83 Beals Street, Brookline, Norfolk, MA," HABS MA-897, www.loc.gov/pictures/collection/hh/item/MA0429/. On the Kennedy household composition, see U.S. Census, 1920, Population Schedules, Brookline; Michael O'Brien, *John F. Kennedy: A Biography* (New York: Griffin, 2005), 24; and von Hoffman, *Birthplace*, 43–44, 102–3, 109–28.

4. Bruce Arlan Phillips, "Acculturation, Group Survival, and the Ethnic Community: A Social History of the Jewish Community of Brookline, Massachusetts, 1915–1940" (Ph.D. diss., University of California, Los Angeles, 1975).

5. On St. Aidan's, see National Park Service, "Kennedy National Historic Site," http://www.nps.gov/history/history/online_books/presidents/site31.htm, and von Hoffman, *Birthplace*, 52–54.

6. C. H. Stearns, "President's Address," *PBHS*, 1911, 8–9; 1914, 9–11; 1917, 9–11.

7. Curtis, *Brookline*, 321–26.

8. Curtis, *Brookline*, 316.

9. Morgan, Cushing, and Reed, *CBD*, 138, 278.

10. Nancy Lurie Salzman and Richard Cheek, *Buildings and Builders: An Architectural History of Boston University* (Boston: Boston University, 1985); Alan Lupo, Frank Colcord, and Edmund P. Fowler, *Rites of Way: The Politics of Transportation in Boston and in the U.S. City* (Boston: Little Brown, 1971); Walter Muir Whitehill, *Boston: A Topographic History* (Cambridge, Mass.: Harvard University Press, 1968), 187–88, 231–32.

11. U.S. Census Bureau, American Fact Finder, http://www.census.gov; Charles K. Bolton, *Brookline: The History of a Favored Town* (Brookline, Mass.: Spencer, 1897). On the challenges facing aging American suburbs in the twenty-first century, see Hayden, *Suburbia*, 230–48.

12. Brookline Assessor's Office Records, http://www.brooklinema.gov.

13. U.S. Census Bureau, American Fact Finder.

14. William Dean Howells, *Suburban Sketches* (New York: Hurd and Houghton, 1871), 12–13.

15. Hayden, *Suburbia*, 10–18.

Index